From Bakunin to Lacan

Anti-Authoritarianism and the Dislocation of Power

Saul Newman

LEXINGTON BOOKS

A division of
ROWMAN & LITTLEFIELD PUBLISHERS, INC.
Lanham • Boulder • New York • Toronto • Plymouth, UK

LEXINGTON BOOKS

A division of Rowman & Littlefield Publishers, Inc.
A wholly owned subsidiary of The Rowman & Littlefield Publishing Group, Inc.
4501 Forbes Boulevard, Suite 200
Lanham, MD 20706

Estover Road
Plymouth PL6 7PY
United Kingdom

British Library Cataloguing in Publication Information Available

The hardback edition of this book was previously catalogued by the Library of Congress
as follows:

Newman, Saul, 1972–
    From Bakunin to Lacan: anti-authoritarianism and the dislocation of
power / Saul Newman.
        p.   cm.
    Includes bibliographical references and index.
        1. Power (Social sciences).   2. Anarchism.   3. Poststructuralism.
    4. Authority.   5. Authoritarianism.   6. Government, Resistance to.
    I. Title

    JC330 .N49 2001
    320'.01—dc21   00-067786

    ISBN-13: 978-0-7391-0240-4 (cloth : alk. paper)
    ISBN-10: 0-7391-0240-0 (cloth : alk. paper)
    ISBN-13: 978-0-7391-2455-0 (pbk. : alk. paper)
    ISBN-10: 0-7391-2455-2 (pbk. : alk. paper)

Printed in the United States of America

♾™ The paper used in this publication meets the minimum requirements of American
National Standard for Information Sciences—Permanence of Paper for Printed Library
Materials, ANSI/NISO Z39.48–1992.

For Suzy, with love

Contents

Foreword

Contemporary political analysis is increasingly centered on the complexities that the multifarious forms of the relation power/resistance show in present day societies. Gone are the times in which the locus of power could be referred to in a simple and unequivocal way—as in the notion of 'dominant class.' Today, the proliferation of social agents and the increasingly complex fabric of relations of domination have led to approaches which tend to stress the plurality of networks through which power is constituted, as well as the difficulties in constructing more totalizing power effects. This, in turn, has led to a transformation of the discursive logics attempting to grasp such plurality and complexity.

One of the merits of Dr. Newman's book is that it presents a clear and precise description of how the various poststructuralist approaches—mainly Foucault, Deleuze and Guattari, Derrida and Lacan—have dealt with this question of the reconfiguration of power in our societies. The central category organizing the whole argument is that of 'essentialism': the various theoretical approaches are discussed in terms of their ability to supersede the foundationalism which had marred most of the traditional approaches to power. A second merit of the book is its attempt at linking the contemporary discussion to the classical formulations of the anarchist critique of Marxism. The anarchist roots of present day libertarian politics are explored in a very rigorous and novel way. The discussion of Stirner, in particular, is highly original. It throws new light on the ways in which the latter's forgotten work represents an important link in the development of a political theory which avoids the pitfalls of both state-centered socialist approaches and anarchist humanism.

The reader will find in Dr. Newman's book a highly rigorous, original, and insightful discussion of some of the most crucial issues in contemporary political theory.

Ernesto Laclau

Acknowledgments

There are a number of people who have advised and guided me along the way, and without whose help this book would never have gotten off the ground. I would like to thank Ephraim Nimni and John Lechte who have worked closely with me over the past few years, and for whose friendship, support, warmth, and encouragement I am eternally grateful. I am also greatly indebted to Ernesto Laclau, who kindly wrote the foreword to this book and whose groundbreaking work in the area of contemporary political theory has had a great impact on my own thinking. I would also like to thank Todd May and Paul Patton for their invaluable advice and feedback. A special mention must go to Aree Cohen for his technical wizardry and assistance in preparing the manuscript. I would also like to thank Trevor Matthews for compiling the index. Gratitude must also go to a certain government department where I worked for a little while, which made my life so miserable that I decided to go back to academia, for better or for worse. Most importantly, I want to thank Suzy Casimiro who has always been there for me, and who has inspired, helped, and encouraged me throughout.

Introduction

The Return of Power

Ultimo día del despotismo
y primero de lo mismo
(The last day of despotism;
the first day of the same thing).[1]

We are always being told that we are living in a time of dramatic, sweeping political and social change. On the one hand this is undoubtedly true. Everything from relatively recent collapse of communist systems in Russia and Eastern Europe, the emergence of a distinctly European political identity, and the explosive growth of new technologies and forms of communication, to the widespread revival of national and ethnic identities, and the wars and genocides that seem to be the consequence of this, would all seem to suggest that ours is a time of radical change.

But on the other hand, one could be forgiven for thinking that things have not really changed that much at all. The same forms of domination and institutional hierarchies seem to appear time and time again, only in different garbs and ever more cunning disguises. With every popular uprising against the state and with every overthrow of some repressive regime or other, there always seems to be a new and more subtle form of repression waiting to take its place. There is always a new discourse of power to take the place of the old. For instance, what does it matter to the Australian Aboriginal, or the township dweller in South Africa, or the prisoner in a Russian jail, or the Latino "illegal immigrant" in the United States, whether he or she has a new set of masters? One is still dominated by a series of institutional practices and discursive regimes which tie him to a certain marginalized and, therefore, subjugated identity. Increased technology seems to go hand in hand with intensified social control and more sophisticated and complex ways of regulating individuals. Freedom in one area always seems to entail domination in others. So there is still, despite these profound global changes, the raw, brutal inevitability of power and authority. Maybe Friedrich Nietzsche was right when he saw history as merely a "hazardous play of dominations."[2]

This is not say, of course, that there have not been significant advancements on a world scale. Nor is it to say that all regimes and modes of political and social organization are equally oppressive. To argue that the postapartheid regime in South Africa, or the now not so new governments in the former Soviet bloc, are as dominating as the ones they replaced, would be ludicrous and insulting. Moreover, we must once and for all stop falling into the pernicious error of advocating a purer or more universal revolutionary theory that would seek to be more complete and sweeping in its paroxysm of destruction. Such a revolutionary strategy only reaffirms, paradoxically, the very power and authority that it seeks to overthrow. The Bolshevik revolution is a good example of this. I will be arguing that the very notion of revolution as a universal, cataclysmic overriding of current conditions should be abandoned. Also I am not trying to be excessively pessimistic or fatalistic by talking about the interminable reaffirmation of power at every turn. However the reality of power is something that cannot be ignored.

For too long power was shrouded in "objective" explanations offered by philosophies like Marxism, or dressed up in some theory or other which allowed it to be neglected. However, power can, and should, now be seen *as* power. It can no longer be seen as an epiphenomenon of the capitalist economy or class relations. Power has returned as an object of analysis to be studied in its own right. I use "return" here in the Lacanian sense of *repetition:* for Lacan, the Real is "that which always *returns* to the same place" [my italics].[3] The real, for Lacan, is that which is missing from the symbolic structure, the indefinable, elusive *lack* that always resists symbolization by "returning": "Here the real is that which always comes back to the same place—to the place where the subject in so far as he thinks, where the *res cogitans*, does not meet it."[4]

The complexities of the Real and lack will be discussed later, yet we may perhaps say here that power is like the real; power inevitably "returns" to the same place, despite various attempts to remove it. It always haunts, by its sheer inability to be defined, by its resistance to representation within political discourse, the very political discourses that have as their aim the overthrow of power.

The point of this discussion is not really to offer a definition of power that has hitherto eluded us, but on the contrary to recognize that power is abstract and indefinable, and to construct a definition precisely through this very resistance to definition. Rather than saying what power is, and proceeding from there, it may be more productive to look at the ways in which theories and ideas of revolution, rebellion, and resistance reaffirm power in their very attempt to destroy it. This logic which inevitably reproduces power and authority, I will call the *place of power*. "Place" refers to the abstract preponderance, and ceaseless reaffirmation, of power and authority in theories and movements that are aimed at overthrowing it. The real "always returns to the same place," and it is this *place*, or more precisely this logic of *return,* that I will be talking about. It is a cruel and malicious logic, but a logic that is nevertheless crucial to the way we think about politics.

So, in light of this, how should we look at the political and social changes that have characterized our recent past and continue to structure the horizons of our present? On the one hand, one might argue that, dramatic as these developments are, they signify that we are still tied to the same essentialist ideas and political categories that have dominated our thought for the past two centuries. For instance, we do not seem to be able to escape the category of the nation state which has been with us since the Treaty of Westphalia in 1648, and more specifically, since the French Revolution. The outbreak of wars fought over ethnic identities indicates, in a most violent and brutal manner, how much we are still tied to the idea that it is best for ethnic and national identities to have their own state. Perhaps in this sense, then, the idea of the state may be seen as a manifestation of the place of power. Moreover, we are still, quite clearly, trapped in essentialist ethnic identities. The idea that one is essentially Croat or Serb or Albanian or Hutu or European, and that one defines oneself in opposition to other, less "pure," less "educated" or "enlightened," less "rational," less "clean," less "hardworking" identities, is still all too evident today. The "changes" that are ceaselessly promulgated have only succeeded in solidifying these essentialist nationalist ideas.

However, the problem of essentialism is broader than the problem of nationalism. Essentialist ideas seem to govern our political and social reality. Individuals are pinned down within an identity that is seen as true or natural. Essentialist identities limit the individual, constructing his or her reality around certain norms, and closing off the possibilities of change and becoming. There is, moreover, a whole series of institutional practices which dominate the individual in a multitude of ways, and which are brought into play by essentialist logics. One has only to look at the way in which social and family welfare agencies and correctional institutions operate to see this. The identity of the "delinquent," "welfare dependent," or "unfit parent" is carefully constructed as the essence of the individual, and the individual is regulated, according to this essential identity, by a whole series of rational and moral norms.

The changes that have taken place on a global scale seem only to have denied the individual the possibility of real change. Not only does essentialist thinking limit the individual to certain prescribed norms of morality and behavior, it also excludes identities and modes of behavior which do not conform to these norms. They are categorized as "unnatural" or "perverse," as somehow "other" and they are persecuted according to the norms they transgress. The logic of essentialism produces an oppositional thinking, from which binary hierarchies are constructed: normal/abnormal, sane/insane, hetero-homosexual, etc. This domination does not only refer to individuals who fall outside the category of the norm [homosexuals, drug addicts, delinquents, the insane, etc]; it is also suffered by those for whom certain fragments of their identity—for identity is never a complete thing—would be condemned as abnormal. We all suffer, to a greater or lesser extent, under this tyranny of normality, this discourse of domination which insists that we all have an essential identity and that that is what we are. We must not think, though, that this domination is entirely forced upon us. While this is no doubt true to a certain extent—think of prisons, mental institutions, the army, hospitals, the workplace—an essentialist identity is also something that we often willingly submit to. This mode of power cannot operate without our consent, without our desire to be dominated. So not only will this discussion examine the domination involved in essentialist discourses and identities—the way they support institutions such as the state and the prison for example—it will also look at the ways in which we participate in our own domination.

The problem of essentialism is the political problem of our time. To say that the personal is the political, clichéd and hackneyed though it is, is merely to say that the way we have been constituted as subjects, based on essentialist premises, is a political issue. There is really nothing radical in this. But it is still a question that must be addressed. Essentialism, along with the universal, totalizing politics it entails, is the modern place of power. Or at least, it is something around which the logic of the place of power is constituted. It will be one of the purposes of this discussion to show how essentialist ideas, even in revolutionary philosophies like anarchism, often reproduce the very domination they claim to oppose. Modern power functions through essentialist identities, and so essentialist ideas are something to be avoided if genuine forms of resistance are to be constructed and if genuine change is to be permitted. The changes of recent times, dramatic as they were, were still tied to these essentialist ways of thinking, particularly with regard to national identity, and to forms of political sovereignty like the state. They did not at all challenge or disrupt these categories, often only further embedding them in political discourse and social reality.

However, modernity, like everything, is a paradox. It is open to a plurality of interpretations and characterized by different implications, voices, and dreams. The changes that I have spoken about can be seen, at the same time, in a different light. While they have consolidated the political categories that continue to oppress us, they have also discovered ways they may be resisted. While they have tightened the parameters of our identity, they have also shown us extraordinary possibilities of freedom hitherto undreamt of. Freedom, I will argue, is a diaphanous idea, often involving its own forms of domination. But it is also something indefinable, like power: it remains constitutively open, and its possibilities are endless.

Like power, freedom may be seen in terms of the real: it always exceeds the boundaries and definitions laid down for it, and the possibility of freedom always "returns," despite the most ardent attempts to suppress it. So our time presents us with an open horizon, a horizon that allows us to construct our own reality, rather than having it constructed for us. Slavoj Zizek talks about the collapse of communist states as characterized by an experience of "openness," of a symbolic moment of the absence of any kind of authority to replace the one just overthrown.[5] It is a *sublime* moment, a moment of emptiness pregnant with possibility; a truly revolutionary moment caught in that infinitesimal lack between one signifying regime and the next. This is the moment in which the place of power becomes an *empty* place. There is no inevitability about domination, but there is always its possibility.[6] The same goes for freedom. Perhaps we too are caught in this empty place, this chasm between one world of power and the next.

Although we are still very much tied to the old political categories, we are beginning to see their limits. We are beginning to see how we can move beyond them. The question is where are we going to next? If we think that we can move to a world without power, then we are already trapped in the world that oppresses us. The dream of a world without power is part of the political language of this world. It is based on essentialist ideas about humanity, ideas which render it nothing more than that—a dream, and a dangerous one at that. While there is no moving completely beyond power, there are, however, possibilities of limiting power, or at least organizing it in such a way that the risk of domination is defused. One of these ways, I will argue, is through a critique of essentialist and totalizing logics.

The idea that we can be completely free from power is based on an oppositional Manichean logic that posits an essential division between humanity and power. Anarchism is a philosophy based on this logic. It sees humanity as oppressed by state power, yet uncontaminated by it. This is because, according to anarchism, human subjectivity emerges in a world of "natural laws" which are essentially rational and ethical, while the state belongs to the "artificial" world of power. Thus man and power belong to separate and opposed worlds. Anarchism therefore has a logical point of departure, uncontaminated by power, from which power can be condemned as unnatural, irrational, and immoral. In the past, radical political theory has always relied on this uncontaminated point of departure in order to present a critique of power, whether it be the power of the state, the power of the capitalist economy, the power of religion, etc. Without this point of departure, it would seem that any kind of resistance against power would be impossible. Where would resistance or revolution come from if this were not the case? Surely it must come from a rational, ethical form of subjectivity which is somehow uncorrupted by the power it confronts.

Now here is the problem—the problem that will haunt our discussion. Let us imagine that the natural human essence, the essential, moral, and rational subjectivity supposedly uncontaminated by power, is contaminated, and indeed, *constituted*, by the power it seeks to overthrow. Moreover, not only is this subjectivity, this pure place of resistance, decidedly impure; it also constitutes, in itself, through its essentialist and universalist premises, a discourse of domination. To put it simply, then, would this not mean that the place of resistance has become a place of power? Using the argument that one needs a pure agent to overthrow power, the possibility of a contaminated agent would only mean a reaffirmation of the power it claims to oppose. In anarchist discourse humanity is to replace the state. But if we were to suggest that humanity is actually constituted by this power and that it contains its own discourses of domination, then the revolution that the anarchists propose would only lead to a domination perhaps more pernicious than the one it has replaced. It would, in other words, fall into the trap of place. This would seem to leave us at a theoretical impasse: if there is no uncontaminated point of departure from which power can be criticized or condemned, if there is no essential limit to the power one is resisting, then surely there can be no resistance against it. Perhaps we should give up on the idea of political action altogether and resign ourselves to the inevitability of domination.

However, the question of the possibility of resistance to domination is crucial to this discussion. The work will explore, through a comparison of anarchism and poststructuralism, the paradox of the uncontaminated place of resistance. I will suggest that the point of departure central to anarchist discourse—the essential human subject and its concomitant morality and rationality—cannot operate in this way because it is actually constituted by power. Moreover, because it is based on essentialist ideas, it forms itself into a discourse of domination—a place of power. I will use the arguments of various thinkers—Stirner, Foucault, Deleuze and Guattari, Derrida, and Lacan—to explore the logic of the place of power. They will be used to show that the human subjectivity of anarchist discourse is constructed, at least partially, by a variety of institutions and discursive regimes, and that therefore it cannot be seen as an uncontaminated point of departure. The politics of poststructuralism is the politics of *dislocation:* the metaphor of war, rift, and antagonism is used to break down the essentialist unity of human subjectivity, showing its dependence on the power it claims to oppose. This idea of dislocation develops the argument up to the logical impasse mentioned before: how can there be resistance to power without a theoretical point of departure outside power? It will remain of the discussion to argue, despite these limits, that a discourse of resistance can be constructed through a non-essentialist notion of the Outside.

Broadly speaking, then, the aim of this work is to explore the logic of the place of power in various political discourses and ideas, and to develop a way of thinking about resistance that does not reaffirm domination. It could be seen as an exercise in anti-authoritarian thought because it tries to resist the temptation of place. It resists, in other words, the desire to find an essential point of resistance, because this will inevitably form itself into a structure or discourse of authority. The discussion tries to develop anti-authoritarian thinking relevant to our time.

It may seem strange, however, that this thinking will be developed through a comparison between anarchism and poststructuralism. At first glance it would seem as though anarchism and poststructuralism have little in common: the former is a revolutionary philosophy born out of nineteenth century humanist ideals, while the latter—can it really be said to be a philosophy?—would appear to reject the very foundations upon which anarchism is based. However it is precisely for this reason that the two are brought together. The fundamental differences between them, particularly on the questions of subjectivity, morality, and rationality, expose, in a most crucial way, the problems of modernity. While anarchism as a revolutionary philosophy would seem to have very little to do with our time, it is based on various essentialist categories which still condition our political reality, and which must be explored if we are to ever move beyond them.

Moreover, anarchism is, as I will argue, a philosophy of power. It is, fundamentally, an *unmasking* of power. In contrast to Marxism, anarchism was revolutionary in analyzing power in its own right, and exposing the place of power in Marxism itself—its potential to reaffirm state authority. For our purposes, anarchism is the philosophy that invented the place of power as a political concept. I will also argue that anarchism itself falls into the trap of the place of power, and this is explored through the poststructuralist critique of essentialism. And it is through this critique that the problems central to radical political theory are brought to the fore. Poststructuralism too is an unmasking of power—an unmasking of the power in discourses, ideas, and practices that we have come to regard as innocent of power. In this sense, then, anarchism and poststructuralism, as different as they are, can be brought together on the common ground of the unmasking and critique of power. However, as I said before, what really makes this comparison interesting and useful is not what they have in common, but rather in the crucial ways in which they differ. So this work is not really a comparison of anarchism and poststructuralism, but rather a bringing together of certain contrasting ideas in order to highlight the questions facing radical political theory today. This "comparison" is merely a device used to think through these questions and problems and, hopefully, to find solutions to them.

It is, however, undoubtedly an unusual comparison, and it is a comparison not often made. I am only aware of one work—Todd May's seminal work, *The Political Philosophy of Poststructuralist Anarchism*—which explores these connections at any great length.[7] This is not to claim any great originality on my part, but rather to suggest that there is a legitimate area of research that remains largely unearthed. Hopefully this discussion will go some way in redressing this. As I said before, however, the purpose of this work is not simply to compare anarchism and poststructuralism, but rather to use this comparison to explore certain theoretical problems which are brought out, in a unique way, through this comparison. I do not apologize for using the word "use," as mercenary as it sounds. I intend to *use* other thinkers to work through certain ideas, and I take my cue from Foucault when he says about interpreting Nietzsche: "For myself, I prefer to utilize the writers I like. The only valid tribute to thought such as Nietzsche's is precisely to use it, to deform it, to make it groan and protest."[8]

In doing this I do not believe I am being unfair to the thinkers I am discussing. On the contrary, the whole point of a philosophy like poststructuralism is that it is there to be utilized. Therefore, I will use the logic of these thinkers to produce new meanings, to raise questions that they might not have raised, and to make connections with other ideas that they may have rejected. Although I discuss certain thinkers at length—I devote a chapter to each poststructuralist thinker—my work is not really about them. It is, as I said, a shameless use of their ideas to advance the argument.

The chapters should not be read as an exposition of each thinker, but rather as crucial stages in the development of the argument I have outlined above. The structure of the book allows each chapter to be taken both as an integral link in the argument, and also as a separate essay with its own conclusions, implications, and directions. In this way, it uses the thinkers to explore and advance the argument, while, at the same time, using the argument to explore the thinkers. But it is never intended to be an exposition of these thinkers, and there are certainly other important aspects to these thinkers that I have deliberately left out because they do not reflect on the issues I am discussing. This does not mean that I sweep under the carpet ideas that are problematic for the argument. These objections are not dismissed but are, on the contrary, used to expand the argument, distort its path, and make it turn down dark alleyways which it might not have otherwise entered.

Chapter Outline

The first chapter is a discussion of the anarchist critique of Marxism. It uses the arguments of the classical anarchists, such as Bakunin and Kropotkin, to unmask the authoritarian currents in Marxism. It looks at the ideas of Marx and Engels, as well as those of modern Marxist theorists such as Althusser, Poulantzas, and Callinicos, and contends that Marxist theory ignored the problem of power, particularly state power, by reducing it to an economic analysis. This would lead to the fate of every Jacobin revolution: as the anarchists predicted, the structure, or *place* of state power would be left intact, and even perpetuated in an infinitely more tyrannical way. The chapter also looks at the broader problem of authority in Marxism—the authority of the vanguard party and the privileging of the industrial proletariat—and it argues that although Marx himself regarded authority as pernicious, he was inescapably indebted to a Hegelian logic which allowed authority to be perpetuated.

The anarchist critique of Marxism, then, is used to construct a theory of the place of power—which anarchists detected in the state—which will become the point of departure for the discussion. Moreover, the dialogue between anarchism and Marxism is important, because it introduces anarchism as a philosophy of power. Anarchism sought to study power in its own right, without shrouding it in an economic or class analysis. This unmasking of power and authority makes it particularly relevant to our discussion.

The second chapter looks at anarchism, not merely as a critique of Marxism, but also as a philosophical system in its own right. It is based on a notion of a natural human essence, and a morality and rationality which emanate from this essence. I suggest that anarchism is a radical humanist philosophy fundamentally influenced by Feuerbach's dream of seeing man in the place of God. Moreover, it is founded on a Manichean political logic that opposes the "artificial" order of state power, to the "natural" order of human essence and organic society. This fundamental division, as I suggested before, leaves open an uncontaminated point of departure based on this natural essence. This point of departure is essential to anarchist discourse if state power, and indeed any kind of institutional power, is to be resisted on moral and rational grounds. It is the basis for most revolutionary political philosophy. Also in this chapter, the idea of the *war model* is introduced. This is an analytical model of antagonism that will be applied throughout the argument to expose the emptiness and rift at the basis of essence.

The next chapter [chapter three] uses the ideas of the largely ignored Max Stirner as a critique of humanist anarchism, in particular of the idea of human essence, which Stirner sees as an oppressive ideological construct denying difference and individuality. His ideas are used as a point of rupture in the discussion because they allow us to break out of the Enlightenment humanist paradigm of essentialism, which informs anarchism, and continues to inform radical political theory to this day. Stirner's critique of Feuerbachian humanism is discussed: he argues that man is merely God reinvented, and that the category of the absolute—the place of religious authority—is left intact in the form of essence. I apply this argument to anarchism, suggesting that in its critique of political authority, it has displaced this authority only to reinvent it within the idea of human essence. This place of resistance to power has become, then, a place of power itself.

Stirner, in talking about the links between power and subjectivity, provides an obvious but hitherto unexplored connection with poststructuralism. Stirner is therefore the link in this discussion between the politics of classical anarchism and the politics of poststructuralism to which it is being compared. The possible connections between Stirner's ideas and those of poststructuralists are startling. I would argue that Stirner is at least as relevant to poststructuralism as Nietzsche, and for this reason it is all the more curious that he has been almost entirely ignored by contemporary theory.[9] The contribution of Stirner to poststructuralist thought remains largely unexplored, and I hope that this discussion of Stirner in this context will inspire some interest in the topic.

The place that Stirner has in this discussion of power and resistance is equally important. He shows that there can be no world outside power, and that the politics of resistance must be engaged within the limits of power. Therefore, the fourth chapter looks at Michel Foucault's discussion of power and resistance, as well as his use of the concept of war to analyze power relations. Foucault's critique of humanism follows on from Stirner's, and he shows that a politics of resistance can no longer be based on a point outside power, as anarchism proposed, because it is constituted by power. Therefore the anarchist idea of an essential human subjectivity, and the rational and moral norms associated with it, becomes itself a discourse of domination. It will be suggested, however, that Foucault is forced, by the logistics of this argument, to incorporate, despite himself, some form of essential exteriority to power in order to explain resistance, leaving certain vital questions about resistance unanswered.

The next chapter [chapter five] explores the conceptual world of Gilles Deleuze and Felix Guattari to try and find some figure or language of resistance that was found lacking in Foucault. It looks at their contributions to our critique of Enlightenment humanism, particularly with regard to subjectivity and representation, which they see as authoritarian discourses. Their notions of the "rhizome" as a model of anti-authoritarian thought, and the "war-machine," are seen to be ways of constructing a discourse of resistance. However, it is found that even Deleuze and Guattari, like Foucault, fall back into the language of essentialism by positing a metaphysical notion of desire as a figure of resistance. While their war-machine, continuing the war metaphor, may be developed as an alternate figure of resistance, it is becoming increasingly apparent that there cannot be any notion of resistance without some notion of an outside to power. The question remains as to whether we can construct a non-essentialist outside.

Chapter six, expands upon the critique of authority by looking at the way in which Jacques Derrida's deconstructive terminology unmasks and interrogates essentialist and metaphysical structures in philosophy. In his attack on logocentric thought, it is found that Derrida does not want to merely reverse the terms of textual hierarchies produced by essentialist ideas, because this leaves the structure of hierarchy—the place of power—intact. Derrida does, however, incorporate a notion of the Outside—as an ethical "realm" of justice—which, while it is seen as being constituted by the Inside, is still problematic in the context of the poststructuralist argument. So where does this leave us? We can no longer posit an essential place of resistance outside power, but it seems that there needs to be some notion of an outside, no matter how momentary, for resistance to be theorized.

Chapter seven proceeds to address the problem of this non-essentialist outside through the ideas of Jacques Lacan. Like Stirner, Lacan will be seen as a pivotal point in the discussion. His arguments about subjectivity, signification, and particularly his notion of lack, will be used as a way of breaking through the theoretical impasse that has arisen. He allows us to go beyond the limits of the poststructuralist paradigm—the limits of difference and plurality—to explore this question of the outside. I use the concept of the lack at the base of subjectivity to formulate a notion of the outside that does not become essentialist or foundational—which does not become, in other words, a place. I also use Lacanian ideas such as the real to contest Habermas' ideal of rational communication. This critique of Habermas is relevant here, not only because the ideal of rational communication, and the communitarian philosophies founded on this, is similar to anarchism; it is also important to show that the universal and essential categories that this communication is based on amount to a totalitarian discourse that is embroiled in the very domination it claims to eschew. Moreover, this Lacanian terminology is applied to the identity of society, and I attempt to reconstruct the notion of political and social identity on the basis of its own impossibility and emptiness. The social is shown to be constructed by its limits, by what makes its complete identity impossible—namely power. However, the identity of power itself is found to be incomplete, so there is a gap between power and identity. But this lack is not from another, natural world, as anarchists would contend. On the contrary, it is produced by the power it limits. This would allow us to conceptualize an outside to power, paradoxically on the inside of power—in other words, a non-essentialist point of resistance.

I argue that resistance must not refer to essentialist foundations if it is to avoid reaffirming domination. This is because, as I will have shown, the place of power is inexorably linked to essentialism: universal and totaling politics that deny difference inevitably flow from essentialist notions. So the next chapter [chapter eight] will try to delineate, using the non-essentialist place I have just developed, a politics of resistance without foundations—a politics which rejects universalizing and totalizing tendencies. The ethical parameters of this politics are provided by the anarchist moral discourse of freedom and equality, which has been freed from its essentialist-humanist foundations. The ethical limits that I am trying to develop remain constitutively open to difference and plurality, while, at the same time, restricting discourses which seek to deny difference and plurality.

The purpose of this chapter, and indeed the whole discussion, is perhaps to show that politics can be thought in both a non-essentialist, non-universal way, and in a way which is productive and not nihilistic. To say this may not sound all that radical or contentious, but it must be remembered that political theory is still, to a large extent, trapped within essentialist and foundational discourses which limit it to certain norms and modes of subjectivity, while dominating and excluding others. The political project that I attempt to outline is an open project, a project defined by its fundamental incompleteness. I can only offer a few suggestions here. The point of this discussion is not really to construct a political project, but rather to show how this political project arises through the limitations of modern political discourse.

This has been nothing more than a brief outline of the argument—the thread I will draw through the discussion. As I said before, the chapters can be read both as stages in an argument, and as separate discussions with their own themes and digressions. I would feel happier if they were taken as both.

I am also aware that there are certain issues that could have been, and perhaps should have been, raised in the discussion, but due to limitations of space were not. One of these is the question of libertarianism. In my discussion of anarchism I mention its possible connection with libertarian philosophy. I also mention this connection with reference to Foucault. I do not go into great length for the reason just mentioned. Libertarianism is an anti-authoritarian, antistate philosophy, which sees political power as an insufferable burden upon the individual, and which seeks to maximize personal freedom and minimize the power of institutions.[10] What is more, it is a philosophy that, if its advocates are to be believed, is becoming more relevant and more prominent in politics today. It is a philosophy, moreover, which cuts across both the left and right, and which informs the radical, anti-authoritarian elements of both. It clearly has links with both anarchism and poststructuralism which, although they approach the problem of authority in radically different ways, still seek to minimize political domination, and maximize personal freedom. Both anarchism and poststructuralism may be seen as forms of left libertarianism. But the problem with this similarity is that, although certain aspects of the libertarian tradition appeal to those on the left—if "left" or "right" still means anything today— libertarianism is, more often than not, considered a right wing philosophy in the sense that it idealizes free market individualism and wants to liberate society from the oppressive burden of the welfare state and its taxes. This cannot easily be dismissed. It must be remembered that anarchists also saw the state as a burden on the natural functioning of society, and they would be equally suspicious of welfare, and Foucault, for instance, was interested in, or at least did not discount, liberalism, which forms the basis of libertarianism, as a critique of excessive government.[11]

Anarchism and poststructuralism both reject the idealized notion of the individual that libertarian philosophy is founded on. For anarchists, the individual cannot be taken out of the context of the natural society that creates him, and, moreover, the free market, which libertarians see as a mechanism that expands individual freedom, anarchists see as a fundamental site of oppression. For poststructuralists, to posit such an abstracted notion of individuality as libertarians do, is to ignore the various dominations that are involved in its construction. In this sense, then, anarchism and poststructuralism, while they are both anti-authoritarian philosophies, and while they both aim at increasing individual freedom, still question the abstracted notion of individuality—where the individual exists in a kind of vacuum of the free market in which he has absolute free choice—that libertarianism propounds. Nevertheless, there are still undeniable links that can be established here with a philosophy that easily gives itself over to right wing politics. Perhaps libertarianism can be seen as a dark potentiality of the critique of authority. To deny this potentiality would be against the spirit of theoretical openness that I hope is imbued in this book. On the other hand, I do not want to emphasize this link too much because the discussion is not about libertarianism. I only mention it here to indicate that the anti-authoritarian categories of anarchism and poststructuralism are not watertight. Their meanings and implications cannot be contained in narrow, clear cut definitions, but rather are contaminated, and very often overflow in directions they might not have counted on, and which they might be opposed to. Without this unpredictability of meaning there would be no such thing as politics.

Definitions

Political definitions are a difficult thing, and rightly so. Nevertheless, I realize that I had better define certain terms that I will be using throughout the discussion. Many of the terms that I have used already like "the lack" and "the real," are Lacanian terms, and will be defined in the chapter devoted to Lacan. However there are other terms that need some explanation.

Power, Domination, and Authority

I realize that I have, to a certain extent, been using these terms interchangeably. Now because these ideas are seen in radically different ways by the different thinkers I am discussing, it will be impossible to offer an overall definition for them here. Moreover, *power* in this discussion, is an intentionally abstract concept. The problem is that although I will be using these interchangeably, by the time we get to Foucault, "power" and "domination" have somewhat different meanings. Although relations of domination arise from relations of power, domination [and authority] is something to be resisted, while power is something to be accepted as unavoidable. For Foucault and, to a certain extent, Stirner, power relations are inevitable in any society, and this is precisely where the problems for anarchism, which posits an essential division between power and society, emerge. So the confusion that arises from Foucault's terminology is a necessary part of the argument, because it not only makes the uncontaminated point of departure a theoretical impossibility—it also renders the place of power itself somewhat ambiguous. However, when I refer to the *place of power*, I still use "power" in the sense of *domination*. Domination is seen as an effect of power, an effect of authoritarian structures. I employ a deliberately broad definition of *authority:* it refers not only to institutions like the state and the prison, etc.; it also refers to authoritarian discursive structures like rational truth, essence, and the subjectifying norms they produce.

Essentialism

Essentialism is the idea that beneath surface differences, there lies one true identity or character. This essential identity, it is claimed, is concealed or repressed by forces external to it.[12] For example, anarchism claims that the essential identity of the individual, defined by a natural morality and rationality, is concealed and distorted by the power of the state and religion. Once these institutions are destroyed, according to this argument, human essence will flourish.

We can see that this argument, which views political forces as external to this essence, constructs this essence as an uncontaminated point of departure, a moral and rational place from which these political forces can be resisted. My argument against this will be twofold. First, I will try to show, using the poststructuralist thinkers mentioned above, that the logic of the uncontaminated point of departure is flawed: in reality, the essential human identity that constitutes this point of departure is already constructed by, or at least infinitely bound up with, the power regimes it claims to oppose. Indeed its identity of opposition to these power regimes is itself constructed by power. Second, essential identity, far from being an identity of resistance, actually becomes an authoritarian signifier: it becomes the norm according to which other identities are persecuted. It becomes the basis of a whole series of binary oppositions that restrict other identities by constructing them as somehow a failure or perversion of the norm. These arguments are developed from the poststructuralist critique that eschews the very idea of an essential identity, seeing identity as nothing more than a dispersed series of surfaces, pluralities, and antagonisms.

Poststructuralism

Poststructuralism is an ambiguous area that requires some explaining. For a start, there is considerable debate as to whether there is any such thing as poststructuralism at all. Many of the "poststructuralist" thinkers I will be discussing would have rejected the title. Poststructuralism is merely a catchphrase, a term of convenience, which groups together a whole series of thinkers and ideas which, in many respects, are quite diverse. So it must be remembered that poststructuralism by no means signifies a unified theory or body of thought. There are, however, among these thinkers, certain shared strands of thinking and philosophical traditions which can be brought out and developed, and it is this which may be termed *poststructuralist*.

Poststructuralism has its origins in the structuralism of Barthes, Levi-Strauss, Althusser, etc.[13] Broadly, structuralism subordinated the signified to the signifier, seeing the reality of the subject as constructed by structures of language that surround it. Thus essentialist ideas about subjectivity are rejected, and in their place is put a wholly determining structure of signification. For instance, Althusserian Marxism saw the subject as overdetermined by the signifying regime produced by capitalism, the subject becoming merely an effect of this process. The problem with this rejection of essentialism was that the all-determining structure of language became, in itself, an essence. The structure becomes just as determining as any essence, just as totalizing and as closed an identity. As Derrida argues, the structure became a *place:* "the entire history of the concept of the structure . . . must be thought of as a series of substitutions of center for center, as a linked chain of determinations of the center."[14] In other words, the all-determining structure becomes merely a substitution for the essential centers—like God, man, consciousness—that it supposedly resisted.

This critique of structuralism may be broadly characterized as "post-structuralist." Poststructuralism goes one step beyond structuralism by seeing the structure itself, to a certain extent, as affected by other forces. At least the identity of the structure is not closed, complete, or pure—it is contaminated, as Derrida would argue, by what it supposedly determines. This makes its identity *undecidable.* There can be no notion, then, of an all-determining, centralized structure like language. For poststructuralists, the subject is constituted, not by a central structure, but by dispersed and unstable relations of forces—power, discursive regimes, and practices. The difference between structuralism and poststructuralism is that: first, for poststructuralists, the forces which constitute the subject do not form a central structure—like capitalism, for instance—but remain decentralized and diffused; second, for poststructuralists, the subject is *constituted* by these forces, rather than determined. One is constituted in such a way that there is always the possibility of resistance to the way one is constituted. It must be remembered, then, that for poststructuralism, as opposed to structuralism, forces, like power, which constitute the subject, are always unstable and open to resistance.

Poststructuralism may be seen as a series of strategies of resistance to the authority of place. Poststructuralists sees structuralism as falling into the trap of place by positing, in the place of God, or man, a structure which is just as essentialist. So poststructuralism is not only a rejection of the essentialism of Enlightenment humanism, but also the essentialism of the structuralist critique of humanism. Apart from this, I am not prepared to define poststructuralism any further. Its definition will be brought out in the discussion. However, as I suggested before, the purpose of the discussion is really not to define or describe, but to use, and this is how I will approach poststructuralism.

It may be noticed that I refer to *poststructuralism* and not *postmodernism.* The two terms are often equated, but they are not the same. Poststructuralists like Foucault would wholly reject the description "postmodernist," and in fact Foucault said that he did not know what "postmodernity" actually meant.[15] For Jean-Francois Lyotard, postmodernity refers not to a historical period, but rather to an a condition of critique of the unities and totalities of modernity—an "incredulity towards metanarratives."[16] This would seem to equate postmodernism with poststructuralism. However, the word "postmodern" has become so clichéd—"We all live in a postmodern world" etc.—that it comes to be seen as an actual stage in history beyond modernity. It is for this reason that I prefer to use the term *poststructuralism.*

Poststructuralism is a strategy, or series of strategies, of resistance to the unities and totalities of modernity—its essentialist categories, its absolute faith in rational truth, morality, and the practices of domination which these are often tied to. However, poststructuralism does not see itself as a stage beyond modernity, but rather a critique conducted upon the limits of modernity. Poststructuralism operates *within* the discourse of modernity to expose its limits and unmask its problems and paradoxes. It presents us with a problem rather than a solution. Modernity is not a historical period but a discourse to which we are still heavily indebted. We cannot simply transcend modernity and revel in a nihilistic postmodern universe. Is this not to fall once again into the trap of place—to replace one discourse, one form of authority, with another? Rather, we must work at the limits of modernity, and maintain a critical attitude, not only toward modernity itself, but toward any discourse which claims to transcend it. This is what I understand "poststructuralism" to mean. It means that our work is yet to be done.

Notes

1. Agustín Cueva, *El proceso de la Dominación Política en Ecuador* (Quito: Solitierra, 1977), 7. Quoted in Peter Worsley, *The Three Worlds* (London: Weidenfeld & Nicholson, 1984), 267.
2. Michel Foucault, "Nietzsche, Genealogy, History," in *The Foucault Reader,* ed. Paul Rabinow (New York: Pantheon, 1984), 76-100.
3. Jacques Lacan, *The Four Fundamental Concepts of Psychoanalysis,* ed. Jacques-Alain Miller (London: Hogarth Press, 1977), 280.
4. Lacan, *The Four Fundamental Concepts of Psychoanalysis,* 49.
5. Slavoj Zizek, *Tarrying with the Negative: Kant, Hegel, and the Critique of Ideology* (Durham: Duke University Press, 1993), 1.
6. The fact that what came after these communist states was even worse—the recurrent pattern of "ethnic cleansing," for example—illustrates this point.
7. See Todd May, *The Political Philosophy of Poststructuralist Anarchism* (University Park, Pa.: Pennsylvania State University Press, 1994). See also May, "Is Post-structuralist Political Theory Anarchist?" in *Philosophy and Social Criticism* 15, no. 3 (1989): 167-181; and Andrew Koch, "Poststructuralism and the Epistemological Basis of Anarchism," *Philosophy of the Social Sciences* 23, no. 3 (1993): 327-351.
8. Michel Foucault, "Prison Talk," in *Power/Knowledge: Selected Interviews and Other Writings 1972-1977,* ed. Colin Gordon (Brighton, Sussex: Harvester Press, 1980), 37-54.
9. This is not, of course, to diminish the importance of Nietzsche, who plays an important role in this discussion, although there is no single chapter devoted to him. In the same way that Derrida sees Marx as the specter that continues to haunt our present, perhaps one could see Nietzsche as the spirit who haunts our discussion. See Jacques Derrida, *Specters of Marx: The State of the Debt, the Work of Mourning, & the New International,* trans. Peggy Kamuf (New York: Routledge, 1994), 4.
10. For a fuller account of libertarianism see David Boaz, *Libertarianism: a Primer* (New York: Free Press, 1997); and Stephen L. Newman, *Liberalism at Wit's Ends: The*

Libertarian Revolt Against the Modern State (Ithaca, N.Y.: Cornell University Press, 1984).

11. See Andrew Barry, ed., *Foucault and Political Reason: Liberalism, Neo-Liberalism and the Rationalities of Government* (Chicago: University of Chicago Press, 1996), 7-8.

12. See Anna Marie Smith, "Rastafari as Resistance and the Ambiguities of Essentialism in the 'New Social Movements,'" in *The Making of Political Identities,* ed. Ernesto Laclau (London: Verso, 1994), 171-204.

13. Michael Peters, "What is Poststructuralism? The French Reception of Nietzsche," *Political Theory Newsletter* 8, no. 2 (March 1997): 39-55.

14. Jacques Derrida, *Writing and Difference*, trans. A. Bass (Chicago: University of Chicago Press, 1978), 279-80.

15. Peters, "What is Poststructuralism?" 40.

16. Peters, "What is Poststructuralism?" 40.

Chapter One

Marxism and the Problem of Power

The conflict between Marxism and anarchism was a pivotal debate that shaped nineteenth century radical political thought. The anarchist Mikhail Bakunin was one of Marx's most formidable opponents, his dissension splitting the First International. The conflict between these two revolutionary forces remains significant to this day. This discussion will not cover all aspects of the debate between Marxism and anarchism, but will center around questions of domination, power, and authority, some of the most pressing questions confronting political theory. Theorists and activists of different shades of opinion are asking themselves how significant social change can be achieved without a perpetuation of the forms of authority and domination that have come to be associated with the notion of revolution. The recently failed communist experiment should, if anything, make one aware of the dangers of institutional power being perpetuated in revolutionary movements. One of the most potentially liberating movements in history ended up reinstating the very institutions it sought to destroy. It was, as Michel Foucault argues, a mere changing of the guard.[1]

However, the experience of the Russian revolution is certainly not enough to indict the whole of Marxist theory. One must take into account the objections of those who say that the Bolshevik revolution was not a true Marxist revolution and that Marx himself would have been turning in his grave. Marxism and the anarchist critique will be looked at on their own terms and judged on the grounds of theory. The discussion will involve the arguments of not only Marx and Engels and the classical anarchists, but also those of contemporary Marxist and anarchist thinkers. The debate between Marxism and anarchism is based around the themes of power, domination, and authority. It will involve, then, the crucial question of the state, and state power. Now, for Marxists, as well as for anarchists, the state is an enemy of human freedom. For Marx and Engels it was essentially the instrument through which one economic class dominated another. The state, then, was something to be transcended. However, Marx is ambiguous on this point. He does not formulate a consistent theory of the state, seeing it at certain times as a tool of economic and class domination, and at other times as a relatively autonomous institution that acts, in some cases, against the immediate interests of the bourgeoisie. The extent of the state's autonomy is crucial to the Marx-anarchist debate and will be expanded upon later.

Marx's point of departure is Hegel, who believed that the liberal state was the ethical agent through which the fundamental contradictions in society could be overcome. Thus in the *Philosophy of Right*, Hegel argued that civil society was racked by rampant egotism and divided by the conflicting interests of self-seeking individuals. Civil society embodied a "universal self-interest."

However, this would be transcended, according to Hegel, by the modern state which would instigate a universal system of law, and unite consciousness, so that the egoism of civil society would be kept out of the political sphere.[2] In other words the particular state—the state that governs on behalf of particular interests in society must be replaced by a universal state—one which governs for the general good. For Hegel, the modern liberal state is the overcoming of contradictions and divisions in society. It is the culmination of morality and rationality.[3] This idea that the state can exist for the general good, for the whole of society, was rejected by Marx. According to Marx, the state is always a particular state that paints itself as universal. Its universality and independence from civil society are only a mask for the particular economic interests—such as private property—that it represents.[4] Marx was later to develop from this the position that the state represented the interests of the most economically dominant class—the bourgeoisie. For Marx, then, unlike Hegel, the state cannot overcome the tensions and contradictions in civil society and must, therefore, be transcended. Thus, Marx talks about the abolition of the state through universal suffrage.[5]

It is this point that those who want to emphasize the anti-authoritarian, antistatist aspect of Marx's thinking, seize upon. However, while Marx ostensibly breaks with Hegelian statism, he remains inexorably caught within its framework.[6] The clearest expression of this contradiction in Marx's thinking is in his advocating the necessity for a transitional state in the postrevolutionary period, and for a centralization of all authority in the hands of this state. Moreover, Marx, for all his celebrated anti-authoritarianism, was unable to really come to terms with the problem of authority, with the more diffuse spheres of domination and hierarchy, such as those within the factory, the party apparatus, and in systems of technology. Indeed, even those who wish to highlight anti-authoritarian tenets within Marx must reluctantly concede that Marxism is inadequate for dealing with the broader problems of power—that is, power which exists outside class conflict and which is not reducible to the economic factors.[7]

Marxist Theory of the State

Critique of Bauer

The idea that economic and class forces generally determine political matters is central to many forms of Marxism. For Marx himself, it was the economic forces of society that determined all historical, political, cultural, and social phenomena.[8] The political system, Marx argues, is a sphere which appears to have a determining effect on society—whereas, in reality, it is social relations based on a particular mode of production that generally determine politics. The origins of this position may be seen in Marx's article, *On the Jewish Question*. This was a response to an article by Bruno Bauer in which he suggested that the state should be used to combat religious alienation. The state, according to Bauer, could emancipate society from the grasp of religion by becoming secular.[9] Marx argued, in response, that if the state became secular and religion became a private matter for the individual, this would not necessarily mean that society would be freed from the hold of religion: "To be politically emancipated from religion is not to be finally and completely emancipated from religion, because political emancipation is not the final and absolute form of human emancipation."[10] The *political* emancipation that Bauer advocates would only further entrench religion in society and exacerbate the division between general and private interests, between the state and civil society—a division that Marx wanted to overcome. It would not do anything to weaken religion's grasp.[11] With Bauer, the emphasis is on the state—its theological character and its power to free society from religion by freeing itself from religion. With Marx, on the other hand, the emphasis is on civil society. The state cannot free society from religious alienation or economic alienation because the state itself is merely a reflection of this alienation. The real power for Marx is within civil society and the forces—like religion and private property—which dominate it.

Economic forces, rather than political forces, are what dominate society, according to Marx. To argue for political emancipation, as Bauer does, is to widen the gap between the state and civil society and to allow impersonal, dominating economic forces to entrench themselves more deeply in society by abdicating political control over them. To argue for less political control was to remove the possibility, according to Marx, of exercising any sort of communal control.

The point of this discussion of *On the Jewish Question* is to suggest that Marx argues from society—and therefore from the economic system—to the state, rather than from the state to society, as Bauer did. Bauer believed that the power to shape society was contained in the state, and claimed that if the state emancipated itself from the religion—if it became secular—then religion itself would be dissipated. Marx, on the other hand, believed that the real domination, the real determining power, lay within civil society: "civil, not political, life is their real tie."[12] Bauer, Marx argued, mistakenly believed that the state was an "independent entity" capable of acting autonomously and determinately. The state was, on the whole, derivative and determined [by economic forces] rather than autonomous and determinant.

Although Bauer was by no means an anarchist, anarchism converges with his position on this very point: the belief that the state is a determinant, autonomous force with its own conditions of existence and the power to shape society. Bauer regarded this power as positive, while anarchists saw it as negative and destructive. However, it is this similarly held belief that political power was the primary determinant force in society that Marx criticized. Marx therefore attacks the anarchist Pierre-Jospeh Proudhon for his suggestion that political power could actually shape the economic system. According to Marx, the state lacks this power because it exists as a mere reflection of the economic conditions which it is purported to be able to change. Bakunin believed that Marx was unable to see the state as anything but an instrument of economic forces: "He (Marx) says 'Poverty produces political slavery, the State,' but he does not allow this expression to be turned around to say 'Political slavery, the State, reproduces in its turn, and maintains poverty as a condition of its own existence; so that in order to destroy poverty, it is necessary to destroy the State'."[13]

The Question of Bonapartism

However, while it is true that Marx saw the state as largely derivative of the economic forces and class interests, he did at times allow the state a substantial degree of political autonomy. For instance, his work *The Eighteenth Brumaire of Louis Bonaparte* describes a coup d'état in France in 1851, in which state forces led by Louis Bonaparte seized absolute power, achieving not only a considerable degree of independence from the bourgeoisie, but often acting directly against its immediate interests. Thus Marx says: "Only under the second Bonaparte does the state seem to have made itself completely independent."[14] However, while this state has achieved a considerable degree of political autonomy, it was still essentially a state that ruled in the economic interest of the bourgeoisie. The Bonapartist state was the monstrous creation of the capitalist class: Bonaparte was put in power by the bourgeoisie to secure its economic interests and quell working class unrest; he then turned on the very bourgeois parliament that brought him into power. The Bonapartist state, according to Marx, was a deformed, hypertrophied expression of bourgeois power—a bourgeois monster that turned on the bourgeoisie itself. It was a case of the bourgeoisie committing political suicide in order to safeguard its economic interests: "that, in order to save its purse, it must forfeit the crown."[15] The bourgeoisie was willing to sacrifice its political power in order to preserve its economic power, and the Bonapartist state was the expression of this "sacrifice."

To what extent, then, does this account of the Bonapartist state allow for the relative autonomy of the state in Marxist theory? There has been considerable debate about this. David Held and Joel Krieger argue that there are two main strands in the Marxist theory of the relation between classes and the state. The first—let us call it (1a)—which is exemplified by Marx's account of Bonapartism, stresses the relative autonomy of the state. It sees state institutions and the bureaucracy as constituting a virtually separate sphere in society; its logic is not necessarily determined by class interests, and it assumes a centrality in society. The second strand (2a) which Held and Krieger argue is the dominant one in Marxist thought, sees the state as an instrument of class domination, whose structure and operation are determined by class interests.[16]

Held and Krieger also argue that these two contrasting traditions in Marxist thought correspond respectively to different revolutionary strategies in regards to the state. The first position (1b) would allow the state to be used as a force for revolutionary change and liberation. Because the state is seen as a neutral institution in the sense that it is not essentially beholden to class interests, it can be used against capitalism and the economic dominance of the bourgeoisie. The second position (2b), on the other hand, because it sees the state as essentially a bourgeois state, an instrument of class domination, demands that the state be destroyed as part of a socialist revolution.[17] This is the position exemplified by Lenin.[18]

This traditional interpretation of the relation between the question of the autonomy of the state and its role in a socialist revolution may be best represented by a table:

The Marxist model

1(a) Autonomous state---------->   1(b) State as tool of revolution

2(a) Determined state----------->   2(b) State to be destroyed in revolution

Now it is this dichotomy of state theories and their concomitant revolutionary strategies that could be questioned. It may be argued that it is precisely the second position (1b)—the view of the state as an instrument of class—that entails the first revolutionary strategy (2a) which allows the state to be used as a revolutionary tool of liberation. Furthermore, one could see the first position (1a) which allows the state relative autonomy—as entailing the second revolutionary strategy (2b) which calls for the destruction of the state in a socialist revolution:

An Anarchist model

1(a) Autonomous state-------->   2(b) State to be destroyed in revolution

2(a) Determined state---------->   1(b) State as tool of revolution

The reason for this rather radical overturning of the accepted logic is that the first position (1a) comes closest to an anarchist theory about the state. Anarchism sees the state as a wholly autonomous and independent institution with its own logic of domination. It is precisely for this reason that the state cannot be used as a neutral tool of liberation and change during the time of revolution. Even if it is in the hands of a revolutionary class like the proletariat—as Marx advocated—it still cannot be trusted because it has its own institutional logic above and beyond the control of the "ruling class." The time of revolution is when the state institution can least be trusted, as it will use the opportunity to perpetuate its own power. To regard the state as neutral, then, as strategy (1b) does, is fatal. According to this anarchist logic, moreover, position (2a)—that which sees the state as an instrument of the bourgeoisie—is the most dangerous because it is this which implies that the state is merely a neutral institution subservient to the interests of the dominant class. It is this position which would actually entail revolutionary strategy (1b)—the use of the state as a tool of revolution when in the hands of the revolutionary class. It is really a dispute over the meaning of *neutrality*: according to the Marxist logic, neutrality would mean autonomy from class interests, whereas for anarchists neutrality would imply precisely the opposite—*subservience* to class interests. This is because the view that the state is determined by class interests does not allow the state its own logic; it would be just a humble servant of class interests and could, therefore, be used as a neutral tool of revolution if it was in the hands of the right class. On the other hand, it is Marx's Bonapartist version of the state—that which sees it as a neutral institution, not beholden to class interests—that is precisely the logic which, for anarchists, paradoxically, denies the neutrality of the state because it allows it to be seen as an autonomous institution with its own logic and which, for this reason, cannot be seen as a neutral tool of revolution.

Anarchists perhaps pursue the logic of Bonapartism much further than Marx himself was prepared to take it, and, in doing so, entirely turn on its head the Marxist conception of state and revolution. The anarchist conception of the state and its relation to class will be expanded upon later. However, it is necessary at this point to show that, while Marx was no doubt opposed to the state, it is precisely the question of how he was opposed to it—as an autonomous Bonapartist institution, or as an institution of bourgeois dominance—and the consequences of this for revolutionary strategy, that is crucial to this debate.

Nicos Poulantzas, who wants to emphasize the relative autonomy of the capitalist state, argues that for Marx and Engels Bonapartism is not merely a concrete form of the capitalist state in exceptional circumstances, but actually a constitutive theoretical feature of it.[19] This would apparently question determinist interpretations of the state in Marxist theory. Ralph Miliband, on the other hand, argues that the state for Marx and Engels was still very much the instrument of class domination.[20] So what are we to make of this disparity in the interpretations of Marx's theory of the state? Marx himself never developed a theory of the state as such, or at least not a consistent theory. There are times when he appears to have a very deterministic and instrumentalist reading of the state. In the *German Ideology* he says: "the state is the form in which the individuals of a ruling class assert their common interests."[21] Also, one reads in the *Communist Manifesto* that "the executive of the modern state is but a committee for managing the common affairs of the bourgeoisie."[22] The *Communist Manifesto* was a political pamphlet, so we cannot place too much emphasis on it. However, it does perhaps give some indication of the general direction of Marx's thinking in regards to the state.

So how should we approach the question of the autonomy of the state? There is no clear answer to this. But at the risk of trying to enforce some cohesion onto Marx's thoughts on this subject, that he himself maybe never intended, perhaps we can say the following: while one can clearly reject the crude functionalist reading of the state, and while allowing the state perhaps a considerable degree of political autonomy, we can still say that, for Marx, the state is, in essence, class domination. By this we mean that, while the state is by no means the simple political instrument of the bourgeoisie, while it clearly does not do everything the bourgeoisie tells it and indeed, often acts against it, the state is still, for Marx, an institution that allows the most economically powerful class—the class which owns the means of production—to exploit other classes. In other words, it is still the state that facilitates the bourgeoisie's domination and exploitation of the proletariat. This interpretation would allow the state a large degree of political autonomy: it could work against the political will of the bourgeoisie, but it still would have to protect the long-term economic interests of the bourgeoisie.

So rather than saying that, for Marx, the state is the instrument of bourgeoisie, it may be more accurate to say that the state is a *reflection* of bourgeois class domination, an institution whose structure is determined by capitalist relations. According to Hal Draper, the state rules in a "class-distorted" way.[23] Its function is to maintain an economic and social order that allows the bourgeoisie to continue to exploit the proletariat. By maintaining the conditions of the capitalist economy in the name of the common good, the state serves the interests of the bourgeoisie. This is what Marx meant by saying that the state was derivative of particular interests in society.

One can see in Marx's account of the state—if there can be said to be an "account" as such—a continuation of the Hegelian critique of the partial state, the state that serves the interests of part, rather than the whole, of society. For Marx, the state has an illusory character: it paints itself as a universal political community that is open to general participation whereas, in fact, it generally acts on behalf of certain sectional interests. It is a veil behind which the real struggles of economic classes are waged and behind which the real misery and alienation of people's lives is concealed. Like Hegel, Marx was concerned with finding an ethical agency, a form of communal control, a legitimate form of power, which would transcend the partial state and embody the interests of the whole of society—something which would overcome the contradiction between public and private life. For Marx the capitalist state was an expression of the alienation in civil society, and the only way this alienation could be overcome was through an agency which did not reflect existing economic and property relations.[24] Unlike Hegel, Marx believed that this agent could not be the modern state as it stands because it was essentially the state of bourgeois relations. While Hegel, then, saw this unifying agent in the ethical principle behind the liberal state, Marx found it in the proletariat.[25]

Dictatorship of the Proletariat

The proletariat is Marx's version of the universal agent sought within the Hegelian tradition—the agent that would overcome the contradictions in society. The emancipation of the proletariat is synonymous with the emancipation of society as a whole. It represented the possibility, according to Marx, of exercising a legitimate ethical authority over society: a society characterized by a lack of public—as opposed to private—authority; a society in which people were alienated from each other, and from the public sphere. Marx, therefore, saw this exercise of public authority, of social power, as a necessary stage in the ushering in of communism.

How was this social power to be organized however? Marx said that it would be organized, temporarily, in the apparatus of the state. The proletariat, in the "transitional period" between capitalist and communist society, will exercise political power through the instrumentality of the state: "There corresponds to this [transitional period] also a political transition in which the state can be nothing but the dictatorship of the proletariat."[26] Marx called, furthermore, in his *Address of the Central Committee to the Communist League* for the workers to strive for "the most decisive centralization of power in the hands of state authority."[27] The coercive power of the state may be used by the proletariat to suppress class enemies and sweep away the conditions of the old bourgeois society. Thus Marx says in the *Communist Manifesto*: "The proletariat will use its political supremacy to wrest, by degrees, all capital from the bourgeoisie, to centralize all instruments of production in the hands of the state."[28] So the state, controlled by the proletariat, has become, for Marx, albeit temporarily, the vehicle which would liberate society from bourgeois domination by representing society as a whole. Thus the aim of the revolution, for Marx, was not to destroy state power, but rather to seize hold of it and to perpetuate it in the "transitional period." It must be remembered that Marx sees this proletarian state as a temporary arrangement, and Engels argued that it would "wither away" when no longer necessary.[29] However, the anarchists argued that to expect the state to just disintegrate on its own was naive. The reason for this will become clear later.

So Marx's strategy in the "transitional" phase of the revolution amasses enormous power in the hands of the state. However, if the state is, as Marx had argued, always the "instrument" of a particular class, or at least a reflection of class domination, how then can Marx see the "transitional state" as acting on behalf of the whole of society? Is not this at variance with Marx's professed antistatism and his departure from Hegel on this question? Anarchists saw this as a major flaw in Marx's thinking. Marx, on the other hand, did not see this as a contradiction at all. Because the transitional state was in the hands of the proletariat—the "universal class"—it would act for the benefit of society as a whole. According to Marx, it was no longer a partial state, as it had been in bourgeois society—it was now a *universal* state. In fact, Marx said that state power will no longer even be political power, since "political power" is defined by its reflection of the interests of a particular class. In other words, because there are no more class distinctions in society, because the bourgeoisie has been toppled from its position of economic and, therefore, political, dominance, there is no longer any such thing as political power: "When, in the course of development, class distinctions have disappeared, and all production has been concentrated in the hands of a vast association of the whole nation, public power will lose its political character."[30] He also says in response to Bakunin's objections to the transitional state: "when class domination ends, there will be no state in the present political sense of the word."[31] For Marx, because political domination and conflict is an expression of class domination, once class domination disappears, then so will political domination: the state will become a neutral institution to be used by the proletariat, until it "withers away."

Let us follow Marx's logic: because political power is the derivative of class and capitalist relations, once these are abolished, then, strictly speaking, political power no longer exists—even though the state has become, in accordance with the Marxist revolutionary program, more centralized and powerful than it ever was in bourgeois society, or in any other society. This claim that the increasingly dominant "transitional" state no longer exercises political power is, argued the anarchists, dangerously naive. It neglects what they see as the fundamental law of state power [or, for that matter, any form of institutional power]: that it is independent of economic forces, and that it has its own logic— that of self-perpetuation. Now it is true that, as we have shown before in the case of the Bonapartist state, Marx allows the state some independence from class will, but the question is whether he has allowed it enough. The anarchists would argue that he has not, and that the evidence for this is precisely Marx's use of the state institution to further revolutionary aims. Anarchism sees the state, *in its essence*, as independent of economic classes, and that for this reason it cannot be trusted to revolutionize society no matter which class controls it. It may be suggested, then, that anarchism pursues to its furthest reaches the possibilities of Bonapartism.

The implication of Marx's thinking is that the state apparatus, because it reflects the interests of class and because it is claimed that it can be used to benefit society if the proletariat—the "universal class"—controls it, is perceived as being merely the humble servant of the political will of the dominant class. While we have shown this to be a crude characterization, Marxist theory, according to Robert Saltman, does, on the whole, see political oppression, not within in the state apparatus itself, but in its subservience to the interests of a particular class.[32]

The Anarchist Theory of the State

This idea that the state can be utilized for revolutionary ends is the result, as we have seen, of the Marxist analysis which works from society to the state— seeing the state as a derivative of social forces, namely the economic power of the bourgeois class. Anarchism works the other way around—it analyzes from the state to society. It sees the state—all states, all forms of political power, the place of power itself—as constituting a fundamental oppression. Marxist theory also sees the state as an evil that is to be eventually overcome, but it is an evil derived from the primary evil of bourgeois economic domination and private property. Anarchism, on the other hand, sees the state itself as the fundamental evil in society.[33]

The state, for anarchists, is a priori oppression, no matter what form it takes. Bakunin argues that Marxism pays too much attention to the forms of state power while not taking enough account of the way in which state power operates: "They (Marxists) do not know that despotism resides not so much in the form of the State but in the very principle of the State and political power."[34] Kropotkin, too, argues that one must look beyond the present form of the state: "And there are those who, like us, see in the State, not only its actual form and in all forms of domination that it might assume, but in its very essence, an obstacle to the social revolution."[35] Oppression and despotism exist in the very structure and symbolism of the state—it is not merely a derivative of class power. The state has its own impersonal logic, its own momentum, its own priorities: these are often beyond the control of the ruling class and do not necessarily reflect economic relations at all. For anarchists, then, political power refers to something other than class and economic relations.

The modern state has its own origins too, independent of the rise of the bourgeoisie. Unlike Marx, who saw the modern state as a creation of the French Revolution and the ascendancy of the bourgeoisie, Bakunin saw the state as the child of the Reformation. According to Bakunin, the crowned sovereigns of Europe usurped the power of the church, creating a secular authority based on the notion of divine right—hence the birth of the modern state: "The State is the younger brother of the Church."[36] Kropotkin, in his discussion of the state, also attributes the rise of the state to noneconomic factors such as the historical dominance of Roman law, the rise of feudal law, the growing authoritarianism of the church, as well as the endemic desire for authority.[37]

Furthermore, it could be argued that the political forces of the state actually determine and select specific relations of production because they encourage certain forces of production which are functional for the state, allowing the development of the means of coercion needed by the state. This turns the base-superstructure model of the state on its head, seeing the determining forces going from top to bottom rather than from the bottom to the top. According to Alan Carter, then, because many Marxists have neglected the possibility of political forces determining economic forces, they have fallen into the trap of the state:

> Marxists, therefore, have failed to realize that the state *always* acts to protect its own interests. This is why they have failed to see that a vanguard which seized control of the state could not be trusted to ensure that the state would "wither away." What the state might do, instead, is back different relations of production to those which might serve the present dominant economic class if it believed that such new economic relations could be used to extract from the workers an even greater surplus—a surplus which would then be available to the state.[38]

So for the anarchists, to view the state, as some Marxists do, as derivative of class power, is to fall victim to the state's deception. The state apparatus in itself appears to be faceless—it appears to lack any inherent values or direction. Marx sees it as an illusory reflection of the alienation created by private property, or as an institution of the bourgeois class. In reality, however, the state has its own origins and operates according to its own agenda, which is to perpetuate itself, even in different guises—even in the guise of the worker's state.

For anarchists, state power perpetuates itself through the corrupting influence it has on those controlling it. This is where the real domination lies, according to Bakunin: "We of course are all sincere socialists and revolutionists and still, were we to be endowed with power . . . we would not be where we are now."[39] Therefore, argued Bakunin, the fact that the proletariat is at the helm of the state apparatus does not mean, as Marx claimed, an end to political power. On the contrary, the Marxist program only meant a massive increase in political power and domination, as well as new lease of life for capitalism. Indeed, Bakunin believed that Marx's revolutionary strategy would lead to a new stage of capitalist development.[40] According to Bakunin, the Marxist workers' state will only perpetuate, rather than resolve, the contradictions in capitalist society. It will leave intact the division of labor, it will reinstate industrial hierarchies, and furthermore, it will generate a new set of class divisions.

Bakunin perhaps represents the most radical elements of Marxist theory. He takes Marx at his word when he says that the state is always concomitant with class divisions and domination. However, there is an important difference. To put it crudely: for Marx the dominant class generally rules through the state; whereas for Bakunin, the state generally rules through the dominant class. In other words, for anarchists, bourgeois relations are actually a reflection of the state, rather than the state being a reflection of bourgeois relations. Unlike Marxism, the emphasis in anarchist theory is on the state itself—a term which includes economic exploitation—rather than on economic relations specifically. Anarchism would seem to have a much broader notion of the state than Marxism. The ruling class, argues Bakunin, is the state's real material representative. In this sense ruling classes are essential to the state, rather than the state being essential to ruling classes. Behind every ruling class of every epoch there looms the state—an abstract machine with its own logic of domination. The bourgeoisie is only one of the state's manifestations. When the bourgeoisie is destroyed the state will create another class in its place, another class through which it perpetuates its power—even in an allegedly classless society.[41] This new bureaucratic class, Bakunin argues, will oppress and exploit the workers in the same manner as the bourgeois class oppressed and exploited them.[42]

It is for this reason, anarchists argued, that revolution must be aimed, not at conquering state power, even if only temporarily, but at destroying it immediately, and replacing it with decentralized, nonhierarchical forms of social organization.[43] It is also for the reasons mentioned before that anarchists argue that the state cannot be trusted simply to "wither away" as Marxists believed. For anarchists it is extremely naive, even utopian, to believe that entrenched political power—and Bakunin's analysis has shown the workers state to be precisely this—will simply self-destruct just because old class divisions have disappeared and relations of production have been transformed.

It must be remembered, though, that Marx ultimately wanted to see a society in which the state was unnecessary and would be abolished. How is it that he came to advocate the use of state power to usher in a stateless society? It would seem to be a blatant contradiction. However, as I have suggested, this results from a Hegelian dialectic to which Marx was inescapably indebted. Each epoch in history creates the conditions for its own transcendence. Marx, following this dialectical approach, believed that the seeds of communist society existed within capitalism and that, consequently, communism will emerge from the foundations of capitalist society.[44] The elements of the old society, such as the state apparatus, may be used to facilitate the transition to the new society. Unlike the anarchists, who did not distinguish between types of states, and considered all states to be equally oppressive whatever form they took, Marx saw some progressive and potentially liberating aspects in the modern liberal state. Marx considered bourgeois representative democracy, for instance, to be an important stage in the development of human emancipation.[45] Anarchists, on the other hand, regarded the modern liberal state with scorn—it was seen as another insidious attempt to mask the brutal, despotic character of the state and was, for this reason, even more pernicious than the autocratic state.[46] Therefore Marxism, unlike anarchism, sees it as possible, and indeed essential, that the struggle for a new society be articulated within the terms and institutions of the old society.

The anarchist response to this is that the forms and institutions of the old society will not simply fall away: they will become entrenched, denying the possibility of genuine liberation. They must therefore be removed straight away—their destruction must be the first revolutionary act. Anarchism is, in this respect, anti-Hegelian. Bakunin rejected the Hegelian tracheotomy: there was no reconciliation between thesis and antithesis, between the Positive and the Negative.[47] In Bakunin's "negative dialectics" the dialectical contradiction is the victory of the Negative. However, in this victory both the Positive and the Negative are destroyed. For Hegel, and indeed for Marx, on the other hand, the thesis and antithesis are transcended—however elements of both are preserved in the synthesis. In the same way, elements of the old society are preserved and form a necessary part of the foundations of the new. For Marx, then, the communitarian, public essence that the state expresses should survive the destruction of the existing society. For anarchists, on the other hand, the new society was to emerge only with the complete destruction of the old.[48]

In contrast to the Hegelian dialectical framework, anarchism works within a dualistic or even Manichean view of the world, seeing the state as essentially evil and society as essentially good. Anarchism is based, to some extent, on the separation central to liberal theory, between the state and society—the very division that Marx wanted to overcome dialectically. Anarchists argue that the state oppresses society, and that if only the state was destroyed, then society could flourish. Marx, on the other hand, argued that the domination is not in the state but in society itself, and that if the state were to be destroyed before socialist economic relations could be established, society would not flourish or be liberated—it would be even more at the mercy of the forces of economic authority.

For anarchists, the liberation of human society must be made by society itself—through libertarian means. Freedom can never come through the agency of authority.[49] For Marx, on the other hand, power and authority are not necessarily something to be embraced, but something to be used in a certain way, with a view to their own transcendence. However, if one takes account of the anarchists' analysis, particularly of state power, power and authority can never be transcended unless they are destroyed immediately.

The Broader Problem of Authority

The anarchist response to Marxism has shown that Marx is trapped within an authoritarian bind—a statist, centralist framework. John Clark argues that while there are certainly some elements of Marxist theory which have anti-authoritarian and decentralist implications, "if the totality of his thought is considered, Marx was attached to centralist and authoritarian structures which are inseparable from statist and bureaucratic forms of domination."[50] Despite Marx's proclaimed anti-authoritarianism and antistatism, he cannot escape a statist way of thinking. There is an authoritarian current that runs throughout the body of classical Marxism.[51]

Class

The debate between anarchism and Marxism over the state, however, has not exhausted the question of authority and power. There are other points of disagreement between the two theories that suggest that the problem of authority in Marxism goes deeper than the question of the state. The question of class, for instance, is another point of difference between anarchism and Marxism. For Marx there is only one class that is truly revolutionary and that is the industrial proletariat. Because the proletariat is tied to a peculiarly capitalist system of production and is defined by its place within the productive process, it is the only class that can overthrow capitalism.[52] By the revolutionary status that Marx attributed to the proletariat, it is endowed with a privileged position, to the exclusion of other classes in society. Marx saw artisans and peasants, for instance, as reactionary. They could only become revolutionary by joining the ranks of the proletariat. As for the *lumpenproletariat* [impoverished workers, vagrants etc.], according to Marx, it is scarcely even worth a mention. He calls it the "social scum, that passively rotting mass thrown off by the layers of the old society."[53] Marx establishes a hierarchy among classes with the industrial proletariat at the top: its moral and epistemological authority defined by its relation to the productive process.

Anarchism, on the other hand, did not exclude other classes just because they had no real connection with the industrial process. In fact this distance from the factory system made other classes possibly even more revolutionary than the industrial working class. These other classes, according to the anarchists, have not been contaminated by capitalist morality which anarchists saw as thoroughly counterrevolutionary. Bakunin, for instance, spoke of "that great rabble which being very nearly unpolluted by all bourgeois civilization carries in its heart, in its aspirations, in all necessities and the misery of its collective position, all the germs of the Socialism of the future, and which alone is powerful enough today to inaugurate the Social revolution and bring it to triumph."[54]

Bakunin includes in this revolutionary rabble peasants, the *lumpenproletariat,* and even intellectuals *déclassé.* This rabble which the classical anarchists spoke of is a class whose very nature is that of a nonclass. In fact Bakunin prefers not to call this a class at all, but a "mass." "Class" implies hierarchy and exclusiveness.[55]

Anarchists argued, moreover, that not only is the industrial proletariat actually numerically small compared to other groups and classes in society [this is obviously more so today], but that it is also thoroughly imbued with bourgeois ethics. Bakunin believed that the small elite of "class-conscious" proletarians constituting the upper echelons of the working class, lived in a relatively comfortable and semibourgeois fashion, and had been, in fact, coopted into the bourgeoisie.[56] Murray Bookchin, a modern day anarchist, argues that Marxist privileging of the proletariat over other groups in society is obsolete and, more importantly, counterrevolutionary. This is because the proletariat has become "an imitation of its masters," adopting the worst aspects of capitalist society: the work ethic, bourgeois morality, and a respect for authority and hierarchy conditioned by the discipline and hierarchy of the factory milieu.[57] Therefore, anarchists argue that the Marxist privileging of the proletariat above other groups as the most revolutionary is a practice which is itself born of a bourgeois mentality and is doomed, as a consequence of this, to perpetuate bourgeois systems of domination. The category of class, for anarchists, is authoritarian in itself: it is a form of subjectivity that ties the worker to the work place and to authoritarian industrial hierarchies.

The Party

The Marxist desire for a unified, disciplined proletariat is, anarchists suggest, a thoroughly authoritarian desire. Tied to this is the requirement for a disciplined, authoritarian party controlling the proletariat.[58] The communist party was subsequently built on hierarchical and authoritarian premises. The role of the communists was defined by Marx in terms of leadership and control. He says: "they have over the great mass of the proletariat the advantage of clearly understanding the line of march."[59] As anarchists argue, this is clearly elitist: the most "class-conscious" of the industrial proletariat leads others in society, and this elite, in turn, is led by the communist party, playing the vanguard role.

The vanguard role of the communist party, furthermore, is based on an epistemological authority—on the claim that it is the sole possessor of knowledge of the movement of history. It is seen as having a monopoly on scientific knowledge that no one else can grasp. Bakunin often criticized Marxists as doctrinaire socialists whose strategy would culminate in a dictatorship of scientists and experts—a domination of science over life. Bakunin believed that scientific dogma, particularly when it was part of the revolutionary program was an authoritarian discourse that mutilated the complexity and spontaneity of life. The Marxist program, he argued, would open the way for a society governed by a new class of scientists and bureaucrats: "It will be the reign of the scientific mind, the most aristocratic, despotic, arrogant and contemptuous of all regimes."[60]

Technology

Another aspect of Marx's centralist thinking was his faith in bourgeois technology.[61] Marx believed that bourgeois industrial technology was progressive because within it lay the seeds of a society in which work was no longer a matter of absolute necessity: technology produced a surplus and it therefore had the ability to liberate man from the need to work.[62] Hierarchically organized systems of industrial technology such as Taylorism were not dominating in themselves, Marx argued—they were dominating because they were used for bourgeois, not socialist, production. It was for this reason that Marx condemned Luddism, a protest against the industrialization during the nineteenth century which involved wrecking industrial equipment. For Marx, machine-breaking as a form of protest was utopian because "they [Luddites] direct their attacks, not against the bourgeois conditions of production, but against the instruments of production themselves."[63] The implication of this is that technology itself is neutral: the domination arises when it is used for bourgeois production. If this same technology were to be used for socialist production, it would be liberating. The Marxist program, therefore, does not call for the destruction of this technology. Rather it seeks a concentration of this technology in the hands of the state.[64] Factory hierarchies and forms of industrial discipline are thus perpetuated. Discipline and authority in the workplace was essential for the Marxist revolutionary program: "Wanting to abolish authority in large scale industry is tantamount to wanting to abolish industry itself, to destroy the power loom in order to return to the spinning wheel."[65]

Anarchists, on the other hand, argued that large-scale industrial technology is never neutral. It is dominating in itself, no matter what form of production it is used for. Furthermore, it destroys individual creativity and independence, tying the worker to the machine and disrupting natural human relationships. To see this technology as neutral is, anarchists argue, another example of the way Marx neglected the problem of power and authority. Moreover, in contrast to large-scale, hierarchically organized production, anarchists like Kropotkin proposed the development of humanly scaled, labor-intensive, decentralized production which would be compatible with individual freedom and self-management.[66] Hierarchical and authoritarian forms of industrial organization form the basis of scientific and bureaucratic elites, anarchists argue, and should therefore be abolished.

Economic Reductionism

The anarchist critique of technology, science, and party hierarchies points to an important aspect in this debate. For anarchists, Marxism has great value as an analysis of capitalism and a critique of the private authority it is tied to. However, in concentrating on this, Marxism neglects other forms of authority and domination, or at least is unable to adequately deal with them because it reduces them to economic authority when they may have their own origins and logic. To reduce everything to economics is to neglect the problem of domination.

Marxism is trapped in an authoritarian framework for this very reason. It is not because Marx believed that authority was necessarily good: indeed Marx believed that domination was dehumanizing and would be transcended. Rather it was the conviction that all forms of domination, particularly political domination, could be reduced to economic domination, which led Marx into this authoritarian bind. Even those who want to emphasize the libertarian aspects of Marx give some credibility to the anarchist viewpoint. According to Rappaport, even within the framework of historical materialism Bakunin was right to predict that socialist authority would become tyrannical.[67] She also argues that: "His [Marx's] tendency to regard all political conflict as grounded in class antagonism led him to underestimate the importance of the political dimension of socialist development."[68] In other words, Marx fell into a fatal trap when he argued that political power would cease to be political when class divisions had been overcome. On the contrary, as anarchists like Bakunin warned, political power may become even more entrenched and dominating with the abolition of old class antagonisms. The political cannot be reduced to the economic for this reason.

This economic determinism is not only the domain of classical Marxism. For instance, while the Marxist theorist Louis Althusser proposed a picture of society radically different from the classical Marxian notion of the social superstructure strictly determined by the economic essence or structure, he nevertheless saw social relations as being determined, *in the last instance*, by the economy. Althusser's intervention did, however, open the possibility, within Marxist discourse, for theorizing the autonomy of the political because it proposed that the economy acts on the social only indirectly. According to Althusser, economic forces are part of the social whole: they do not constitute a privileged core outside the social superstructure. In other words, political formations can act on the economy, just as they can be acted on by the economy. He calls this symbiotic relationship, "overdetermination."[69] This rejection of the base-superstructure thesis has much in common with classical anarchism. Althusser would seem, then, to be approaching the anarchist position because he allows for a greater emphasis to be placed on the autonomy of the political, and other noneconomic forms of power. However, despite this, Althusser structured his conception of the social around the economy: the economy is the "structure in dominance," the organizing principle in society.[70] While political and social formations were not directly, in every instance, determined by the economy, they were still *dominated* by it. The prerogatives of the economy still took precedence, *in the last instance* [in a time of revolution, for example] over other social formations. Althusserian Marxism is, therefore, not entirely removed from classical Marxism. In its essence it is a reaffirmation of the theoretical predominance of economic power over other forms of power.

More recently, Alex Callinicos has defended classical Marxism against the potential challenge it faced from Althusser. For Callinicos, Althusser's rejection of the Hegelian social whole culminates in an affirmation of difference—a multiplicity of social practices that cannot be *dialecticized* back into an original unity.[71] It is this potential openness to the notion of difference and plurality, according to Callinicos, which has caused the "crisis of Marxism." Instead what must be reaffirmed is the classical Marxist notion of the social totality, centrally determined by the economy. It is only this perspective, Callinicos argues, that allows for the possibility of the class struggle. However, it is precisely this perspective which negates the possibility of other sources of power in society, that is being challenged by anarchism.

Bob Jessop tries to develop within the Marxist framework a contingent theory of political power and the state. He argues that in Marxist theory there are three main ways of approaching this question: the first sees the relationship between economic interests and institutional systems purely in terms of function; the second approach stresses the way in which the institutional form of different systems reflects or corresponds to the structural needs of economic systems; the third approach rejects the economic determinism of the last two and sees the relationship between institutions and economic systems to be based on *"contingent articulatory practices."*[72] The second, and possibly even the first, approach is represented by Callinicos who sees the social and political as centrally determined by economic relations. The third strand of Marxist thought is perhaps best reflected by Althusser who, on the surface, seems to put forward a contingent approach to the relationship between the political and the economic which allows the political considerable autonomy. However, as we have seen, even in this sort of analysis the political is still, ultimately, dominated by the economy. Therefore, it could be argued that for a genuinely contingent and autonomous theory of political and noneconomic power, it means going beyond Marxism. The problem of political power cannot be adequately answered within the Marxist theory. As Rappaport says: "It does . . . require going beyond Marx in developing a theory capable of explaining political relationships which do not have their foundations in material scarcity."[73] Hence the importance of anarchism today.

Some Marxists have in the past been too ready to blame things like "bureaucratic deformation" and "bourgeois revisionism" for what happened in the Soviet Union. Foucault, for instance, condemns those Marxists who refuse to question the actual texts of Marx when looking at what happened in the USSR, and who try to explain away the persecutions and the Gulag by putting it down to a betrayal of the "true theory" through "deviation" or "misunderstanding." "On the contrary," says Foucault, "it means questioning all these theoretical texts, however old, from the standpoint of the Gulag. Rather than searching in those texts for a condemnation in advance of the Gulag, it is a matter of asking what in those texts could have made the Gulag possible."[74]

In other words, although Marx obviously cannot be held responsible for what happened, one must nevertheless question his ideas—they must be studied for possible links. There can be no absolute separation between theory and practice: one clearly informs the other, even if not directly. As we have seen, there are links which can be made, certain connections to be found, sometimes explicit, sometimes more subtle, between the authoritarian tendencies in Marx's work and the growth of totalitarianism in Russia. It is these connections, these authoritarian undercurrents, which I have tried to unearth in this debate between Marx and the anarchists.

This debate has revolved around the question of the place of power. Marxism, through its economic reductionism, has neglected the place of power. It dismantles one form of power, the bourgeois state, but re*places* it with another kind of power, the workers' state. Thus, power itself—its mechanisms, its operation—remains unhindered. In fact, power is only reaffirmed and perpetuated by Marxism. This is what one learns from the anarchist critique of Marxism. Marxism failed to revolutionize power. It has failed to overcome the place of power—it has succeeded only in *renaming* it. A Marxian revolution is, therefore, only a changing of the guard, the anarchists argue. Because Marxism reduces social phenomena to the capitalist economy, it neglects, to its peril, other autonomous sources of power in society. Moreover, this economic reductionism has its roots in a Hegelian historicism: state power cannot be destroyed immediately in a socialist revolution because its existence is a necessary part of the historical process. Anarchism, on the other hand, tries to escape, to some extent, this dialectical determinism by establishing a moral place of subjectivity. This moral place will be the subject of the next chapter.

Notes

1. See Michel Foucault, ed.,"Revolutionary Action: 'Until Now,' " in *Language, Counter-Memory, Practice* (Oxford: Basil Blackwell, 1977), 218-233.

2. Paul Thomas, *Karl Marx and the Anarchists* (London: Routledge & Kegan Paul, 1980), 22.

3. Georg Wilhelm Friedrich Hegel, *The Philosophy of Right,* trans. T. M. Knox (Chicago: Encyclopaedia Britannica, 1952), 155-156.

4. Karl Marx, *Critique of Hegel's* 'Philosophy of Right,' ed. Joseph O'Malley (Cambridge, U.K.: Cambridge University Press, 1970), 107.

5. Marx, *Critique of Hegel's* 'Philosophy of Right,' 1.

6. See Thomas *Karl Marx and the Anarchists,* 22.

7. See Elizabeth Rappaport, "Anarchism and Authority," *Archives Europeenes de Sociologie (European Journal of Sociology)* 17, no. 2 (1976): 333-343.

8. See Karl Marx, *Capital* (New York: International Publishers, 1967), 1:82.

9. Karl Marx, "On the Jewish Question," in *The Marx-Engels Reader,* 2d ed., ed. Robert C. Tucker (New York: W. W. Norton, 1978), 26-52.

10. Marx, "On the Jewish Question," 32.

11. Marx, "On the Jewish Question," 35.

12. Karl Marx and Friedrich Engels, "The Holy Family," in *Collected Works*, vol. 4, (London: Lawrence & Wishart, 1975), 9-211.

13. Mikhail Bakunin, *Marxism, Freedom and the State,* trans. K. J. Kenafick (London: Freedom Press, 1950), 49.

14. Marx, "The Eighteenth Brumaire of Louis Bonaparte," in Karl Marx and Friedrich Engels, *Collected Works*, vol. 11 (London: Lawrence & Wishart, 1975), 99-197.

15. Marx, "The Eighteenth Brumaire of Louis Bonaparte," 143.

16. David Held and Joel Krieger, "Theories of the State: Some Competing Claims," in *The State in Capitalist Europe,* ed. Stephen Bornstein, et al. (Winchester, Mass.: George Allen & Unwin, 1984), 1-20.

17. Held and Krieger, "Theories of the State: Some Competing Claims," 4.

18. See Vladimir Ilich Lenin, *The State and Revolution: The Marxist Theory of the State and the Tasks of the Proletariat in the Revolution* (Moscow: Progress Publishers, 1965).

19. Nicos Poulantzas, *Political Power and Social Classes* (London: Verso, 1978), 258.

20. Ralph Miliband, *The State in Capitalist Society* (New York: Basic Books, 1969), 5.

21. Karl Marx, "The German Ideology," in *The Marx-Engels Reader*, 2d ed., 187.

22. Karl Marx, "Manifesto of the Communist Party," in *The Marx-Engels Reader*, 2d ed., 469-500.

23. Hal Draper, *Karl Marx's Theory of Revolution, vol.1: State and Bureaucracy* (New York: Monthly Review Press, 1977), 249.

24. Thomas, *Karl Marx and the Anarchists*, 71.

25. Karl Marx, "Contribution to the *Critique of Hegel's Philosophy of Right:* Introduction," in *The Marx-Engels Reader*, 2d ed., 16-25.

26. Karl Marx, "Critique of the Gotha Program," in *The Marx-Engels Reader*, 2d ed., 525-541.

27. Karl Marx and Friedrich Engels, "Address to the Central Committee of the Communist League," in *The Marx-Engels Reader*, 2d ed., 501-511.

28. Marx, "Manifesto," 490.

29. Friedrich Engels, *Anti-Duhring* (Moscow: Progress Publishers, 1969), 333.

30. Marx, "Manifesto," 490.

31. Karl Marx, "After the Revolution: Marx Debates Bakunin," in *The Marx-Engels Reader*, 2d ed., 542-548.

32. Robert Saltman, *The Social and Political Thought of Michael Bakunin* (Connecticut: Greenwood Press, 1983), 69.

33. This point of difference is summarized by Engels: "Bakunin maintains that it is the state which has created capital, that the capitalist has his capital *only by the grace of the state*. As, therefore, the state is the chief evil, it is above all the state which must be done away with and then capitalism will go to blazes of itself. We, on the contrary, say: Do away with capital . . . and the state will fall away of itself." See Friedrich Engels, "Versus the Anarchists," in *The Marx-Engels Reader*, 2d. ed., 728-729.

34. Mikhail Bakunin, *Political Philosophy: Scientific Anarchism*, ed. G. P. Maximoff (London: Free Press of Glencoe, 1984), 221.

35. Peter Kropotkin, *The State: Its Historic Role* (London: Freedom Press, 1943), 9.

36. Mikhail Bakunin, *From Out of the Dustbin: Bakunin's Basic Writings 1869-1871*, ed. Robert M. Cutler (Ann Arbor, Mi: Ardis, 1985), 20.

37. Kropotkin, *The State*, 28. Also Bookchin elaborates an anarchist critique of the Marxist conception of the State and its relation to class: "Each State is not necessarily an institutionalized system of violence in the interests of a specific ruling class, as Marxism would have us believe. There are many examples of states that *were* the 'ruling class' and whose interests existed quite apart from—even in antagonism to—privileged, presumably 'ruling' classes in a given society." See Murray Bookchin, *Remaking Society* (Montreal: Black Rose Books, 1989), 67.

38. Alan Carter, "Outline of an Anarchist Theory of History," in *For Anarchism: History, Theory and Practice*, ed. David Goodway (London: Routledge, 1989), 176-197.

39. Bakunin, *Political Philosophy*, 249.

40. Mikhail Bakunin, *On Anarchism*, ed. Sam Dolgoff (Montreal: Black Rose Books, 1980), 336-337.

41. Bakunin, *Marxism, Freedom and the State*, 32.

42. Bakunin, *Political Philosophy*, 228.

43. Mikhail Bakunin, *Selected Writings*, ed. Arthur Lehning (London: Cape, 1973), 169.

44. Marx "Critique of The Gotha Program," in *The Marx-Engels Reader,* 2d ed., 529.

45. Thomas, *Karl Marx and the Anarchists,* 344.

46. Bakunin, *Political Philosophy,* 209.

47. See Bakunin, *From Out of the Dustbin,* 18.

48. Bakunin, *Selected Writings,* 11.

49. Bakunin, *Political Philosophy,* 288.

50. John Clark, *The Anarchist Moment: Reflections on Culture, Nature and Power* (Montreal: Black Rose Books, 1984), 91.

51. This is sometimes quite explicit, as this passage by Engels shows: "A revolution is certainly the most authoritarian thing there is; it is an act whereby one part of the population imposes its will upon the other part by means of rifles, bayonets and cannon, all of which are highly authoritarian means." See Friedrich Engels, "On Authority," in *The Marx-Engels Reader,* 2d ed., 730-733.

52. Marx: "Of all the classes that stand face to face with the bourgeoisie today, the proletariat alone is a really revolutionary class." See Marx, "Manifesto," 481-482.

53. Marx, "Manifesto," 482.

54. Bakunin, *Marxism, Freedom and the State*, 48.

55. Bakunin, *Marxism, Freedom and the State*, 47.

56. Bakunin, *Marxism, Freedom and the State*, 47.

57. Bookchin, *Remaking Society*, 188.

58. Bookchin, *Remaking Society*, 188.

59. Marx, "Manifesto," 484.

60. Bakunin, *Selected Writings*, 266.

61. Clark, *The Anarchist Moment*, 88.

62. Clark, *The Anarchist Moment*, 55.

63. Quoted in Clark, *The Anarchist Moment*, 50.

64. Marx, "Manifesto," 490.

65. Engels, "On Authority," 713.

66. See Peter Kropotkin, *Fields, Factories and Workshops Tomorrow* (London: Allen & Unwin, 1974).

67. Rappaport, "Anarchism and Authority," 343.

68. Rappaport, "Anarchism and Authority," 343.

69. Louis Althusser, *For Marx*, trans. Ben Brewster (London: NLB, 1977), 101.

70. Louis Althusser, "The Object of *Capital*," in *Reading Capital,* eds. Louis Althusser and Etienne Balibar (London: Verso, 1979), 71-198.

71. Alex Callinicos, *Is There A Future for Marxism?* (London: Macmillan Press, 1982), 62-64.

72. Bob Jessop, *State Theory: Putting Capitalist States in their Place.* (Cambridge, U.K.: Polity Press, 1990), 80.

73. Rappaport, "Anarchism and Authority," 343.

74. Michel Foucault, "Power and Strategies," in *Power/Knowledge,* 134-145.

Chapter Two

Anarchism

The previous chapter discussed the anarchist critique of Marxism and introduced an anarchist theory of power. The anarchist critique exposed Marxism's inadequacy in dealing with questions of noneconomic power and authority: by reducing political power to economic power, by seeing the economy as ultimately determining, Marxism has failed to take account of other autonomous sources of power and has thereby neglected their dangers. It has fallen into the trap that power lays for political theory—the ruse of power. It has, in other words, merely reaffirmed the place of power. Anarchism, on the other hand, has, through its confrontation with Marxism, opened the way for a critique of these noneconomic forms of power. By breaking the hold economic determinism had on radical political theory, anarchists have allowed power to be studied in its own right. Anarchism has freed political power from the economic, and this makes it important for political theory. However, anarchism is more than just a critique of Marxism. It is a philosophical system that incorporates theories of power, subjectivity, history, freedom, ethics, and society. This chapter will explore this system in greater depth.

Anarchism is the story of man: his evolution from an animal-like state to a state of freedom and enlightenment, of a rational and ethical existence—in other words, to a state of humanity, in which man can finally see himself as fully human. Concomitant with this is also a critique of power and authority: power exists in an oppressive and antagonistic relationship with man, destroying his relationship with society, and stultifying the development of his rational and moral attributes. Humanity, if it is to flourish, cannot coexist with state power—only one can live. For the Russian anarchist Peter Kropotkin:

> Either the State will be destroyed and a new life will begin in thousands of centers . . . or else the State must crush the individual and local life, it must become master of all domains of human activity, must bring with it wars and internal struggles for the possession of power, surface revolutions which only change one tyrant for another, and inevitably, at the end of this evolution—death.[1]

History, for anarchists, is this struggle between humanity and power.

The Uncontaminated Point of Departure

Natural and Artificial Authority

This struggle can be understood only through the concept of *natural authority* and its opposition to *artificial authority*. Anarchists do not reject all forms of authority as the old cliché would have it. On the contrary, they declare their absolute obedience to the authority embodied, as Mikhail Bakunin argues, in "natural laws." Natural laws are essential to man's existence, according to Bakunin. He believes that they surround us, shape us, and determine the physical world in which we live. One is therefore determined by these laws. There is no escaping this form of authority. The more one tries to resist natural laws, Bakunin argues, the more one finds oneself subjected to them: "Nothing can free him, from their domination; he is their unconditional slave."[2] However, anarchists argue that this is not a form of slavery because these laws are not external to man. They are, on the contrary, what constitute man—they are his essence. Man is constituted in a natural system; he is part of nature and is thus subject to its laws.[3] Man is ..nextricably part of a natural, organic society: "Man did not create society; society existed before Man," claims Kropotkin.[4] Therefore, natural authority [natural laws] is not external to human beings: "those laws are not extrinsic in relation to us, they are inherent in us, they constitute our nature, our whole being physically, intellectually and morally."[5] Natural laws make up human nature according to Bakunin. They determine human essence.

Anarchism is based on a specific notion of human essence. For anarchists there is a human nature with essential characteristics. This human nature is distinguished by two faculties according to Bakunin: "the thinking faculty and the urge to rebel," as well as "free will."[6] Moreover, morality has its basis in human nature, not in any external source: "the idea of justice and good, like all other human things,* must have their root in man's very animality."[7] Furthermore, Bakunin defines this essential, natural human morality as "human respect" by which he means the recognition of "human rights and of human dignity in every man."[8] This notion of human rights is part of anarchism's humanist vocabulary, and provides a standpoint around which a critique of power is based.

For Bakunin, natural authority is fundamentally opposed to "artificial authority." By artificial authority Bakunin means power: the political power enshrined in institutions such as the state and the church and in man-made laws. This external authority exists, says Bakunin, in "pneumatic machines called governments" which, instead of embodying "a natural organic, popular force" were, on the contrary, "entirely mechanical and artificial."[9] This power is external to human nature and an imposition upon it. Moreover, this external power stultifies the development of humanity's innate moral characteristics and intellectual capacities. It is these capacities, the anarchists argue, which will liberate man from slavery and ignorance. For Bakunin, then, political institutions are "hostile and fatal to the liberty of the masses, for they impose upon them a system of external and therefore despotic laws."[10]

In Bakunin's analysis of political authority, power [artificial authority] is external to the human subject. The human subject is oppressed by this outside power, but remains uncontaminated by it because human subjectivity is a creation of a natural, as opposed to a political, system. Anarchism is based on this clear, Manichean division between artificial and natural authority, between power and subjectivity, between state and society. Furthermore, political authority is fundamentally oppressive and destructive of man's potential. For Bakunin, "the State is like a vast slaughterhouse and an enormous cemetery, where under the shadow and the pretext of this abstraction (the common good) all the best aspirations, all the living forces of a country, are sanctimoniously immolated and interred."[11] Human society, argue the anarchists, cannot develop until the institutions and laws which keep it in ignorance and servitude, until the fetters which bind it, are thrown off. Anarchism must, therefore, have a place of resistance: a moral and rational place, a place uncontaminated by the power that oppresses it, from which will spring a rebellion against power. It demands a pure place of revolution, and it finds it in natural essence, in an essential human subjectivity. It is the deep wells of nature and the natural, essential qualities that lie dormant in man that will produce a revolution against power. The innate morality and rationality of man will counteract political power that is seen as inherently irrational and immoral. According to anarchist theory, natural law will replace political authority; man and society will replace the state.

This idea of essential human subjectivity being the pure place of resistance, the uncontaminated point of departure for anarchist revolutionary theory, is problematic: it derives from an Enlightenment humanist framework whose basis will be challenged in subsequent chapters. In particular, anarchism derives from Feuerbachian humanism, which sought to restore man to his rightful place at the center of the philosophical universe. This place had hitherto been usurped by God, to whom man was now subordinated. For Feuerbach, God is an illusion, a hypostatization of man: it is an abstraction upon which man abdicates his good qualities such as love, virtue, and benevolence, thereby alienating himself, and subjecting himself to an authority outside him. This is the ruse of religion, according to Feuerbach: "Thus in religion man denies his reason . . . his own knowledge, his own thoughts, that he may place them in God. Man gives up his personality . . . he denies human dignity, the human ego."[12]

Anarchism applies this logic to political theory. In the same way that man was subjugated under God, he is now subjugated under the state. The state becomes the new wheel upon which man is broken, the new altar upon which human freedom is sacrificed. The principle of religious authority sanctions the principle of political authority. The two forms of logic are fundamentally linked: "We are convinced that theology and politics are both closely related, stemming from the same origin and pursuing the same aim under two different names; we are convinced that every State is a terrestrial Church, just as every Church with its Heaven—the abode of the blessed and the immortal gods—is nothing but a celestial State."[13] Bakunin shows the way in which Christianity's premise of man's original sin justifies state domination.[14] This is the theory of social contract, the Hobbesian paradigm whose basic premise is that man is essentially selfish and egotistical, and that, in a state of nature, his desires necessarily bring him into conflict with others: this is the war of "all against all." The Hobbesian predicament necessitates the creation of a strong state, an absolute power above society, which will arbitrate amongst men, temper their desires, and protect others from their excesses. Anarchism is fundamentally opposed to this theory of the social contract. Anarchists argue, to the contrary, that man has an innate morality and rationality, but that this has been stolen from him, through the artifice of religion, and turned against him. The morality of man has become the morality of the state—the *raison d'état*—and any crime or atrocity carried out by the state is justified by this: "black becomes white and white becomes black, the horrible becomes humane, and the most dastardly felonies and most atrocious crimes become meritorious acts."[15]

Anarchists counter this moral hypocrisy of the state with what they consider to be the simple, natural morality of man. They argue that the true domain of morality and rationality is human essence and natural human society. This is the religion of humanity that Bakunin talks about, and which he says will have to be founded upon the ruins of the religion of divinity.[16] Thus Bakunin calls for humanity to reclaim the moral and rational essence which has become abstracted, through religion, into an external, metaphysical essence—into, as Feuerbach would say, an "essence of nature outside nature; the essence of man outside man."[17] For anarchists, morality is the essence of man. It is innate to human nature, an essential part of human subjectivity. Man must, therefore, re-establish himself as the ground, the place, of morality and rationality. Man must, in other words, seize for himself the category of the divine, the infinite, thereby usurping God. This has always been a motif of Enlightenment humanism, of which anarchism has been its most radical political expression. As Bakunin says: "You are mistaken if you think that I do not believe in God . . . I seek God in man, in human freedom, and now I seek God in Revolution."[18] In this way anarchism establishes the human subject as a pure place of resistance, an uncontaminated point of departure: first, in the sense that humanity becomes the moral and rational standard from which to condemn the immorality and irrationality of the state; and second, in the sense that the natural morality and rationality latent in human nature and human society makes the artificial power of the state unnecessary, as the existence of the state is premised on the theory of man's essential wickedness. Therefore, anarchism can look beyond the state. Because it posits an essential point of departure outside the state, anarchism, unlike Marxism and liberal political theories based on the social contract, is not caught within the paradigm of the state: it is not trapped by the immanent question of what will replace the state if it is destroyed. Anarchism, it seems, has an answer to this.

The question of *what replaces the state?, what replaces power?,* has haunted and continues to haunt radical political theories which have as their eventual goal the overcoming of political power. It is a question that must therefore be addressed. As we have seen in the previous chapter, Marxism was unable to come to terms with this question and ended up reaffirming state power. For the anarchist Kropotkin, all political struggles must have an end in mind: "No destruction of the existing order is possible, if at the time of the overthrow, or of the struggle leading to the overthrow, the idea of what is to take the place of what is destroyed is not always present in the mind."[19]

For Kropotkin, anarchism can think beyond the category of the state, beyond the category of absolute political power, because it has a place, a ground from which to do so. Political power, according to this anarchist logic, has an outside from which it can be criticized and an alternative with which it can be replaced. This is precisely the proposition that will be questioned. However, anarchism is based on a radical picture of human nature and human society. Kropotkin is thus able to envisage a society in which the state no longer exists, nor is needed; a society "in which all mutual relations of its members are regulated, not by laws, not by authorities, whether self-imposed or elected, but by mutual agreements between members of that society."[20] Such a society is possible, according to anarchists, because of the fundamental morality, goodness, and cooperativeness latent in human nature.[21]

Mutual Aid: Anarchist Morality

For anarchists, then, man is born with essential moral and rational capacities and it is this potential which Kropotkin sets out to explore in his study, *Ethics*. Kropotkin argues that to discover the true basis of morality one must apply scientific learning to it: morality must be studied as a science so that it can be freed from metaphysical superstition.[22] Kropotkin argues that it was Darwin who first discovered an instinctive sociability in animals, a "permanent instinct" found in most animals, particularly in humans.[23] This instinct Kropotkin calls mutual aid, the instinct of cooperation amongst species.[24] Thus, Kropotkin argues that "Mutual aid is the predominant fact of Nature."[25] This, however, puts him at odds with various social Darwinists who, Kropotkin argues, misappropriate Darwin to support their claim that warfare and selfish competition—"survival of the fittest"—are the natural condition of animal and human society. For Kropotkin, on the contrary, mutual aid does not run against the principle of self-preservation; rather it is its most effective weapon.[26]

Kropotkin applies these arguments to human society. He argues that the natural and essential principle of human society is mutual aid, and that man is naturally cooperative, sociable, and altruistic, rather than competitive and egotistic. This is the principle that naturally governs society, and it is out of this organic principle that notions of morality, justice, and ethics grow. Morality, Kropotkin argues, evolves out of the instinctive need to band together in tribes, groups—and an instinctive tendency towards cooperation and mutual assistance. As Kropotkin says then: "Nature has thus to be recognized as the *first ethical teacher of man*. The social instinct innate in men as well as in all the social animals—this is the origin of all ethical conceptions and all the subsequent development of morality."[27]

Kropotkin concludes, then, that morality has its basis in nature, in the instinctive principle of mutual aid and competition. Every individual, Kropotkin argues, has this capacity, even criminals. In his study on the prison system, he argues that it is the brutality of prisons that breeds crime: "Prisons are the nurseries for the most revolting category of breaches of moral law."[28] Crime, he argues, is environmental: it is socially created, not a natural condition. He calls, therefore, for crime to be treated not as an evil, but as a disease, a physical defect, something which can be treated scientifically and cured through "moral hygiene."[29] Kropotkin's ideas on crime and punishment might seem somewhat antiquated. However, as we shall see from Stirner and Foucault in subsequent chapters, this humanistic treatment of crime has had an impact on modern systems of punishment and criminology, and this highlights the political problem of humanist power today.[30] Moreover, as Stirner and Foucault will argue, the treatment of crime as a disease to be cured is merely a reapplication in a new guise, no matter how well intended, of moral domination over a deviant form of behavior.

For Kropotkin, however, crime could be more or less abolished by appealing to a sense of humanity within the individual, by appealing to one's instinctive morality and sociability. This natural sociability, this capacity for mutual aid is, according to Kropotkin, the principle whose evolution drives society. It binds society together, providing a common basis upon which daily life can be conducted. Society, anarchists argue, thus has no need for the state: it has its own regulating mechanisms, its own natural laws. State domination only poisons society and destroys its natural mechanisms. The anarchist William Godwin, who also believed in mutual assistance, said of governments: "They lay their hand on the spring there is in society, and put a stop to its motion."[31] Mutual assistance is the "spring there is in society," and it will become the basis upon which society is organized once the state is abolished. It is therefore the principle of mutual aid that will naturally replace the principle of political authority. A state of "anarchy," a war of "all against all" will not ensue the moment state power has been abolished. This is the hackneyed, old bugbear that has always been laid at the door of anarchism. For anarchists, a state of "anarchy" exists *now*: political power creates social dislocation, it does not prevent it. What is prevented by the state is the natural and harmonious functioning of society.

The Social Contract

Anarchist political philosophy is, therefore, based on an essentially optimistic conception of human nature: if individuals can have a natural tendency to get on well together, then there is no need for the existence of a state to arbitrate between them. On the contrary, the state actually has a pernicious effect on these natural social relations. Anarchists reject political theories based on the notion of the social contract. Hobbesian theories of the social contract rely on a singularly negative picture of human nature. They argue that individuals are naturally selfish, aggressively competitive, and egotistic and that in a state of nature they are engaged in a war of "every man, against every man" in which their individual drives necessarily bring them into conflict with one another.[32] Let us call this, for the moment, the *conflict model* of society, as opposed to the *harmony model* of society which anarchists propound. The two models would appear to be diagrammatically opposed. According to the social contract theory, society, in a state of nature, is characterized by a radical dislocation: there is no common bond between individuals; there is in fact a perpetual state of war between them, a constant struggle for resources.[33] Society is therefore characterized by a lack—a lack of social order, an absence of any kind of authority or even common social ground upon which it can be built. There is no *place* for authority. In order to put a stop to this state of permanent war, individuals come together to form a social contract upon which some kind of authority can be established. They agree to sacrifice at least part of their freedom in return for some kind of order, so that they can pursue their own individual ends more peacefully and, therefore, more profitably. They agree on the creation of a state with a mandate over society, which shall arbitrate between conflicting wills and enforce a state of peace and order. This would heal the rift in society—the lack that rends society apart.

The extent of the state's authority may vary from the liberal state whose power is supposedly tempered by the rule of law, to the absolute state power—the Leviathan dreamed up by Hobbes. While the models may vary, however, anarchists argue that the result of this social contract theory is the same: a justification of state domination, whether it be through the rule of law or through an arbitrary imposition of force. For anarchists, any form of state power is an arbitrary imposition of force. Bakunin argues, then, that the social contract theory is a fiction, a sleight of hand that legitimates political domination:

> A tacit contract! That is to say, a wordless and consequently a thoughtless and will-less contract! A revolting nonsense! An absurd fiction, and what is more— a wicked fiction! An unworthy hoax! For it presupposes that while I was in a state of not being able to will, to think, to speak, I bound myself and my descendants—simply by reason of having let myself be victimized without any protest—into perpetual slavery.[34]

Bakunin points out here the essential paradox in the theory of the social contract: if, in a state of nature, individuals subsist in a state of primitive savagery, then how can they suddenly have the foresight to come together and create a social contract? If there is no common bond in society, no essence within humans which brings them together, then upon what basis can a social contract be formed? Anarchists argue that there is no such agreement, that the state was imposed from above, not from below, by various elites that formed in society. The social contract tries to mystify the brutal origins of the state: war, conquest, and self enslavement, rather than rational agreement. The state, says Kropotkin, was imposed by force, not created freely and consensually by society. The state is based on violence: it is a disruption of, and an imposition upon, a harmoniously functioning, organic society.[35] Society has no need for a social contract. It has its own contract with nature, governed by natural laws: "Society is the natural mode of existence of the human collective, and is independent of any contract. It is governed by customs or traditional usages and never by laws . . . There are many laws which govern society . . . but those are natural laws, inherent in the social body, just as physical laws are inherent in material bodies."[36]

Libertarianism

There is an interesting parallel that could be drawn here between anarchism and libertarianism, even the right wing kind that rejects any state intervention in the economy. Both anarchism and libertarianism amount to an absolute rejection of the state and any form of social contract theory that leads to a justification of the state. Anarchists and libertarians both argue that all forms of political authority and coercion are an unfair burden upon the freedom of the individual and should therefore be resisted. They both view the state as a parasitic institution preying on society and disrupting its natural harmony. Stephen L. Newman sums up the libertarian view point:

> Libertarianism is distinguished by its extreme hostility toward political power and its refusal to consider public interest as anything but a cruel hoax. Libertarians define political power as coercion or the threat of coercion. To exercise political power, then, is to employ the coercive potential of the state against the citizenry . . . by implication, political power is incompatible with liberty.[37]

Libertarianism begins to sound like pure anarchism, and while there are important differences—anarchism emphasizes free collectivism, while libertarianism emphasizes the individual and free markets—it is clear that the two theories converge in a fundamental rejection of political power and in the view that society has an essential harmony which political power stultifies. Both theories are informed, then, by a Manichean logic that opposes the natural authority of society to the "artificial" authority of political power. It could be argued that they are based on the essential liberal division between society and the state, the division which both Hegel and Marx, in their own ways, tried to overcome. However, both anarchism and libertarianism would reject social contract theories that see the state as a necessary antidote to the rapacious conflict of the state of nature: they see this argument as highly fraudulent. They reverse the Hobbesian paradigm, seeing individuals as essentially cooperative, and this leads to the conclusion that rather than the state being a necessary institution which protects the individual—as Hobbes would argue—it actually constitutes a threat to the individual. So both anarchism and libertarianism have an essentially positive view of human nature, and a great faith in the ability of people to interact with each other without the interference of the state.

Now while it might seem curious that we are bringing together a generally left wing, and a generally right wing, theory in this way, it is apparent that there are definite parallels which could perhaps be addressed. This proximity of libertarianism to anarchism suggests that there are other directions this discussion can take. Philosophies like anarchism [and, as we will see later on, poststructuralism] which seek to challenge power and authority, and maximize personal freedom, do not fit into such neat little political categories. As I suggested before, the political implications of these ideas cannot be contained within the boundaries originally laid down for them and often overlap with philosophies like libertarianism. So perhaps libertarianism may be seen as the dangerous excess of the critique of authority: an antistate philosophy which is logically linked to anarchism, and indeed poststructuralism, and which continually haunts these discourses.

So anarchists [and indeed libertarians] argue that the social contract theory is a fiction, moreover a dangerous fiction. The interesting thing is, however, that the social contract was never intended to be anything other than a fiction. Let us look more closely at Hobbes. He paints a picture of the state of nature as being characterized by a "continual fear and danger of violent death."[38] However, for Hobbes the "state of nature" was not an actual historical situation, but rather a hypothetical situation that could exist given the predisposition of human nature.[39] In other words, it is a picture of what society would be like without government: "Where there is no common power, there is no law: where no law, no injustice."[40] It is, in other words, a polemic model invented by Hobbes to justify the existence of the state. It is merely an attempt to construct a legitimate ground for the state, to ground it in law, consensus, and contract. A legitimate ground for political power must be constructed because none exists—there is no legitimate place of power in the state of nature. Paradoxically, then, Hobbes shares with the anarchists one crucial point: the recognition that the state is based on a fiction and it has no absolute, legitimate ground in society. Hobbes does not try to shroud the state in ideals such as divine right, patriotism, religion, or morality. He does not glorify the state or make it sacred.[41] There is no covenant with God but rather with an earthly sovereign.[42] Nor does the state exist at the behest of the nobility: everyone is equally subjected under the Leviathan.[43] The Leviathan exists for purely pragmatic reasons—the suppression of violence and disorder—and there is no justification for the state beyond this. In other words, with Hobbes, there is no attempt to see the state as anything other than it is—pure power.

While *The Leviathan* is a justification of the state, it is, at the same time, an *unmasking* of the state. This is the point at which Hobbesian state theory converges with anarchist political philosophy. Both theories—while they start from different premises and while they support different solutions—point to one thing: the arbitrariness of the state, the arbitrariness of power. Both theories, in opposite ways, show the absence of any absolute ground for power.

In Hobbes' case, absolute political power is based on a lack, on the absence of any kind of social order. Hobbes sought to impose some kind of order upon society, hence the Leviathan. This absolute power, however, does not have any positive content. It is justified in purely negative terms, as putting a stop to disorder. This is because, as Ernesto Laclau and Lilian Zac suggest, the other of power, according to this Hobbesian logic, is disorder, and hence, power becomes legitimate in itself, independent of its actual content.[44] For Hobbes, the political content of the state is unimportant as long as it quells unrest in society. Whether there be a democracy, or a sovereign assembly, or a monarchy, it does not matter: "the power in all forms, if they be perfect enough to protect them, is the same."[45] Like the anarchists, Hobbes believes that the guise taken by power is irrelevant. Behind every mask there must be a pure, absolute power. Hobbes' political thought is centered around a desire for order, purely as an antidote to disorder. And for Hobbes, the extent to which individuals suffer under this order is incomparable to the suffering caused by war.[46]

For Hobbes, then, state sovereignty is a necessary evil. There is no attempt to make a fetish of the state: it does not descend from heaven, preordained by divine will. It is pure sovereignty, pure power, and it is constructed out of the emptiness of society, precisely in order to prevent the warfare immanent in the state of nature. For anarchists, on the other hand, the state is an *unnecessary* evil. Rather than preventing perpetual warfare between men, the state engenders it: the state is based on war of conquest, rather than embodying its resolution. Therefore, while anarchists share with Hobbes certain perspectives on state power, they disagree fundamentally on this one point: whether the natural state of man and society is one of sociability and potential harmony—thus making the state unnecessary and harmful—as the anarchists argue; or whether it is a state of constant warfare engendered by man's untempered desires and selfishness—thus making the state absolutely necessary—as Hobbes argues. Anarchism can reject the state because it argues from the perspective of an essential place—natural human society—and the morality and rationality immanent within it. It can, therefore, conceive of an alternative to the state. Hobbes, on the other hand, has no such point of departure: there is no standpoint that can act as an alternative to the state. Society, as we have seen with Hobbes, is characterized by rift, antagonism, and war. In fact, there is no essential society to speak of—it is an empty place. Society must therefore be constructed artificially in the shape of the absolute state. While anarchism can rely on natural law, Hobbes can only rely on the law of the state. At the heart of the anarchist paradigm there is the essential fullness of society, while at the heart of the Hobbesian paradigm there is nothing but emptiness and dislocation.

However it might be argued that anarchism is a mirror image of Hobbesianism in the sense that they both posit a commonality that derives from their indebtedness to the Enlightenment. They both emphasize the need for a fullness or sociality, some legitimate place of authority around which society can be organized. Anarchists see this place in the natural law which informs society and human subjectivity, and which is impeded by the state. Hobbes, on the other hand, sees this place as an absence, an empty place that must be filled by the state. In other words, the authority which anarchists see as naturally occurring does not exist for Hobbes, and must therefore be artificially created.

Hobbes' thought is caught within the paradigm of the state. The state is made necessary by the constant threat of the warfare and dislocation that will reign supreme without it. The state is the absolute conceptual limit, outside of which are the perils of the state of nature. Liberal political theories based on the social contract are haunted by the little argument that says: "if you get rid of the state then society will revert back to a state of nature." Anarchism, on the other hand, because it proceeds from the *harmony model* of society, claims to be able to transcend this quandary. But can it? Anarchism operates within a Manichean political logic: it creates an essential, moral opposition between society and the state, between humanity and power. Natural law is diagrammatically opposed to artificial power; the morality and rationality immanent in natural human society comes into conflict with the fundamental irrationality and immorality of the state.

Manicheism

With anarchism, as we have seen, there is an essential antithesis between the pure, uncontaminated place of resistance—constituted by essential human subjectivity and natural human society—and the place of power. Jacques Donzelot argues that this Manichean logic is endemic to radical political theory: "Political culture is also the systematic pursuit of an antagonism between two essences, the tracing of a line of demarcation between two principles, two levels of reality which are easily placed in opposition. There is no political culture that is not Manichean."[47]

Moreover, anarchism, in subscribing to this logic, and making power the focus of its analysis, instead of economics as Marxism did, has perhaps fallen into the same trap as Marxism. Has it not merely replaced the economy with the state as the essential evil in society, from which other evils are derived? As Donzelot argues:

> No sooner has one decided on good or bad grounds—no matter which—that capitalism is not the unique or even principle source of evil on earth that one rushes to substitute for the opposition between capital and labor that between State and civil society. Capital, as foil and scapegoat, is replaced by the State, that cold monster whose limitless growth 'pauperizes' social life; and the proletariat gives way to civil society, that is to say to everything capable of resisting the blind rationality of the State, to everything that opposes it at the level of customs, *mores*, a living sociability, sought in the residual margins of society and promoted to the status of motor of history.[48]

Can we not see, then, that by pitting "living sociability" against the state, in the same way that Marxism pitted the proletariat against capitalism, anarchism shows, perhaps, that it has been unable to transcend the traditional political categories which bound Marxism? As Donzelot argues, Manicheism is the logic that skewers all these theories: it is the undercurrent that runs through them and circumscribes them. It does not matter if the target is the state, or capital, or anything else; as long as there is an enemy to destroy and a subject who will destroy it; as long as there is the promise of the final battle and final victory. Manichean logic is, therefore, the logic of place: there must be an essential place of power and an essential place of resistance—the point of departure from which issues forth the revolution against power. This is the binary, dialectical logic that pervades anarchism: the place of power—the state—must be overthrown by the pure subject of resistance, the essential human subject. Has not anarchism merely fallen prey to the logic of place? By replacing the economy with the state as the privileged point of analysis and the primary evil in society, has it not failed to dismantle the very logic of place? Has it not, in other words, fallen into the same reductionist trap as Marxism?

The Manichean logic of place, moreover, involves a reverse mirroring operation: the place of resistance is a reflection, in reverse, of the place of power. In the case of anarchism, human subjectivity is essentially moral and rational, while the state is essentially immoral and irrational. According to Bakunin: "The State never had and never will have any morality . . . The State is the complete negation of humanity, a double negation: the opposite of human freedom and justice, and the violent breach of the solidarity of the human race."[49]

Can we not see, then, that in anarchist discourse the state is essential to the existence of the revolutionary subject, just as the revolutionary subject is essential to the existence of the state? The place of resistance depends upon the place of power, and vice versa. One defines itself in opposition to the other. The purity of revolutionary identity is only defined in contrast to the impurity of political power. Revolt against the state is always prompted by the state. As Bakunin argues: "there is something in the nature of the state which provokes rebellion."[50] While the relationship between the state and the revolutionary subject is one of clearly defined opposition, the two antagonists could not exist outside this relationship. They could not, in other words, exist without each other.

Nietzsche would call this a relationship of *ressentiment*: "this need to direct one's view outward instead of back to oneself—is the essence of ressentiment: in order to exist, slave morality always first needs a hostile external world; it needs, physiologically speaking, external stimuli in order to act at all—its action is fundamentally reaction."[51] Nietzsche sees this outlook as distinctly unhealthy, emanating from a position of weakness and sickness. Moreover, Nietzsche talks of "anarchists" as the ones who are permeated with this morality of the slave. While this is perhaps rather unfair of Nietzsche, it does point to a certain tenet of ressentiment within Manichean philosophies such as anarchism. Pure revolutionary identity in anarchist philosophy is constituted through its essential opposition to power. However, like the "reactive man" that Nietzsche speaks of, revolutionary identity purports to be unpolluted by power: human essence is seen as moral where power is immoral, natural where power is artificial, pure where power is impure.

The Power Principle

Anarchism is based around this notion of the purity of the revolutionary identity. Human essence and natural human society is anarchism's uncontaminated point of departure, the pure place of resistance that will overcome power.

Because, as I have indicated, this subjectivity is constituted within a system of natural law—as opposed to artificial law—it is a point which, while it is oppressed by power, remains outside power and unpolluted by it. But is it? Bakunin himself throws some doubt on this when he talks about the "power principle." This is the natural lust for power which, Bakunin argues, is innate in every individual: "Every man carries within himself the germs of the lust for power, and every germ, as we know, because of a basic law of life, necessarily must develop and grow."[52] He says, moreover, that: "the instinct to command others, in its primitive essence, is a carnivorous, altogether bestial and savage instinct—it is this principle alone that has produced all the misfortunes, all the crimes, and the most shameful facts of history."[53]

The *power principle* means that man cannot be trusted with power, that there will always be this desire for power at the heart of human subjectivity. While Bakunin intended to warn others of the corrupting danger inherent in power, he has perhaps unconsciously exposed the hidden contradiction that lies at the heart of anarchist discourse: namely that, while anarchism bases itself upon a notion of an essential human subjectivity uncontaminated by power, this subjectivity is impossible to achieve. The idea of a pure revolutionary identity is torn apart, subverted by a "natural" desire for power, by the lack which is at the heart of every individual. Bakunin indicates that this lack, this desire for power is an essential part of human subjectivity. Perhaps the implication of Bakunin's power principle is that the subject will always have a desire for power, and that the subject will be incomplete until it grasps power. Kropotkin, too, talks about the desire for power and authority. He argues that the rise of the modern state can be attributed in part to the fact that "men became enamoured of authority."[54] He implies, then, that state power is not completely an imposition from above. He talks about self-enslavement to law and authority: "Man allowed himself to be enslaved far more by his desire to 'punish according to law' than by direct military conquest."[55] Does the desire to "punish according to law" grow directly out of humanity's natural sense of morality? Can human essence still be seen, then, as unpolluted by power, as an uncontaminated point of departure? While anarchism's notion of subjectivity is not totally dismantled by this contradiction, it is nevertheless destabilized by it: it is made somewhat ambiguous, incomplete, open to question. Subjectivity is constituted by lack and desire—the desire for power—and this makes it unstable and dangerous. The place of resistance is in danger of becoming *dis-placed*.

The possibility, then, that the place of resistance is unstable and not completely constituted, forces one to question anarchism's notion of a revolution of humanity against power. If, as Bakunin and Kropotkin argue, humans have an essential desire for power, then how can one be sure that a revolution aimed at destroying power will not turn into a revolution aimed at capturing power? How can one be sure, in other words, that an anarchist revolution will be any different from a Marxist vanguard revolution?

The War Model

Another implication of the instability of the place of resistance is that it opens the possibility for an alternate conception of social relations. Anarchism, as I argued, rejects the traditional Hobbesian "state of nature" model in favor of the harmony model of social relations. The social harmony model has now, however, been thrown into uncertainty: while individuals are naturally moral and sociable, and while society is, therefore, essentially harmonious, individuals also have a dark side—an insatiable desire for power and authority—which jeopardizes this harmony. This apparent contradiction does not mean that the harmony model of social relations should be rejected out of hand. It does, however, cast some doubt on it and forces us to consider other ways of approaching the problem.

This need to question the social harmony model is not prompted by the charge of naiveté: the harmony model of human relations, which claims that humans are essentially sociable and altruistic, is no more unrealistic than the Hobbesian model, which claims that individuals are essentially selfish and competitive. They are the two sides of the same idealist coin—in a sense, they are mirror images of each other. However, what if we were to apply the Hobbesian conflict model to social relations? What if we were to take this model, not in the sense of its essentialist assumptions about human nature, but rather in the sense of its use of war as a metaphor for social relations? The *war model* sees social relations as characterized by constant antagonism, rift, and dislocation. However, one does not use "war" here in the way that Hobbes meant, to describe a state of nature in which individuals are constantly at war with one another. I use it here, rather, to attack this very essentialist notion of society. The war model can perhaps be used against Hobbes, to reject the very idea of "society" as a concept, or at least the idea of there being an essence in society. Perhaps society should be seen as an empty place, an unstable, incomplete identity, characterized by constant antagonism, and consequently, open to continual reinterpretation.

This refers to the Nietzschean idea of war as being the struggle of values and representations. Social reality, according to Nietzsche, is not governed by the evolution of natural law as anarchists argue, but by a constant struggle of a multitude of forces which inscribe themselves in law. Even natural law is an interpretation of force and conquest. Nietzsche says then:

> whatever exists, having somehow come into being, is again and again reinterpreted to new ends, taken over, transformed, and redirected by some power superior to it; all events in the organic world are a subduing, a *becoming master*, and an all subduing and becoming master involves a fresh interpretation, an adaptation through which any previous "meaning" and "purpose" are necessarily obscured or even obliterated.[56]

According to this, society itself can have no stable meaning—no origin, and no grand dialectical movement towards a conclusion—because meaning itself is open to continual change and reinterpretation. This calls into question both anarchism *and* Hobbesianism because they both envisage a complete society, free from conflict and antagonism. As I will argue in later chapters, particularly with reference to Lacan, identity—social or individual—can never be completely constituted: it is always grounded in a lack [which Bakunin has perhaps unintentionally exposed], preventing it from achieving fullness. It is always limited by rift and antagonism. As Nietzsche would argue, no society can be free of antagonism and conflict because antagonism and conflict are, in a sense, all society consists of. The very notion of society is based on the conquest and unstable domination of certain forces over others. Hobbes, for instance, sees the rule of law as suppressing hostilities. However, law, as Nietzsche argues, is a continuation of struggle, not a halt to it: "A legal order thought of as sovereign and universal, not as a means in the struggle between power complexes, but as a means of preventing all struggle in general would be a principle *hostile to life.*"[57]

Life, for Nietzsche, is the recognition and acceptance of struggle: the acceptance that there are no fixed meanings, essences, or stable identities. At the base of these is always a conflict of forces making them inherently unstable and open to reinterpretation. Apollo is always haunted by Dionysius. Apollo is the god of light, but also the god of illusion: he "grants repose to individual beings . . . by drawing boundaries around them." Dionysius, on the other hand is the force that occasionally destroys these "little circles," disrupting the Apollonian tendency to "congeal the form to Egyptian rigidity and coldness."[58] Society is the illusion, perhaps, that hides the struggle and antagonism behind the scenes— behind the "veil of the *maya.*"[59] War is the reality: the dark, turgid, violent struggle of silent forces; the conflict of the multitude of representations which are precariously held in check by notions such as human essence, morality, rationality, and natural law. The "instinct for power," for instance, is the dark, volatile force which threatens the purity and stability of the anarchist subject. The subject who pits himself against power is the same subject who secretly lusts after power. His identity is therefore precarious.

The war model, or the "genealogical" model as Nietzsche would see it, unmasks rift behind closure, discord behind harmony, war behind peace. It has revealed the emptiness at the heart of place. Anarchism relies on essence: on the notion of an essential, natural human subjectivity; on there being a natural essence in social relations that will be able to take the place of the state, the place of power. This idea of essence constitutes anarchism's point of departure, its place of resistance which is uncontaminated by power. The war model, however, jeopardizes this idea of essence: it claims that essence itself is merely a temporary and precarious domination of certain forces over others, and there is nothing transcendental or permanent about it. Max Stirner continues this assault on the idea of an essential place. He will apply the war model, in his own way, to show that the notion of human essence constituting a pure revolutionary identity is not only dubious, but that its continued use in radical political philosophy is immanently dangerous. This will be the subject of the next chapter.

Notes

1. Kropotkin, *The State,* 44.

2. Bakunin, *Political Philosophy,* 239.

3. Bakunin, *Political Philosophy,* 239.

4. Kropotkin, *The State,* 12.

5. Bakunin, *Political Philosophy,* 239.

6. Bakunin, *Political Philosophy,* 84.

7. Bakunin, *Political Philosophy,* 121.

8. Bakunin, *Political Philosophy,* 147.

9. Bakunin, *Political Philosophy,* 212.

10. Bakunin, *Political Philosophy,* 240.

11. Bakunin, *Political Philosophy,* 207.

12. Ludwig Feuerbach, *The Essence of Christianity,* trans. G. Eliot (New York: Harper), 27-28.

13. Bakunin, *Political Philosophy,* 143-144.

14. Bakunin says: "The State, then, like the Church, starts with this fundamental assumption that all men are essentially bad and that when left to their natural liberty they will tear one another apart and will offer the specter of the most frightful anarchy wherein the strongest will kill or exploit the weaker ones." See Bakunin, *Political Philosophy,* 144.

15. Bakunin, *Political Philosophy,* 141.

16. Bakunin, *Political Philosophy,* 142.

17. Ludwig Feuerbach, *The Fiery Brook: Selected Writings of Ludwig Feuerbach,* trans. and ed. Zawar Hanfi (New York: Anchor, 1972), 157.

18. Quoted in Eugene Pyziur, *The Doctrine of Anarchism of Michael A. Bakunin* (Milwaukee, Wis.: The Marquette University Press, 1955.

19. Peter Kropotkin, *Revolutionary Pamphlets,* ed. Roger N. Baldwin (New York: Benjamin Blom, 1968), 156-157.

20. Kropotkin, *Revolutionary Pamphlets,* 157.

21. As Bakunin says: "The moral law . . . is indeed an actual law, which will triumph over all the conspiracies of all the idealists of the world, because it emanates from the very nature of human society, the root basis of which is to be sought not in God but in animality." See Bakunin, *Political Philosophy,* 156.

22. Peter Kropotkin, *Ethics: Origin and Development,* trans. L. S. Friedland (New York: Tudor Publishing, 1947), 5.

23. Kropotkin, *Ethics,* 15.

24. Kropotkin, *Ethics,* 14.

25. Kropotkin, *Ethics,* 14.

26. Kropotkin, *Ethics,* 14.

27. Kropotkin, *Ethics,* 45.

28. Peter Kropotkin, *In Russian and French Prisons* (London: Ward & Downey, 1887), 336.

29. Kropotkin, *In Russian and French Prisons,* 338.

30. Larry Tifft and Louis Stevenson argue for a reappraisal of Kropotkin's ideas and their possible application for criminology today. See "Humanistic Criminology: Roots from Peter Kropotkin," *Journal of Sociology and Social Welfare* 12, no. 3 (September 1985), 488-520.

31. William Godwin, *Anarchist Writings,* ed. Peter Marshall (London: Freedom Press, 1968), 92.

32. Thomas Hobbes, *Leviathan* (Oxford: Basil Blackwell, 1947), 83.

33. To quote Hobbes, life is "solitary, poor, nasty, brutish and short." See Hobbes, *Leviathan*, 82.

34. Bakunin, *Political Philosophy,* 165.

35. Kropotkin, *The State,* 37.

36. Bakunin, *Political Philosophy,* 166.

37. Newman, *Liberalism at Wit's End,* 41.

38. Hobbes, *Leviathan*, 82.

39. April Carter, *The Political Theory of Anarchism* (London: Routledge & Kegan Paul), 14.

40. Hobbes, *Leviathan*, 83.

41. Carter, *The Political Theory of Anarchism*, 20.

42. Hobbes, *Leviathan*, 114.

43. Hobbes, *Leviathan*, 120.

44. Ernesto Laclau and Lilian Zac, "Minding the Gap: The Subject of Politics," in *The Making of Political Identities*, 11-39.

45. Hobbes, *Leviathan*, 120.

46. Hobbes: "not considering that the state of man can never be without some incommodity or other; and that the greatest, that in any form of government can possibly happen to the people in general, is scarce sensible in respect of the miseries, and horrible calamities, that accompany a civil war, or that dissolute condition of masterless men, without subjection to laws, and a coercive power to tie their hands from rapine and revenge." See *Leviathan*, 120.

47. Jacques Donzelot, "The Poverty of Political Culture," *Ideology and Consciousness* 5 (Spring 1979): 73-86.

48. Donzelot, "The Poverty of Political Culture," 74.

49. Bakunin, *Political Philosophy,* 224.

50. Bakunin, *Political Philosophy,* 145.

51. Friedrich Nietzsche, *On the Genealogy of Morals,* ed. and trans. Walter Kaufmann (New York: Vintage Books, 1989), 36-37.

52. Bakunin, *Political Philosophy*, 248.

53. Bakunin, *Political Philosophy*, 248.

54. Kropotkin, *The State,* 28.

55. Kropotkin, *The State,* 17.

56. Nietzsche, *On The Genealogy of Morals,* 77.

57. Nietzsche, *On The Genealogy of Morals,* 76.

58. Friedrich Nietzsche, *Birth of Tragedy, and The Case of Wagner,* trans. W. Kaufmann (New York: Vintage Books, 1967), 72.

59. The "veil of the *maya*" is the illusion that Apollo wraps man in to protect him from the harsh reality of existence. See Allan Megill, *Prophets of Extremity: Nietzsche, Heidegger, Foucault, Derrida* (Berkeley: University of California Press, 1985), 39.

Chapter Three

Stirner and the Politics of the Ego

"Man is the God of to-day, and fear of Man has taken the place of the old fear of God." [1]

The previous chapter suggested that anarchism, like Marxism, had fallen victim to a theoretical ruse: instead of seeing the principal source of oppression in society in capitalism, as Marxism did, anarchism saw oppression emanating mostly from the state. Both fell victim, therefore, to a reductionist logic— Marxism fell into the trap of economism, while anarchism fell into the trap of *statism.* This still leaves the problem of power unanswered. Moreover, in the last chapter we found that anarchism relies on an uncontaminated point of departure, a place of pure resistance that will overthrow state power. However, as we have seen, this pure place, embodied in human essence, is possibly unstable and open to the temptation of power. Anarchism, therefore, cannot achieve a complete theoretical closure, and this leaves it open to various theoretical interventions. This chapter will look at one possible intervention— that of Stirner. It will use his ideas to explore this opening left by anarchism.

Anarchism, like Marxism, has failed to grasp two fundamental problems: the problem of power, and the problem of place. Anarchism remains buried within an Enlightenment political paradigm that is inadequate for dealing with questions of power today. Perhaps what is needed is a rethinking of the relationship between power and the subject. This is where the work of Max Stirner comes in. Although writing in the nineteenth century, he presents us with a critique of modern forms of power, particularly ideology. His book *The Ego and His Own* [*Der Einzige und sein Eigenthum*] shows the way in which ideas can become, in themselves, a form of domination—a proposal which was never fully grasped by either traditional anarchist or Marxist theory. He discovers a new arena of power, going beyond the epistemological categories that bound both Marxism and anarchism. Perhaps the most important question for Stirner was not how power comes to dominate us, but why we allow power to dominate us—why we willingly participate in our own domination. These were problems that neither anarchism nor classical Marxism could address. Above all, Stirner was concerned with the problem of place, the problem which has plagued radical political theory: how can one be sure that in acting against a particular form of power one does not merely put another in its place? Stirner argues that humanist philosophies such as anarchism fall very neatly into this dialectic which constantly reproduces power. Like poststructuralist thinkers who were writing over a century later, Stirner is troubled by the whole question of essentialism. I argue that he uses a war model of relations, like the one constructed in the previous chapter, to untangle the modern bind of power, identity, and essence, and to unmask the domination and antagonism behind its serene humanist veneer. It is for this reason that Stirner is relevant to our analysis: he represents a decisive break with the Enlightenment rationality that informed Marxism and anarchism, placing himself within an altogether different problematic—one which anticipates, as we shall see, poststructuralism.[2]

Stirner, like Nietzsche who was clearly influenced by him, has been interpreted in many different ways.[3] One possible interpretation of Stirner is that he is an anarchist. Indeed, he has much in common with the anarchist position—particularly in his rejection of the state and political authority. Stirner argues that the state is an apparatus that denies the individual the right of self-realization, the expression of his value: "The State does not let me come to my value, and continues to exist only through my valuelessness."[4] It is a despotism wielded over the individual: "The State always has the sole purpose to limit, tame, subordinate, the individual—to make him subject to some generality or other."[5] For Stirner, the state is the new church—the new place of power, the new authority wielded over the individual. Moreover, it operates through the same moral hypocrisy—now shrouded in legal codes.[6] Stirner, therefore, displays an anti-authoritarianism that shares much with anarchism. He wants to lay bare the vicious, oppressive nature of political power: to unmask its underlying morality that might is right, and to examine its effect—to stultify and alienate the individual, instilling in him a dependence on the state.

Rejection of the State

Like the anarchists, moreover, Stirner attacks state power itself—the very category or place of the state—not just the different forms that it assumes. What must be destroyed is the "ruling principle."[7] Stirner is therefore against revolutionary programs, such as Marxism, which have as their aim the *seizure* of state power. He shares anarchism's distrust of the Marxist workers' state: it would just be a reaffirmation of the state in a different guise—a "change of masters."[8] Stirner suggests, then, that: "war might rather be declared against the establishment itself, the *State*, not a particular State, not any such thing as the mere condition of the State at the time; it is not another State (such as a 'people's State') that men aim at."[9]

Revolutionary action has been trapped, according to Stirner, by the paradigm of the state—it has remained caught within the dialectic of place. Revolutions have only succeeded in replacing one form of authority with another. This is because, as Stirner argues, they do not question the very condition, the category, the *idea* of state authority and, therefore, remain within its hold.[10] The state can never be reformed, Stirner argues, because it can never be trusted and this is why the place of power itself must be destroyed. Stirner rejects Bruno Bauer's notion of a democratic state which grows out of the "power of the people" and which is always subordinated to the people. For Stirner, the state can never really be brought under the control of people—it always has its own logic, and it will soon turn against the will of the people.[11]

Stirner's notion of the state put him at odds with Marxism. Stirner, like the anarchists, believed that the state was an independent entity. This is particularly so in its relation to economic power. Stirner analyzes *noneconomic* forms of repression, and he believes that the state, if it is to be fully understood, must be considered independently of economic arrangements. The power of bureaucracy, for instance, constitutes a noneconomic form of oppression: its operation cannot be reduced to the workings of the economy.[12] This is contrary to the Marxist position, which, I have argued, sees the state as largely reducible to the workings of the capitalist economy and subject to the interests of the bourgeoisie. Stirner suggests, for instance, that while the state protects private property and the interests of the bourgeoisie, it also stands above them and dominates them.[13] For Stirner, as with the anarchists, the political power enshrined in the state has predominance over economic power and its related class interests. The state is the primary source of oppression in society, not the capitalist economy as Marxists would argue.

Stirner reveals himself as an anti-authoritarian thinker *par excellence.* Moreover, his critique of the politics of place is useful in a number of ways. Not only does he continue the critique of Marxism elaborated in the first chapter, he also applies the same logic to anarchism itself—he allows us to think beyond the epistemological categories which inform anarchism.

It is clear that Stirner's antistate philosophy has a great deal in common with anarchism, particularly his rejection of the Marxist conception of state power as being subordinated to class interests, and his implied critique of Marxist revolutionary politics. However Stirner sits almost as uncomfortably with anarchism as he does with Marxism. It will become increasingly clear that Stirner cannot be confined within the category of traditional anarchism. He breaks with this category on several grounds: he rejects the notions of human and social essence which are the foundation of anarchist thought; he eschews the moral and epistemological discourses which are based on this essence; and this leads him to an entirely different conception of revolutionary action. These points however will be discussed later. First we must look at the philosophical background which gave rise to Stirner's thought.

Stirner's Epistemological Break

Critique of Feuerbach

Stirner's thought developed in the shadows of Feuerbach's *The Essence of Christianity.* It was this work which Stirner came to reject—and in doing so, he broke decisively with the theoretical category of humanism. In *The Essence of Christianity* Feuerbach applied the notion of alienation to religion. Religion is alienating because it requires that man abdicate his own qualities and powers by projecting them onto an abstract God, beyond the grasp of humanity. In doing so, man displaces his essential self, leaving him alienated and debased. Man's qualities, according to this argument, become the characteristics of God.[14] Feuerbach argued that the predicates of God were, therefore, really only the predicates of man as a species being. God was an illusion, a hypostatization of man. While man should be the single criterion for truth, love, and virtue, these characteristics are now the property of an abstract being who becomes the sole criterion for them. In claiming, however, that the qualities which we have attributed to God or to the absolute are really the qualities of man, Feuerbach has made man into an almighty being himself. Feuerbach sees will, love, goodness, and thought as essential qualities in man—he wants to restore these abstracted qualities to man. Man becomes, in Feuerbach's eyes, the ultimate expression of these qualities. He becomes almighty, sacred, perfect, infinite—in short, man becomes God. Feuerbach embodies the Enlightenment humanist project of restoring to man his rightful place at the center of the universe. Feuerbach's intention was to make the "human the divine, the finite the infinite."

It is this attempt to replace God with man, to make the finite infinite, that Stirner condemns. According to Stirner, Feuerbach, while claiming to have overthrown religion, merely reversed the order of subject and predicate, doing nothing to undermine the place of religious authority itself.[15] The alienating category of God is retained and solidified by entrenching it in man. Man thereby usurps God, capturing for himself the category of the infinite, the place of God. Man becomes the substitute for the Christian illusion. Feuerbach, Stirner argues, is the high priest of a new religion—humanism: "The HUMAN *religion* is only the last metamorphosis of the Christian religion."[16]

Let us follow Stirner's argument here: it will be the key to the critique of essentialist politics that I am trying to construct. Stirner starts by accepting Feuerbach's critique of Christianity: the infinite is an illusion, being merely the representation of human consciousness. The Christian religion is based on the divided, alienated self—the religious man seeks after his alter ego that cannot be attained because it has been abstracted onto the figure of God. In doing so he denies his concrete, sensual self.[17]

However, Stirner argues that by seeking the sacred in "human essence," by positing an essential man and attributing to him certain qualities that had hitherto been attributed to God, Feuerbach has merely reintroduced religious alienation. The individual finds himself alienated within the symbolic order: he is subjected to a series of signifiers—man, human essence—that imposes an identity on him which only half represents him, and which is not of his own creation or choosing. This is similar to Lacan's theory of subjectification, and will be discussed in later chapters. Stirner shows that by making certain characteristics and qualities essential to man, Feuerbach has alienated those in whom these qualities are not found. And so man becomes like God, and just as man was debased under God, so the concrete individual is debased beneath this perfect being, man. Like the Marxist revolution that only reaffirmed state power, Feuerbach's "insurrection" has not destroyed the place of religious authority—it has merely installed man within it, replacing God. For Stirner, man is just as oppressive, if not more so, than God: "Feuerbach thinks, that if he humanizes the divine, he has found truth. No, if God has given us pain, 'Man' is capable of pinching us still more torturingly."[18] The essential man of Feuerbachian humanism is a new ideological construct, a new deception which, according to Stirner, oppresses and denies the individual. It is a mutilating, alienating idea—a "spook," or a "fixed idea," as Stirner calls it—something that desecrates the uniqueness of the individual by comparing him to an ideal which is not of his own creation. This is Christian alienation all over again, according to Stirner: "To God, who is spirit, Feuerbach gives the name 'Our Essence.' Can we put up with this, that 'Our Essence' is brought into opposition to *us*—that we are split into an essential and unessential self? Do we not therewith go back into the dreary misery of seeing ourselves banished out of ourselves?"[19]

Stirner's critique of the idealism latent within Feuerbachian humanism had a resounding effect on Marxism. It forced Marx to take account of the ideological constructions in his own notions of human essence that he derived to some extent from Feuerbach. Although Stirner never directly criticized Marx, *The Ego and His Own* inspired criticism of Marx's latent humanism from many quarters.[20] Marx himself was shocked by Stirner's work into what is seen by some Marxists as a decisive break with humanism and with the notion of a moral or humanistic basis for socialism. He was clearly troubled by Stirner's suggestion that socialism was tainted with the same idealism as Christianity and that it was full of superstitious ideas like morality and justice. This is manifested in the relentless, vitriolic, and sarcastic attack on Stirner, which the largest part of the *German Ideology* is devoted to. The *German Ideology* represents a cathartic attempt by Marx to tarnish Stirner with the same brush that he himself had been tarnished with—that of idealism—while, at the same time trying to exorcise this demon from his own thought.[21] Marx saw the application of Stirner's work for his own revolutionary socialism and he used Stirner's critique of idealism while, at the same time, accusing Stirner himself of idealism. Stirner showed Marx the perils of Feuerbachian humanism, forcing Marx to distance himself as much as possible from his earlier stance.

The early humanism of Marx, found in the *Economic and Philosophical Manuscripts of 1844*, stands in contrast to his later materialism. The *Manuscripts* are founded on the notion of the "species being" and they describe the way in which private property alienates man from his own species. There is a notion of human essence—an image of a happy, fulfilled man who affirms his own being through free, creative labor.[22] Marx's early humanism bears the unmistakable imprint of Feuerbach. For Marx, man is estranged from his "species being" by abstract forces such as private property, and it is with the overthrow of private property that man reclaims himself—thus everything becomes "human."[23] For Marx, man is essentially a communal, social creature—it is in his essence to seek the society of others. Man and society exist in a natural bond in which each produces the other. Man can only become complete, become the "object" when he affirms this social essence, when he becomes a *social being*.[24]

Marx relies on an essentialist conception of man and an anthropological notion of species. Stirner, as we have seen, rejects these categories, seeing them as religious postulates. For Stirner—and this is the crux of his critique of the humanist Marx—man creates himself. There is no essential human nature—it is merely a construct. Stirner wants to strip away the layers of human existence. He wants to go beyond "essences" till one finds the *individuum*. This is the foundation for what Stirner terms the "creative nothing," "the unique one."[25] Rather than there being a set of essential characteristics at the base of human existence, there is a nothingness, something that cannot be defined, and it is up to the individual to create something out of this and not be limited by essences—by what is "properly human." This idea of emptiness or lack at the base of identity will be crucial to the theorization of a non-essentialist politics of resistance. As Stirner will show, the old Enlightenment-based politics founded on an essential identity—like anarchism and Marxism—is no longer relevant to today's struggles; it can no longer adequately resist modern forms of power which work, as we shall see, through an essential identity. The lack that Stirner finds at the base of identity will allow the individual to resist this modern subjectifying power.

Beyond Humanism

Stirner's implied critique of Marx is expressed in an antidialectic that he constructs to challenge the Hegelian dialectical process that culminates in the freedom of humanity. Stirner, in opposition to this, charts the development of humanity in relation to the political institutions that it corresponds to, and instead of this culminating in freedom, it ends with the enslavement of the individual. The analysis starts with liberalism, or what Stirner calls "political liberalism," characterized by equality before the law, political equality, and political liberty. As Stirner shows, however, political liberty merely means that the state is free, in the same way that religious liberty means that religion is free.[26] He writes: "It does not mean *my* liberty, but the liberty of a power that rules and subjugates me."[27]

Stirner's differences with Marx become more apparent in his dissection of the second stage of the dialectical process—"social liberalism" or socialism. Social liberalism comes about as a rejection of political liberalism, which is perceived as too egoistic.[28] For Stirner, on the other hand, political liberalism was characterized not by too much egoism, but by too little, and he sees the enforced equality in socialism as a further destruction of the ego, a further desecration of the individual. Instead of the "property"—or the *ego*—of the individual being possessed by the state, it is now possessed by society.[29] Once again, according to Stirner, the individual has been subordinated to an abstract power, a place outside him: first the state, and now society. Society has become the new place of power to which the individual is subjugated. Stirner, in opposition to Marx, does not believe in society: he sees it as another abstraction, another illusion like God and human essence. They are all ideological devices that the individual is sacrificed to. The individual is not an essential part of society, as Marx believed. Society means nothing more to the egoistic individual than God or the state: "That society is no ego at all, . . . that we owe society no sacrifice, but, if we sacrifice anything, sacrifice it to ourselves—of this the Socialists do not think, because they—as liberals—are imprisoned in the religious principle, and zealously aspire after—a sacred society, such as the State was hitherto."[30]

For Stirner, then, socialism is just another extension of liberalism: both are systems that rely on an ideal or essence deemed sacred—the state and law for political liberalism, and society for social liberalism—and which the individual ego is subordinated to. Stirner then proceeds to examine the third and final form of liberalism in this dialectic: "humane liberalism" or, for our purposes, humanism. Humane liberalism is based on a critique of both political and social liberalism. For the humanist, these two liberalisms are still too egoistic: the individual should act for selfless reasons, purely on behalf of humanity and one's fellow man.[31] However, as we have seen, humanism is based on a notion of human essence that, as Stirner has shown, is fictional. Moreover, it is an ideological device used to judge and condemn individuals who do not conform to this "essence." The discourse of humane liberalism is centered around this standard of judgement. As Stirner argues, humanism forces everyone to be human beings and to conform to a human essence. It contends that everyone has within them an essential kernel of humanity that they must live up to: if they transgress this essence they are deemed "inhuman." The humanist insists, for instance, that if one goes beyond the surface differences between individuals, one finds that we all share a common human essence—we are all men.[32] Stirner, on the other hand, wants to assert the individual's right to be an individual: to be different, to not be part of humanity—to eschew human essence and recreate oneself. Man is a religious ideal, according to Stirner, an ideological construct that restricts individuality—it is a "fixed idea" that oppresses the ego. It is this religious ideal, however, which has become, in the discourse of humanism, the principle governing the individual's activity: the only labor which will now be tolerated is "human labor," labor which glorifies and benefits man, and which contributes to the development of one's essential humanity.[33]

For Stirner, then, humane liberalism is the final stage in both the liberation of man and enslavement of the individual ego. The more man frees himself, through "human labor," from the objective conditions which bind him—such as the state and society—the more individual ego, the "self-will," is dominated. This is because man and human essence, have conquered the last bastion of the ego, the individual's thoughts or "opinions." Political liberalism tried to destroy "self-will," Stirner argues, but it gained refuge in private property.[34] Socialism abolished private property, making it the domain of society, and so the ego then found refuge in what Stirner calls "self ownership"—the individual's opinions. Humanism now seeks to abolish even this domain of the individual, making personal opinion refer to a generality—man. Personal opinion becomes "general human opinion," and individual autonomy is thus effaced.[35] The humanist Enlightenment fantasy of man's liberation, now fulfilled, is therefore concomitant with the slavery of the individual. At the heart of this dialectic of liberation there is nothing but domination.

The Un-Man

However the supremacy of man is always threatened by what Stirner calls the "un-man," that element of the individual that refuses to conform to human essence, to the ideal of man.[36] This is the other of man, a Dionysian force that cannot be contained—both a creation of man and a threat to it. As Stirner says, then: "Liberalism as a whole has a deadly enemy, an invincible opposite, as God has the devil: by the side of man stands the un-man, the individual, the egoist. State, society, humanity, do not master this devil."[37] The un-man may be seen as a figure of resistance against the subjectifying power of Enlightenment humanism: it is something which makes problematic the idea of the essential human subject by transgressing its narrow boundaries and thus breaking them open. This idea of excess has many connections with poststructuralist thought: Derrida's notions of "supplementarity" and "difference," Deleuze and Guattari's figure of the "war-machine," and Lacan's idea of "lack," can all be seen as examples of this desire to find a point of transgression and resistance to subjectification. This convergence between Stirner and poststructuralism will be explored in subsequent chapters, but it is clear already that he shares with poststructuralism a fundamental rejection of essentialism and dialectical thought.

Stirner's critique is important here because liberalism has the same ontological framework as anarchism. Indeed "humane liberalism" may be seen as a kind of anarchism. Anarchism is based, as I have shown, on a notion of human essence—this is its point of departure. Anarchism is part of the Enlightenment tradition, which has as its goal the liberation of man and human consciousness from oppressive external conditions. It is deeply influenced by Feuerbach's humanist insurrection against God. Anarchism is the most radical expression of humanism, and it is therefore possible to apply Stirner's critique of humanism to anarchism, to uncover its essentialist postulates. Stirner's rejection of human essence is particularly important here. For anarchists, human essence is the point of departure from which state power will be overthrown. However, Stirner has shown that human essence is thoroughly questionable. He has argued, first, that human essence is a fiction, an abstraction invented through Feuerbach's "theological insurrection." Human essence has not broken with the religious categories it purported to overthrow. On the contrary, it has become installed within these categories: man has become just as much a fiction as God, an ideological construct which alienates and oppresses individuals. Anarchism contends that human essence is the true basis for individual activity. However as Stirner argues: "Intercourse resting on essence is an intercourse with the spook, not with anything real."[38] If we accept Stirner's critique of man, then the entire philosophy of anarchism is based on a religious illusion—it falls victim to the very idealism which it claimed to transcend.

Second, Stirner argues that not only is human essence an illusion, but it is also a pernicious illusion. It is linked fundamentally to state power—it is the discourse through which this power operates, and it is itself a structure which oppresses individuals. Just as God was a power that subjugated the individual, now it is man and "the fear of Man is merely an altered form of the fear of God."[39] Man and human essence have become the new criteria by which individuals are judged and punished: "I set up what 'Man' is and what acting in a 'truly human' way is, and I demand of every one that this law become norm and ideal to him; otherwise he will expose himself as a 'sinner and criminal.' "[40]

Thus, human essence, which for anarchists contains the seeds of revolution and liberation, is seen by Stirner to be the new machine of punishment and domination; the basis of a binary discourse which persecutes those individuals who do not measure up and conform. Human essence is the new norm that condemns difference. Kropotkin's treatment of crime as a disease to be cured is an example of the way that this punitive discourse functions. As Stirner argues: "'curative means' always announces to begin with that individuals will be looked on as 'called' to a particular 'salvation' and hence treated according to the requirements of this 'human calling.'"[41] In other words, crime being treated as a disease, as the anarchists propose, is no better than crime being seen as a sin: crime is still seen in terms of a failing, a lack of some kind—only this time it is condemned as a failing of human essence, as a transgression against "human calling." For Stirner there is no difference between cure and punishment—it is a reapplication of the old moral prejudices in a new guise.[42] This is precisely Foucault's argument about the modern formula of punishment: a formula in which medical and psychiatric norms are only the old morality in a new guise. For Stirner, punishment is only made possible by making something sacred. Anarchism, in making human essence sacred, in making it an uncontaminated point of departure, has perhaps only recreated in a new form, the authoritarian discourse it was meant to destroy. Maybe it has created, in Stirner's words, "a *new* feudalism under the suzerainty of 'Man.'"[43]

Humanist Power

Moreover, for Stirner, human essence being posited as a point of departure uncontaminated by power is naive and politically dangerous. Human essence is not a pure place untouched by power: on the contrary, state power has already colonized human essence. For example, Stirner posits a theory of state power that is altogether different from that of anarchism: while anarchists argue that state power subjugates and oppresses man, Stirner suggests that the state rules through "man." Man is constructed as a site of power, a political unit through which the state dominates the individual: "The kernel of the State is simply 'Man,' this unreality, and it itself is only a 'society of men.'"[44] The state and man are not opposed as the anarchists would argue. On the contrary, they are part of the same political discourse in which one depends on the other: the state relies on a conception of man and human essence in order that its rule be legitimized. In other words, the state subjectifies the individual: it demands that the individual be man, be human, so that he can be made part of state society and thus dominated: "So the State betrays its enmity to me by demanding that I be a man . . . it imposes being a man upon me as a *duty.*"[45]

Stirner here has defined a new operation of power that completely eluded political theories like anarchism. He describes a process of subjectification in which power functions, not by repressing man, but by constructing him as a political subject and ruling *through* him. It is precisely this fundamental undermining of Enlightenment humanist ontology that will allow Foucault, and Deleuze and Guattari, to see political action in an entirely new way. He has broken with traditional political theory in seeing the individual and human essence as separate. Human essence is not a transcendental place created by natural laws which power comes to oppress. Rather it is a fabrication of power, or, at least, a discursive construct that can be made to serve power.

Stirner's rejection of essence, then, has dealt classical anarchism a severe blow. First, it has made impossible anarchism's notion of a pure point of departure, a place of revolution uncontaminated by power. Power, argues Stirner, has already colonized this place and uses it for it own purposes—it is no longer a place outside power. Second, Stirner has shown that in subscribing to a Manichean political logic which conceives of a place of resistance outside the realm of power, anarchism has failed to grasp the new functioning of power: domination through subjectification, rather than repression. The implications of this are enormous: the reliance of revolutionary theory on human essence is not only questionable, but immanently dangerous.

Ideology

Stirner has shown, moreover, that in order to study state power one must analyze it at its more minute levels: what is important is not necessarily the institution of the state itself, but the way it functions, and the sites—like human essence and man—through which it operates. There is exactly the same emphasis in Foucault's study of power. In particular, Stirner stresses the importance of ideas, "fixed ideas"—like human essence and man—as sites of power. He is talking about a hitherto neglected area of power, namely *ideology*.

An important site of ideological domination is morality. Morality, Stirner argues, is a "fixed idea"—a fiction derived from Christian idealism, which dominates the individual. Morality is merely the leftover of Christianity, only in a new humanist garb, and as Stirner argues: "Moral faith is as fanatical as religious faith!"[46] This is what Stirner objects to, not morality itself, but the fact that it is a sacred, unbreakable law. Stirner exposes the will to power, the cruelty and the domination behind moral ideas: "Moral influence takes its start where *humiliation* begins; yes, it is nothing else than this humiliation itself, the breaking and bending of the temper down to humility."[47] It is based on the desecration, the breaking down, of the individual will—the ego. Morality mutilates the individual: the individual must conform to prevailing moral codes, otherwise he becomes alienated from his "essence." For Stirner, moral coercion is just as vicious as the coercion carried out by the state, only it is more insidious and subtle—it does not require the use of physical force. The warden of morality is already installed in the individual's conscience. Morality is fundamentally linked to political domination, legitimating the continued existence of the police state.[48] Stirner's critique of morality has implications for anarchism because, as we have seen, anarchism relies on a moral discourse to distinguish man from the power that oppresses him: human subjectivity is essentially moral, while political power is fundamentally immoral. However, Stirner has shown that not only does the discourse of morality subjugate the individual, it is also inextricably related to the very power it is meant to oppose.

This may also be applied to rationality, which anarchists claimed to act in the name of. Rational truths are always held above individual perspectives, and Stirner argues that this is another way of dominating the individual ego. As with morality, Stirner is not necessarily against truth itself, but rather the way it has become sacred, absolute, removed from the grasp of the individual and held over him: "As long as you believe in the truth, you do not believe in yourself, and you are a—*servant*, a—*religious man*."[49] Rational truth, for Stirner, has no real meaning beyond individual perspectives—it is something that can be used by the individual. Its real basis, as with morality, is power and to ignore this, as anarchism does, is extremely perilous.

Stirner's critique of human essence, morality, and rational truth has enormous implications for anarchism, and indeed any Enlightenment-based political theory. It has shown the danger in not questioning these ideas, in neglecting their malleability—the fact that they can be used as much by power, as they can against it. Above all, Stirner points to the fact that power operates at the level of the subject and his ideas, and that power relies on us allowing it to dominate us. This was something which anarchism was unable to fully come to terms with. Stirner is not so much interested in power itself, but in the reasons why we allow ourselves to be dominated by power: he wants to study the ways in which we participate in our own oppression. He wants to show that power is not only concerned with economic or political questions—it is also rooted in psychological needs. It has embedded itself deep within our conscience, in the form of fixed ideas such as the state, human essence, and morality. For instance, the dominance of the state, Stirner argues, depends on our willingness to let it dominate us:

> The State is not thinkable without lordship and servitude (subjection); for the State must will to be lord of all that it embraces, and this will is called the 'will of the State' . . . He who, to hold his own, must count on the absence of will in others is a thing made by these others, as a master is a thing made by the servant. If submissiveness ceased, it would be all over with lordship.[50]

Stirner argues that the state itself is essentially an abstraction, a fiction much like God, and it only exists because we allow it to exist, because we abdicate to it our own authority, in the same way that we create God by abdicating our authority and placing it outside ourselves. What is more important than the institution of the state, is the "ruling principle"—it is the idea of the state that dominates us.[51] Stirner does not discuss the mechanics of the state. The state's power is really based on our power. Is it not undeniable that any kind of rule depends on our willingness to let it rule us? Political power cannot rest solely on coercion. It needs our help, our willingness to obey. It is only because the individual has not recognized this power, because he humbles himself before the sacred, before authority, that the state continues to exist.[52] The dominance of the state is based on the moral and ideological indoctrination of its subjects and Stirner argues that if this indoctrination can be exposed, then this is the first stage in the state's destruction.

Marx argues that this is an example of Stirner's idealism. For Marx, Stirner lives in the world of his own illusions, mistaking them for reality.[53] This idealism, Marx argues, ignores and, thus, leaves intact the real materiality of the state. However, this is a serious and deliberate misreading of Stirner. Rather than dismissing the reality of political power, Stirner actually sees it as the predominant force in society—more so even than economic power. Rather than Stirner's conception of the state breeding inaction and apathy as Marx argues, it could actually have the opposite effect—it may give individuals a realization of their power over the state. Is it really possible, then, to say that Stirner frivolously neglects reality by stressing the importance of ideas? On the contrary, it may be that Marx, because he is trapped within the narrow confines of materialism and because he neglects the importance of ideas and their grip on the psyche, is doomed to perpetuating existing reality rather than changing it. As it was suggested in the first chapter, Marxism is limited by its economic reductionism: it neglects other arenas and sources of domination. Stirner merely argues that the state is based on illusory premises, like morality, which he intends to expose.

Stirner believes, then, that the state must be overcome as an idea before it can be overcome in reality. What must be attacked is the *desire* for authority. The state does not repress desire—rather it channels it to itself: "The State exerts itself to tame the desirous man; in other words, it seeks to direct his desire to it alone, and to content that desire with what it offers."[54] It is this desire for authority, this love for the state, which perpetuates its power. People are dominated, Stirner suggests, because they desire it. Deleuze and Guattari are interested in the same phenomenon. Self-subjection and its relation to desire is a problem that Marx as well as the anarchists did not foresee. It is the specter that haunts revolutionary theory. Stirner was among the first to recognize that statism exists as much in our heads and hearts, as it does in reality. It is only by getting rid of this internalized authoritarianism—this place of power—that one can ensure that the state is not perpetuated. As long as the idea of the state is left intact there is always the danger of it lurking around every corner.

Insurrection and the Politics of the Self

For Stirner, revolutionary action in the past has been a dismal failure. It has remained trapped within the paradigm of authority, changing the form of authority but not its place: the liberal state was replaced by the workers' state;

God was replaced with man. But the category of authority itself has remained unchanged, and has often become even more oppressive. Perhaps, then, the idea of revolution should be abandoned: it is based on essentialist concepts and Manichean structures which always end up perpetuating, rather than overcoming, authority. Stirner has unmasked the links between human essence and power, and has shown the dangers in building a revolutionary theory around this notion. Perhaps, therefore, revolutions should be about escaping subjectification—rejecting the enforced identity of human essence and man. Perhaps, as Stirner argues, revolution should become insurrection:

> Revolution and insurrection must not be looked upon as synonymous. The former consists in an overturning of conditions, of the established condition or *status*, the State or society, and is accordingly a *political* or *social* act; the latter has indeed for its unavoidable consequence a transformation of circumstances, yet does not start from it but from men's discontent with themselves, is not an armed rising but a rising of individuals, a getting up without regard to the *arrangements* that spring from it. The Revolution aimed at new arrangements; insurrection leads us no longer to *let* ourselves be arranged, but to arrange ourselves, and sets no glittering hopes on 'institutions.' It is not a fight against the established, since, if it prospers, the established collapses of itself; it is only a working forth of me out of the established.[55]

It may be argued, then, that insurrection starts with the individual refusing his enforced identity, through which power operates: it starts "from men's discontent with themselves." Insurrection does not aim at overthrowing political institutions themselves. It is aimed at the individual, in a sense overthrowing his own identity—the outcome of which is, nevertheless, a change in political arrangements. Insurrection is therefore not about becoming what one is— becoming human, becoming man, as the anarchist argues—but about becoming what one *is not*. Stirner's notion of individual rebellion involves, then, a process of becoming. It is about continually reinventing one's own self—an *anarchism of subjectivity*, rather than an anarchism based on subjectivity. The self, or the ego, is not an essence, a defined set of characteristics, but rather an emptiness, a "creative nothing," and it is up to the individual to create something out of this and not be limited by essences. The self exists only to be consumed: "I on my part start from a presupposition in presupposing myself; but my presupposition does not struggle for its perfection like 'Man struggling for his perfection,' but only serves me to enjoy it and consume it . . . I do not presuppose myself, because I am every moment just positing or creating myself."[56]

The Ego as Subject

Many argue that Stirner posits an essential subjectivity—the ego—one which is entirely selfish.[57] However this is clearly untrue: Stirner does posit a self, but it is a self which is empty, undefined, and contingent. As Kathy Ferguson argues, the self, for Stirner, is a process, a continuous flow of self-creating flux.[58] This is a process that eludes, to some extent, the imposition of fixed identities and essences: "no concept expresses me, nothing that is designated my essence exhausts me."[59] There is always an excess, then, which escapes identity. This excess may express itself in the un-man, the other of man, but even this is only an ephemeral identity [or nonidentity]: the un-man exists only as a brief flicker of resistance to man. It too will die and change once this binary of man/un-man is overcome. The importance of Stirner's notion of *becoming* for politics, particularly poststructuralist politics, is great indeed: he has shown that resistance to power will never succeed if it remains trapped within fixed, essential identities.

The other side to this question would be the argument that Stirner does *not* concede a stable identity and that for this reason he should be condemned: if he does not allow a stable identity, then how can there be any notion of ethics or ethical action? This is the same critique that has been directed against various poststructuralist thinkers, as we shall see. For Stirner, however, ethical action does not necessarily depend on there being a fixed, stable identity, or an identity that is dialectically mediated. On the contrary, the possibility of ethics would depend on the very openness, contingency, and instability of identity that his critics denounce. Although Stirner does not set down any ethical guidelines— this would be against the very *spirit* of Stirner—it could be argued that ethical action would involve questioning morality, unmasking the domination involved in morality; an *ethical* critique of morality, in other words. An ethical self eschews a fixed moral and rational identity and remains open to change and contingency. This would be Stirner's political and ethical identity of resistance: it is political, not because it affirms a fixed political or moral stance, but rather because it rejects all such fixed positions and the oppressive obligations attached to them.

Ownness

Related to the notion of self is the question of freedom. Freedom has always been the final goal of all revolutionary movements: the freedom of humanity, the freedom of man, the freedom of the self. Freedom still plays a dominant role in political discourse today. Anarchism is founded on the desire for man's liberation from the oppressive external conditions, namely political power and economic exploitation. If man is to fully develop his humanity, anarchists argue, he must first be free. However, in response to this discourse of liberation, Stirner asks, what it is that should be freed—man, human essence? If, as Stirner has shown, human essence is a fabrication of power as well as a discourse of domination, then does not the desire for freedom play right into the hands of power? If what is being freed is itself an authoritarian structure, then does not this only facilitate further domination? This is what happens, Stirner argues, under humane liberalism. Man has been freed from external forces such as the state and society, and has thus gained a virtual supremacy over the individual ego. Surely, Stirner suggests, what should be freed is not human essence from external conditions, but the self from human essence, from fixed identities. The self must be freed from the self. Because the idea of freedom is linked fundamentally to the liberation of man, Stirner suggests that one should, instead, be seeking *ownness*:

> What a great difference between freedom and ownness! . . . 'Freedom lives only in the realm of dreams!' Ownness, on the contrary, is my whole being and existence, it is I myself. I am free from what I am rid of, owner of what I have in my power to control. . . . To be free is something that I cannot truly *will*, because I cannot make it, I cannot create it: I can only wish it and—aspire toward it, for it remains an ideal, a spook.[60]

Freedom is only negative freedom, while ownness is a positive freedom, by which Stirner means freedom to reinvent oneself. Ownness means that one can be free even in the most oppressive situations, because it is a form of freedom that starts with the individual. Stirner believes that freedom must be seized by the individual for himself—if it is handed to him then it is always limited by oppressive conditions.[61] This is because freedom is a diaphanous term: it is always someone's particular idea of freedom which the individual is forced to conform to. It is a freedom, then, which entails further domination. Freedom is a "beautiful dream," whose true basis is power. The individual must therefore seize or invent his own freedom, based on his own power: "only the freedom one takes for himself, therefore the egoist's freedom, rides with full sails."[62] Stirner, however, does not believe that the concept of freedom should be completely abandoned. On the contrary, he wants to see the concept of freedom expanded to include *positive* freedom, which is contingent and is open to the individual to define. Freedom is not a fixed, transcendental concept: it is part of a struggle between the individual and authority, and it is constantly redefined within this struggle. Foucault will employ a similar notion of freedom in the next chapter. Freedom, then, cannot be separated from antagonism and power: ownness is the realization and, indeed, the affirmation, of this.

Society without Essence

The idea of antagonism is prevalent in Stirner's work: he perpetuates the war model discussed in the last chapter. The war model, I have argued, is not a celebration of actual war, but rather a model of analysis that eschews essences and unities, and seeks out differences and pluralities. It revels in dislocation, disunity, and radical openings at the level of representations. It could be argued that Stirner applies the war model to the question of identity: he finds emptiness, rather than essence, at the base of subjectivity. This, however, is a creative emptiness—a radical opening which the individual can use to create his own subjectivity and not be limited by essences. Stirner says, then: "The essence of the world, so attractive and splendid, is for him who looks to the bottom—emptiness."[63]

Stirner also applies the model of war to the identity of the social. Society is a fictional collectivity—it has no essence: "Who is this person that you call 'All'?—It is 'society'!—But is it corporeal, then?—*We* are its body!—You?

Why, you are not a body yourselves. . . . Accordingly the united society may indeed have bodies at its service, but no one body of its own."[64] For Stirner, society is an ideological construct that imprisons the individual within a collectivity. Stirner sees this collectivity, moreover, as a unit through which state power is perpetuated. While anarchists see society as a natural communality that is oppressed and stultified by the state, Stirner sees the state and society as part of the same oppressive collectivity.[65] "The people" is a collectivity created by power—it has no ego.[66] If we accept Stirner's argument, social essence cannot be the basis for resistance to domination, as it is for anarchists. Following this logic, we can question the idea of the social altogether: the social is not an essential organism but rather a discursive arrangement that, because it is based on a lack or constitutive emptiness, is always open to different articulations. This is an idea that will be explored later. However, Stirner's critique of essentialist logic has forced us to abandon the idea of society as a stable, essential unity.

Stirner is not opposed to all forms of mutuality: he wants to see mutual arrangements between individuals which are freely formed by individuals, instead of being imposed from above, and which do not deny the autonomy of the individual. He speaks of the "union of egoists" as such an arrangement.[67] Society, argues Stirner, is a false tie: it is based on a notion of the *sacred* and is, therefore, a forced intercourse between individuals. The union, on the other hand, is based on nothing but the desires of the individuals who enter it: it is solely a relationship of expedience and utility, which dissolves any notion of essence.[68]

What Stirner is against, then, is the *obligation* to be part of a community, to live together. He is not necessarily against the notion of community itself. This is perhaps the same for morality, rationality, society, humanity. Stirner is not necessarily opposed to these ideas at all, if only they did not become abstract, sacred concepts; if only they were not taken out of the grasp of the individual and turned into an obligation. Domination lies, not in these concepts themselves, but in the way that they have consumed the individual. This is why Stirner talks about ownness: he does not mean ownership of material possessions, but rather the bringing down to the level of the individual these concepts which have become abstracted from him. They must become the property of the individual, something that can be reinvented by the individual. Stirner calls for these ideas to become contingent, open to change and redefinition. Stirner's application of the war model has, therefore, not destroyed ideas such as morality, society, and humanity: it has merely freed them from essences, from the sacred. It has placed them within a field of struggle and contingency.

Creative Nihilism

Stirner's use of the war model, because it finds emptiness rather than essence at the base of existence, is nihilistic; but the nihilism that it produces is a *creative* nihilism. It creates a theoretical opening for a play of differences in interpretation. Gilles Deleuze sees Stirner as *"the dialectician who reveals nihilism as the truth of the dialectic."*[69] He exposes the nihilism, the closure, the denial of difference and plurality that essentialism and dialectical logic produce. However, for Stirner, the way to counter these discourses is not through simple transgression, not by affirming immorality over morality, irrationality over rationality, the un-man over man. This kind of transgression merely reaffirms, in a negative sense, the authority of the dominant idea. Crime, for instance, only reaffirms the law that it has transgressed against.[70] Similarly to Nietzsche, Stirner argues that it is only by thinking outside the binaristic logic of authority and its transgression that one can escape the oppressive dialectic of place, the constant replacement of one form of authority with another—the movement from God to man, from the state to society, from religion to morality. It is by inventing new ideas—like uniqueness and egoism—rather than reacting to the established ones, which allows thought, particularly political thought, to escape its own authoritarian tendencies.

It is perhaps this aspect of Stirner's thinking that prompted John P. Clark's criticism of him from the anarchist perspective. Clark argues that Stirner's egoism leads him to defend the very authoritarianism that he would seem to denounce. Stirner's position, claims Clark, would lead to a valorization of the will to power and individual domination.[71] Furthermore, Clark argues that Stirner's rejection of social totalities and essences, and his positing of an ego which Clark sees as wholly autonomous and fictitious, precludes him from having any political or social relevance.[72] This is in contrast to anarchism which, Clark argues, because it has a clear picture of human nature, of the self as essentially a social being, is ethically and politically valid today.[73] In this chapter, however, I have argued precisely the opposite. The first criticism that Clark makes can be rejected: we have seen that Stirner's egoism, and his use of the war metaphor, is more about achieving power over oneself—through the idea of ownness—than power over others. As to the second criticism, I have argued that it is precisely through Stirner's rejection of essence and totality that we are able to engage in political action. Stirner has opened up a theoretical space for politics that was hitherto confined by the limits of essentialism and rationality. His critique of human essence has enabled us to theorize a political identity that is contingent and open to reinvention by the individual. So rather than classical anarchism, with its Enlightenment humanist paradigm of essence, being the way forward as Clark argues, it is precisely this paradigm that holds us back, theoretically and politically. Stirner's fundamental break with this paradigm allows us to reinvent politics in ways that are not limited by essence.

I have argued so far that anarchism is reliant on an uncontaminated point of departure outside power, which is embodied by an Enlightenment notion of essential human subjectivity. Now, in light of Stirner's critique, this whole paradigm of power and resistance needs to be rethought. Stirner's rejection of humanism has shown that not only is the notion of human essence an illusion, it is also intimately linked to state authority and practices of domination. Stirner explores, in a way unprecedented, the subtle connections between identity, politics, and power. He rejects the old humanist politics based on essential identity, moral absolutism, and unquestioned rational truth, and forces us to look at the inadequacies of revolutionary political theory—its hidden perils; its silent authoritarian murmurings. Stirner thus goes beyond both Marxism and anarchism, creating the possibility for a new way of theorizing politics—a possibility which will be developed by poststructuralism.

Stirner occupies a point of rupture in this discussion: the point at which anarchism can no longer deal adequately with the very problematic that it created—the problem of the place of power. He is the catalyst, then, for an epistemological break, or perhaps more accurately, a break with epistemology altogether. Above all, Stirner's explorations into the nature of power, morality, and subjectivity, have made it impossible to continue to conceptualize an uncontaminated point of departure, the pure place of resistance which anarchism relied so heavily upon. There is no longer any place outside power which political theory can find sanctuary in. Politics must now work *within* the confines of power—and this is where the ideas of Michel Foucault will be important. It is to his work that we now turn our attention.

Notes

1. Max Stirner, *The Ego and Its Own*, trans. S. Byington (London: Rebel Press, 1993), 185.

2. See Andrew Koch, "Poststructuralism and the Epistemological Basis of Anarchism," in *Philosophy of the Social Sciences* 23, no. 3 (1993): 327-351.

3. Stirner has been seen as a nihilist, a libertarian, an anarchist, an individualist, an existentialist, and even, rather unfairly, as a protofascist.

4. Stirner, *The Ego*, 254.

5. Stirner, *The Ego*, 227.

6. Stirner: "If the Church had *deadly sins*, the State has *capital crimes*; if one had *heretics*, the other has *traitors*; the one *ecclesiastical penalties*, the other *criminal penalties*; the one *inquisitorial processes,* the other *fiscal*; in short, there sins, here crimes, there inquisition and here—inquisition." See *The Ego*, 23.

7. Stirner, *The Ego*, 226.

8. Stirner, *The Ego*, 229.

9. Stirner, *The Ego*, 224.

10. Stirner: "little scruple was left about revolting against the existing State or overturning the existing laws, but to sin against the *idea* of the State, not to submit to the *idea* of law, who would have dared that?" See *The Ego*, 87.

11. Stirner, *The Ego*, 228.

12. Frank Harrison, *The Modern State: An Anarchist Analysis* (Montreal: Black Rose Books, 1983), 62.

13. Stirner, *The Ego*, 115.

14. Feuerbach, *The Essence of Christianity,* 27-28.

15. Stirner, *The Ego*, 58.

16. Stirner, *The Ego*, 176.

17. Stirner, *The Ego*, 33.

18. Stirner, *The Ego*, 174.

19. Stirner, *The Ego*, 32.

20. Among them, Arnold Ruge and Gustav Julius who were both influenced by Stirner and who used Stirner's critique, ccused Marx of the Feuerbachian humanism and

idealism that Stirner had linked to religious alienation. Following Stirner's critique of socialism, Julius saw the socialist as a modern day version of the Christian, possessed with a religious fervour, and denouncing egoism as the Christian would have denounced atheism. See R. K. W. Paterson, *The Nihilistic Egoist Max Stirner* (London: Oxford University Press, 1971), 108.

21. See Karl Marx, "The German Ideology: 'III Saint Max,'" in *Collected Works* vol. 5, 117-427. It is interesting that, given Marx's vitriolic attack on *The Ego*, it was initially welcomed by Engels. In a letter to Marx he wrote: "You will probably have heard of, if not read, Stirner's book . . . this work is important, far more important than Hess believes, for instance . . . the first point we find is true that, before doing whatever we will on behalf of some idea we have first to make it our cause, personal, egoistic . . . it is equally from egoism that we are communists . . . Stirner is right to reject the 'Man' of Feuerbach . . . since Feuerbach's Man is derived from God." Engels was to change his opinion shortly afterwards upon receiving Marx's reply. However it is interesting that Engels' initial view was that Stirner's work could have some relevance to communism in separating it from various forms of idealistic socialism. Stirner would argue that any form of revolutionary action must be made not in the name of ideals like man, or justice, or morality—it must be made by the worker for purely selfish reasons. See Paterson, *The Nihilistic Egoist Max Stirner*, 103.

22. John Carroll, *Break-Out from the Crystal Palace; The Anarcho-Psychological Critique; Stirner, Nietzsche, Dostoyevsky,* (London: Routledge & Kegan Paul, 1974), 62.

23. Karl Marx, "Economic and Philosophic Manuscripts of 1844," in *The Marx-Engels Reader,* 2d ed., 66-125.

24. Marx, "Manuscripts of 1844," 87.

25. Stirner, *The Ego*, 39.

26. Stirner, *The Ego*, 107.

27. Stirner, *The Ego*, 107.

28. Stirner, *The Ego*, 107.

29. Stirner, *The Ego*, 117.

30. Stirner, *The Ego*, 123.

31. Stirner, *The Ego*, 124.

32. Stirner, *The Ego*, 126.

33. Stirner, *The Ego*, 131.

34. By "property" Stirner does not necessarily mean material possessions, but rather an integral part of the individual—that which belongs to the individual as part of his individuality: this may be expressed in material possessions, or in something more indefinable. Stirner uses this capitalist terminology perhaps as a way of subverting it, but perhaps also because private property does guarantee the individual at least some freedom. It is this terminology of Stirner's that has led some people—including Marx— to see him as a libertarian capitalist. While this is a little unfair, there is still a possible connection here.

35. Stirner, *The Ego*, 128.

36. Stirner, *The Ego*, 177.

37. Stirner, *The Ego*, 140.

38. Stirner, *The Ego*, 189.

39. Stirner, *The Ego*, 185.

40. Stirner, *The Ego*, 204.

41. Stirner, *The Ego*, 240.

42. Stirner: *"Curative means* or *healing* is only the reverse side of *punishment,* the *theory of cure* runs parallel with the theory of punishment; if the latter sees in action a sin

a

against right, the former takes it for a sin of the man *against himself*, as a decadence from his health." See *The Ego*, 240.

43. Stirner, *The Ego*, 314.
44. Stirner, *The Ego*, 180.
45. Stirner, *The Ego*, 179.
46. Stirner, *The Ego*, 46.
47. Stirner, *The Ego*, 81.
48. Stirner, *The Ego*, 241.
49. Stirner, *The Ego*, 353.
50. Stirner, *The Ego*, 195-196.
51. Stirner, *The Ego*, 226.
52. Stirner: "from this moment State, Church, people, society, and the like, cease, because they have to thank for their existence only the disrespect that I have for myself, and with the vanishing of this undervaluation they themselves are extinguished." See *The Ego*, 284.
53. See Marx, "The German Ideology: 'III Saint Max,'" 161.
54. Stirner, *The Ego*, 312.
55. Stirner, *The Ego*, 316.
56. Stirner, *The Ego*, 150.
57. See John P. Clark, *Max Stirner's Egoism* (London: Freedom Press, 1976), 38.
58. Kathy Ferguson, "Saint Max Revisited: A Reconsideration of Max Stirner," *Idealistic Studies* 11, no. 3 (September 1982), 279.
59. Stirner, *The Ego*, 366.
60. Stirner, *The Ego*, 157.
61. Stirner: "The man who is set free is nothing but a freed man, a *libertinus*, a dog dragging a piece of chain with him: he is an unfree man in the garment of freedom, like the ass in the lion's skin." See *The Ego*, 168.
62. Stirner, *The Ego*, 167.
63. Stirner, *The Ego*, 40.
64. Stirner, *The Ego*, 116.
65. Stirner: "What is called a State is a tissue and plexus of dependence and adherence; it is a *belonging together*, a holding together, in which those who are placed together fit themselves to each other, or, in short, mutually depend on each other." See Stirner, *The Ego*, 223.
66. Stirner, *The Ego*, 232.
67. Stirner, *The Ego*, 313.
68. Stirner, *The Ego*, 306.
69. Gilles Deleuze, *Nietzsche and Philosophy*, trans. H. Tomlinson (London: The Athlone Press, 1992), 161.
70. Stirner, *The Ego*, 202.
71. Clark, *Max Stirner's Egoism*, 93.
72. Clark, *Max Stirner's Egoism*, 97-98.
73. Clark, *Max Stirner's Egoism*, 99-100.

Chapter Four

Foucault and the Genealogy of Power

Stirner expanded the scope of the problematic opened by anarchism. He has pushed the critique of authority and power to its furthest conclusion, beyond the very limit constructed by anarchism itself: namely, the essential human subject as the uncontaminated point of departure. Anarchism relied on this pure place in order to define power, and define resistance to it. Power had to have a limit that it could not transgress, and this limit was human essence. Stirner's critique, however, went beyond this limit and, in doing so, destroyed it. Human essence, which was seen by the anarchists to be beyond the reach of power, was found by Stirner to be constructed by it. Moreover, human essence was not only a construct of power, but a discourse which came to dominate the individual. Thus the limit which supposedly repelled power and authority was found to be an authoritarian limit itself, a limit which stultified resistance against power, which doomed revolutions to perpetuating power. It was a limit that reaffirmed, in other words, the place of power. Stirner broke fundamentally with the humanist categories that bound anarchism and, to a great extent, Marxism. He showed that human essence, constituted by a "natural" morality and rationality, can no longer be the rallying cry of the revolution against power. It cannot remain the pure place of resistance because it is colonized by the very power it professes to oppose. Stirner discovered a new arena of political theory—one without guarantees, and in which resistance can no longer rely on an uncontaminated point of departure as a fundamental limit to power. Stirner thus opens the way for poststructuralist ideas—particularly those of Michel Foucault.

Foucault argues that it is futile for political theory to continue to think in terms of essential limits to power, of uncontaminated points of departure. The game of politics must now be played within the confines of power. However, these "confines" are not inexorable and in fact open up unimaginable possibilities for freedom. This chapter, therefore, will discuss—using this theoretical space created by Stirner—Foucault's contribution to the question of power and resistance. It will focus on Foucault's *genealogical*, or war analysis of power, an analysis which finds power to be dispersed rather than centralized, and productive rather than repressive. This has tremendous implications for political theory, and it will enable us to further engage the possibility of resistance to power.

A New Theory of Power

Beyond Reductionism

While Foucault is by no means an anarchist—at least not in the accepted meaning of the term—he does, however, like Stirner, have certain similarities with the anarchist position. This is particularly so in his critique of Marxism. He argues, as I did in the first chapter, that there is a link that can be established between Marx's ideas and the authoritarian system developed in the Soviet Union. He sees the Gulag, for instance, as the ultimate and logical conclusion of Marxism, refusing to explain it away as the result of a deviation from the true letter of Marx. For Foucault, if the Gulag is to be truly challenged and resisted, one must start with Marx's texts.[1] Like the anarchists, Foucault suggests that there are hidden authoritarian currents within Marx's texts themselves, and that these have found their reality in political domination. Marxists can no longer hide behind theory, or separate theory from practice because, as Foucault as well as the anarchists argue, theory *is* practice. For Foucault, then, Stalinism "was the truth, rather naked, admittedly, of an entire political discourse which was that of Marx and of other thinkers before him . . . Those who hoped to save themselves by opposing Marx's real beard to Stalin's false nose are wasting their time."[2]

Foucault's criticism of Marxism bears out the anarchists' prophecy of the place of power. Foucault, like the anarchists, believes that Marxism has only reaffirmed the place of power. This is because it has neglected the question of power by reducing it to an economic analysis: "So long as the posing of the question of power was kept subordinate to the economic instance and the system of interests which this served, there was a tendency to regard these problems as of small importance."[3]

Foucault, therefore, shares with anarchism a critique of Marx's economic and class reductionism. For Foucault, power cannot be reduced simply to the interests of the bourgeoisie or capitalist economics: power does not flow from the bourgeoisie, but from institutions, practices, and discourses that operate independently of the bourgeoisie. The problem, for Foucault, in explaining every strategy of power through the convenient mechanism of class domination is that it is too easy.[4] It neglects other arenas of power—such as the prison, the family, psychiatric discourse—which have their own strategies and logic.

Foucault would agree, then, with the anarchist position that the Marxist revolution is only a changing of the guard: it does not undermine the place of power, it only changes the form and distribution of power in society. In other words, Marxism leaves power itself intact.[5] For Foucault, as well as for the anarchists, any attempt to replace one institution with another is doomed to perpetuate it: "If you wish to replace an official institution by another institution that fulfils the same function—better and differently—then you are already being reabsorbed by the dominant structure."[6] This is the logic of the place of power. For anarchists, the place of power was the state: any revolution that did not involve the immediate dismantling of state power would ultimately perpetuate this power—it would get caught within the logic of place. Foucault, while his conception of state power differs from that of the anarchists, nevertheless acknowledges the dangers of a revolution that leaves the place of power—embodied by the state—intact.[7] A Marxist revolutionary politics that neglects the autonomy of state power by reducing it to an economic analysis is bound to perpetuate this power: it will not simply "wither away." Foucault argues then: "One can say to many socialisms, real or dreamt: Between the analysis of power in the bourgeois state and the idea of its future withering away, there is a missing term: the analysis, criticism, destruction, and overthrow of the power mechanism itself."[8] Like the anarchists, then, Foucault believes that power must be studied in its own right, not reduced to a mere function of the capitalist economy or class interest. Power demands a new area of study and new tools of analysis. If it is continually subordinated to an economic analysis, then the problem of power will never be addressed and will continue to perpetuate itself.

Foucault sought a new method of analyzing power—one that went beyond the economic reductionism of Marxism. Given the limitations of Marxist theory—namely those discussed in the first chapter—new analytical tools are needed. However, one finds that political theories like anarchism, which see power solely in terms of the domination of the state, are employing a reductionism of their own. Instead of reducing power to the workings of the capitalist economy, they reduce it to the operation of the state: power is centralized within the state and emanates from it. This is part of the Manichean logic that informs anarchism: it relies on an essential division between the state and society, where the state represses society and the individual. In this way power has once again, according to Foucault, become subordinated to a generality, an institution of some kind whether it be the economy, the state, the bourgeoisie, etc. This is perhaps another means of avoiding the problem of power: by relegating the question of power to another generality, another place, power is once again neglected and, therefore, perpetuated. Perhaps the only way to subvert the place of power itself is to avoid explanations that confine power to a place.

So Foucault would argue that the Marxist and anarchist conceptions of power are two sides of the same coin. Both political philosophies are caught within a traditional "juridico-discursive" notion of power: namely that power is a commodity that can be possessed, and which is centralized within the figure of the sovereign, the place of authority, be this the king, the state, the bourgeoisie, etc. In other words, it is power attributed to an institution, a place. For Foucault, this is an outdated and naive idea of power that no longer has any relevance to political theory. What is needed, Foucault argues, is a new mechanism for political analysis that is not based on the figure of the sovereign: "what we need . . . is a political philosophy that isn't erected around the problem of sovereignty. . . . We need to cut off the King's head: in political theory that has still to be done."[9]

A "Microphysics" of Power

For Foucault, power can no longer be confined within the institution of the state, or indeed in any institution. Power is a polyvalent force that runs through multiple sites throughout the social network. It is dispersed, decentered power, diffused throughout society: it may run through the prison or the mental asylum, or through various knowledges and discourses such as psychiatry or sexuality. As Foucault says: "power is everywhere because it comes from everywhere."[10] While power can be colonized by the state, it should not be seen as belonging to or deriving from the state as the anarchists believed. Power, for Foucault, is not a function of the institution; rather the institution is a function, or an effect, of power. Power flows *through* institutions, it does not emanate from them. Indeed, the institution is merely an assemblage of various power relations. It is, moreover, an unstable assemblage because power relations themselves are unstable, and can just as easily turn against the institution which "controls" them. Flows of power can sometimes become blocked and congealed, and this is when relations of power become relations of domination.[11] These relations of domination form the basis of institutions such as the state.

Power is to be thought of as a series of ongoing strategies, rather than a permanent state of affairs—as a "mode of action upon the action of others."[12] Foucault is interested in the *microphysics* of power: power which operates at the level of minute and previously unobserved discourses and practices. These may extend from the function of psychiatric norms in the asylum, to the governmental practices of the state. The latter is a good example: for Foucault the state has no essence itself, but is rather a function of the practice of government.[13] Government is not an institution but a series of practices and rationalities, which Foucault calls *governmentality* or the "art of government."[14]

Therefore, for Foucault, the state is not an institution that exists above and beyond the sum total of its operations, as the anarchists suggested. Its operations, discourses, practices—which Foucault is more interested in—*are* the state. Anarchist and Marxist conceptions of the state are two expressions of what Foucault considers the excessive emphasis placed on the problem of the state. Anarchism sees the state as the primary oppressive and evil force in society, which must be destroyed in a revolution. Marxism, while it sees the state through the reductionist lens of its economic analysis, still overvalues the importance of the state in maintaining capitalist productive relations. In other words, both political philosophies make the state the main target of the revolution—anarchism sees it as a target to be destroyed, while Marxism sees it as a target to be seized and utilized.[15] Both see the state as a unified institution that can be assailed. However, as Foucault argues, the state, "no more probably today that at any other time in its history, does not have this unity, this individuality, this rigorous functionality, nor, to speak frankly, this importance; maybe, after all, the state is no more than a composite reality and a mythicized abstraction, whose importance is a lot more limited than many of us think."[16] Perhaps an interesting link can be made here with Stirner, who also sees the state as an abstraction, whose formidable omnipresence exists mostly in our minds and in our subconscious desire to be dominated. In any case, Foucault suggests that the problem of the state needs to be rethought. Perhaps what one should be looking at is not the state itself, but the practices of power that make the state possible.[17]

It is clear that Foucault's conception of power is fundamentally different from that of the anarchists. While anarchism sees power as starting from the institution, Foucault sees the institution as starting from power. While anarchists see power as centralized within the state and radiating downwards to the rest of society, Foucault sees power as thoroughly dispersed throughout the social fabric, moving in a multitude of directions from a multitude of sites. As Foucault says: "relations of power are not in a position of exteriority with respect to other types of relationships [economic processes, knowledge relationships, sexual relations] but are immanent in the latter."[18] It is clear, moreover, that Foucault's notion of power poses a fundamental problem for anarchism, and indeed for any kind of revolutionary philosophy: if power is so dispersed, revolutionary theories like anarchism are deprived of their main target. Anarchism depends on having a state to attack, a centralized power that defines society in opposition to itself. If power is dissipated throughout the social, as Foucault claims, then one can no longer simply confront the state with the social, as anarchism does. Foucault's notion of power undermines this Manichean division between society and power. Anarchism saw society as an essential, natural organism, which was therefore outside the order of power. However, according to Foucault, to see society in this way is dangerous: it disguises the fact that power has already infiltrated it. Revolutionary theory has generally avoided the problem of the social, because if it acknowledged that power has permeated the social itself, then the very notion of revolution—as the overthrow by society of power—would become redundant. Foucault's notion of dispersed power therefore renders the idea of revolution as the final, dialectical overturning of power an anachronism. This applies to the vanguardist revolution of Marxism, as well as to the anarchist revolution.

Perhaps the whole idea of revolution should be abandoned for a form of resistance to power which is, like power itself, nebulous and dispersed. After all, for Foucault, power is a kind of strategy: "it is the name that one attributes to a complex strategic situation in a particular society."[19] Resistance to power must, therefore, be equally strategic. In fact as Foucault argues, power and resistance always exist in a relationship of *agonism*, a perpetual battle, a relationship of mutual provocation. Foucault does not completely discount the possibility of revolution: he argues that just as power relations can be arranged on a mass scale, so to can resistances.[20] However Foucault wants to explore relations of power and resistance at their most minute level. In order to do this he must employ different tools, different models of analysis. The idea of revolution refers to the juridico-discursive model of power that Foucault wants to eschew. Moreover, it is based on the possibility of a dialectical overcoming of power. Foucault argues that power relations can never be completely overcome: all that can be hoped for is a reorganization of power relations—through struggle and resistance—in ways that are less oppressive.

War Model of Politics: Power beyond Place

This nondialectical notion of power is based on the metaphor of war and struggle. This is a way of counteracting theories which subordinate power to a mere function—of the state, of the economy—and which are, therefore, deficient in their explanation of power. It is a way of devoting political analysis to the study of power itself, avoiding reductionist explanations.[21] Power is not stagnant oppression but rather an ongoing struggle of forces pervading all aspects of life. Foucault thus continues the application of the war model developed by Hobbes, and used by Stirner: it is a mode of analysis that eschews essence. For these proponents of the war model, history is nothing but the ceaseless clash of representations—essence itself is a representation, nothing more. As Foucault suggests, maybe antagonism—or the absence of essence—is the essential condition: "Must we regard war as a primary and fundamental state of things in relation to which all the phenomena of social domination, differentiation and hierarchization are merely derivative?"[22] This Hobbes-like paradigm, as I have argued, is not a celebration of war, but rather a rejection of essence. Power, for Foucault has no essence: it is not a commodity, or a strength that one is endowed with. It is simply a relation between certain forces.

Foucault reverses Clausewitz's assertion that war is politics continued by other means: for Foucault, politics is war continued by other means. This war is perpetual: it does not culminate in a dialectical reconciliation of forces, in a final peace which, according to the anarchists, would ensue after the revolution. Peace is simply another form of warfare—not a reconciliation but a relationship of domination due to a temporary disequilibrium of forces. For Foucault then: "Humanity does not gradually progress from combat to combat until it arrives at a universal reciprocity. Humanity settles each one of its violences within a system of rules, and thus goes from domination to domination."[23]

War is simply recodified in institutions, laws, economic inequalities, and even in language. Political power is this process of recoding: it is, according to Foucault, an "unspoken" warfare.[24] Foucault employs this Nietzschean war analysis, which he calls *genealogy*, to "awaken beneath the form of institutions and legislations the forgotten past of real struggles, of masked victories or defeats, the blood that has dried on the codes of law."[25] The war model thus undermines or, at least, displaces the juridico-discursive model which is based on law and which sees law as an antidote to war. For the genealogist, law and political power are merely other forms of warfare.

The genealogist also recognizes that there can never be any escape from power, from the "hazardous play of dominations."[26] Life is a constant struggle of forces, a struggle Nietzsche says, "of egoisms turned against each other, each bursting forth in a splintering of forces and a general striving for sun and for the light."[27] Stirner sees the world in similar terms, as a struggle of egos. However, it must be emphasized that this form of analysis is not a valorization of actual warfare, but rather an attempt to see the world without the comforting gaze of essentialism and unity. Genealogy is a project of *unmasking*: it seeks to expose the antagonism, disunity, and disequilibrium of forces at the heart of essence. As Foucault argues, behind history there is not a "timeless and essential secret, but the secret that things have no essence or that their essence was fabricated in a piecemeal fashion from alien forms."[28] Genealogy attempts to dismantle place— the place of power and the place of resistance—seeing both as an essentialist facade hiding the antagonism behind. In other words, genealogy unmasks the displacement behind place—the *non*place at the heart of place. The forces that struggle are forces of absolute difference, and the struggle occurs in a "nonplace," "a pure distance, which indicates that the adversaries do not belong to a common space."[29] This would seem to reject anarchism's notion of a social essence, a commonality which, in its Manichean schema, is fundamentally opposed to the state. Moreover, for Foucault, "only a single drama is ever staged in this 'nonplace,' the endlessly repeated play of dominations."[30] Therefore the place of power is not a *place*: "This relationship of domination is no more a 'relationship' than the place where it occurs is a place."[31] Power, as we have seen, does not reside in the state, or in the bourgeoisie, or in law: its very place is that of a "nonplace" because it is shifting and variable, always being reinscribed and reinterpreted.

Productive Power: Power/Knowledge

Foucault's conception of power as operating in a nonplace—in other words, as diffuse, variable, and decentralized—is aimed at undermining the juridico-discursive model of power which, as I have said, sees power in terms of law: in other words, as repression and prohibition.[32] Anarchism, which subscribes to this model, claims that power, enshrined in the state, represses human essence within the individual: it denies the individual the realization of his essential morality and rationality, the realization of himself as a human being. Foucault argues, in contrast to this, that power is not repressive—rather it is *productive*— and that to see power entirely in terms of repression is to fundamentally misunderstand it. More insidiously, the "repressive hypothesis" as Foucault calls it, disguises the way power actually operates.[33] Foucault argues, for instance, that power produces, rather than represses, knowledge. Power and knowledge are not hostile, as the anarchists believed. Anarchists such as Kropotkin and Bakunin saw knowledge and rationality as emancipative discourses.[34] Foucault is not quite as enthusiastic about the liberating effects of knowledge. Knowledge has, at best, an ambiguous relationship with power: power works through and produces knowledge, and knowledge in turn perpetuates power.[35]

Knowledge and rationality are not necessarily subversive; they are, on the contrary, fundamentally related to power and must be treated cautiously. According to Foucault, rational truth is a product of power; it is one of the axes around which power operates. Truth does not exist in a realm outside power, as anarchists and other classical political theorists believed. To speak the truth about power relations is also to be fundamentally embroiled in them: "the political question . . . is not error, illusion, alienated consciousness or ideology; it is truth itself."[36] This argument is shared by Stirner, who, as we have seen, rejects the idea that truth is beyond the realm of individual perspective and struggle. There is not one Truth, but many truths, as many as there are individual perspectives. Truth is a weapon in a power game.[37] It can be used against power but it can at the same time perpetuate the very power it professes to oppose. According to this war model of analysis, then, truth is entirely implicated in processes of struggle and power. The point, however, is not to discard knowledge, rationality, and truth, according to Foucault. One must, however, recognize the link between these discourses and power, and be aware of their dangers. This perhaps exemplifies the poststructuralist stance on these discourses: not a rejection, but rather a questioning, a certain incredulity.

Morality also is not innocent of power: it does not constitute a critical site outside power, as the anarchists believed. Kropotkin argued, for instance, that the prison was an affront to any code of human morality: "Prisons do not moralize their inmates."[38] However, Foucault is against the prison precisely because it does moralize the inmate. What must be resisted, for Foucault, is not only the practices of domination which make up the prison, but also the morality which justifies and rationalizes these practices. [39] Therefore the main focus of Foucault's attack on the prison is not necessarily on the domination within, but on the fact that this domination is justified on moral grounds. Foucault wants to disrupt the "serene domination of Good over Evil."[40] Stirner's critique of morality also applies here. He argues, as we have seen, that morality is merely a new form of Christianity now in humanist garb. Moreover, it is based on domination, cruelty, and humiliation.[41] Both Foucault and Stirner would argue that morality is an idea that has become absolute and sacred, and this is its problem. Neither is necessarily against moral conduct itself, merely its abstraction. Foucault and Stirner want to place morality within the struggle of representations and the realm of power. Ideas like morality and justice do not somehow transcend the world of representation and struggle. They operate as discourses within the limits of power, and may be as easily used as a tool of domination as a tool against it.[42]

For Foucault then, morality, truth, and knowledge do not enjoy the privilege of being beyond the grasp of power. They are not pure sites uncontaminated by power but, on the contrary, are effects of power: they are produced by power, and they allow power itself to be produced. Foucault has thus gone against the political rationality of the Enlightenment, which promoted these ideals as tools in the struggle against tyranny: morality, rationality, and truth were seen as an antidote to the immorality, irrationality, and distortion of absolute power. This is the political logic that informed anarchism. Foucault's critique, as well as the interventions of Stirner, question the emancipative potential of these ideals, and thus deny political theories such as anarchism a privileged point of departure outside power. As Foucault says: "It seems to me that . . . one is never outside [power], that there are no margins for those who break with the system to gambol in."[43]

Foucault's critique of the "repressive hypothesis" undermines Enlightenment humanism and the political theories like anarchism, which it spawned, in a more crucial way: it denies the autonomy of human subjectivity from power. The repressive hypothesis, which Foucault considers obsolete, sees essential human subjectivity as repressed by power. Anarchism, as we have shown, is based on a fundamental notion of human essence that is subjugated by power, yet *outside* the order of power. This is the uncontaminated point of departure that anarchism relies upon in order to theorize resistance to power. Stirner, on the other hand, saw human essence itself as an abstraction, an ideological construct that dominates the individual. Foucault, continuing this critique of humanism, rejects any essentialist notions, seeing human subjectivity as an effect of power. Power, for Foucault, is productive rather than repressive: it does not repress human subjectivity, as political theorists have hitherto argued—rather it produces it. This denies the possibility of an uncontaminated point of departure outside power, because the human subject who hitherto constituted this "pure" place is contaminated by power.

This, argues Foucault, is the ruse of power: the fact that power tricks us into thinking that we are repressed, so that we try to assert our essence, but in doing so we play right into the hands of the power we are supposed to be resisting. This is because human essence is not an essence at all but a product of power/knowledge. Therefore, humanist political strategies like anarchism, which call for the liberation of human essence, fall victim to the trap power has laid for them in the same way that Marxist revolutionary strategy, according to the anarchists, is ensnared by the logic of the state. For Foucault then, "The man described for us, whom we are invited to free, is already in himself the effect of a subjection much more profound than himself."[44]

Foucault talks about the way that the subjectivity of the prisoner and the delinquent is constructed within the prison. In *Discipline and Punish*, he argues that the purpose of the prison is not to put a stop to crime: as with sexuality, the old language of repression and prohibition does not apply here. Rather, the purpose of the carceral system is to reproduce a steady flow of delinquency in order to justify the prison's continued existence. Moreover, the prison produces a discourse of criminology that focuses on the prisoner as an individual case to be studied. In this way, the prisoner is pinned down within a constructed identity of "delinquent." Foucault suggests that these techniques of subjection are not confined to the prison but are at work at all levels of society. Moreover, within the prison, through various techniques of surveillance, the "soul" of the prisoner is constructed: if the prisoner believes that he is always being watched, even when he is not, then he becomes his own moral warden. Thus the guilty "soul" of the prisoner is constructed as a tool of self-subjection.

This internalized self-surveillance and self-subjection is the central feature of Foucault's description of modern power. There is no need for a massive, repressive power, because the individual represses himself. With the Panopticon, for instance, there is no need for anyone to be in the watchtower, as long as the prisoner believes there is someone watching him.[45] This, it could be argued, is truly power without essence, without place. Power itself may be an empty place, like the empty watchtower, and it may function without agents. All it needs are subjects who participate in their own domination by believing they are repressed. Power may operate from below, not from above.[46]

It may be interesting here to compare Kropotkin's discussion of the prison and criminology with Foucault's. Kropotkin argues that the prison is ineffectual against crime because it dehumanizes the prisoner—robs him of his humanity—inculcating within him a greater propensity for crime. Instead of treating crime, then, as a sin to be punished, it should, Kropotkin argues, be treated as a sickness to be cured.[47] The criminal should therefore be taken out of the prison and treated humanely, in order to restore to him a sense of humanity and morality. On the surface, Kropotkin's ideas are liberating; they are aimed at emancipating the essential humanity of the prisoner that is supposedly crushed by the prison. However, Foucault, as a genealogist, wants to unmask the domination behind such ostensibly progressive ideas. He argues that the domination of the prison does not repress human essence: on the contrary, it operates through it. We know from Stirner that humanism is a discourse that oppresses the individual. Human essence, seen to be so redeeming and liberating by Kropotkin, is found by Foucault to be the standard of "normalization" by which individuals are judged and condemned.[48] Foucault thus continues Stirner's critique of humanism: man and humanity are discursive constructs, standards according to which individuals are judged and judge themselves—a standard which rationalizes in the name of what is "truly human," the persecution of those who do not fit in.

Foucault does not see Kropotkin's proposal that the criminal should be cured rather than punished, as any more liberating either. The strategy of cure is simply the strategy of punishment under a different name: it is still an application of the same moral and rational norms to an identity that does not measure up. In other words, whether crime or madness is considered either as a sin to be punished or a sickness to be cured, it is still a form of condemnation—an attribution of some kind of lack, or failing to these experiences.[49] Stirner also sees punishment and cure as two sides of the same coin: "if the latter sees in an action a sin against right, the former takes it for a sin of the man *against himself*, as a decadence from his health."[50] Stirner and Foucault force us to ask the question: what right do rationality and morality have to "cure" irrationality and immorality?

As I suggested earlier, this conflict between Foucault's and Kropotkin's ideas about crime and punishment is not an outdated one: anarchist ideas are still being used as a basis for proposals for the reform of criminology.[51] The arguments for reform are based on various essentialist ideas about what constitutes human subjectivity and what human needs are. The differences between Kropotkin and Foucault, then, go to the heart of the debate between humanism and antihumanism or *posthumanism*. For radical humanists, human essence is repressed by institutions such as the prison; and this essence must be liberated if people are to be free. For antihumanists, on the other hand, like

Foucault and Stirner, human essence is not only an effect of domination, but also a tool of it. Individuals are dominated, in prison, and in other ways, because they do not conform to this constructed notion of human essence. Like Stirner's un-man, and like Foucault's delinquent, mad, and perverse, they are persecuted because of their difference from a norm constructed around the notion of what constitutes a human being. Therefore, political reforms and struggles that are based around the notion of liberating human essence are often concomitant with further domination.

Humanism and Power

Stirner's and Foucault's critique of humanism has pointed to the operation of a new kind of power—humanist power—which is based on the denial of our own power, on our abdication of power over ourselves. Foucault sees humanism as "everything in Western civilization that restricts the desire for power."[52] Humanism is a discourse in which we have become trapped: it claims to free individuals from all sorts of institutional oppressions while, at the same time, entailing an intensification of the oppression over ourselves and denying us the power to resist this subjection. In humanism the individual has only "pseudo-sovereignty." Humanism claims to hold sovereign, "consciousness (sovereign in the context of judgement, but subjected to the necessities of truth), the individual (a titular control of personal rights subjected to the laws of nature and society), basic freedom (sovereign within, but accepting the demands of an outside world and 'aligned with destiny')."[53]

In other words, within the humanist language of rights and freedoms there is, according to Foucault, a trap: rights and freedoms are granted to the individual in return for the relinquishment of power, power over oneself. And, as Stirner has shown, rights and freedoms are meaningless without power. Therefore, for Foucault, humanism is based on the individual's abdication of his power. Stirner shares this condemnation of humanism. He argues, for instance, that humanism's claim of freeing the consciousness means only a further subjection to rational truth: "If thoughts are free, I am their slave."[54] Stirner's analysis of humanism has shown that it is concomitant with the domination of the individual ego. While humanism is couched in terms of rights and freedoms, these are granted to man—who is an abstraction—not to the individual. Therefore, Stirner and Foucault see humanism as a discourse that frees man while enslaving the individual.

What Foucault and Stirner oppose in humanism is the absolutization of man. Stirner, as we have seen, talks about the way in which Feuerbach's "theological insurrection" of man against God—which is the basis of humanism—has reproduced man *as* God. Man becomes the very place of authority that it once opposed. The individual in humanist discourse is now subordinated under man, in the same way that man was subordinated under God. Man has killed God, as Nietzsche claimed, but he has also become God. Foucault too, believes that man is not only an effect of power—produced in the ways described—but he is also an institution of domination, a place of power. Man has become, in the past couple of centuries, the dominant figure within scientific, medical, sociological, and political discourses. This absolutization of man, and the power/knowledge regimes associated with it, are oppressive. They tie the individual to a certain identity—the criminal, the insane, the homosexual, the heterosexual, man, woman, etc.—which is limiting and oppressive, and which further subjects the individual to various strategies of power. The figure of man establishes itself as a norm that functions in a binary way, constructing identities and their dialectic opposites: sane/insane, innocent/guilty, normal/perverse, and it is according to these discursive constructions that individuals are dominated.

Foucault argues that this process of pinning down individuals within certain categories and identities is the way that modern power functions. It is not aimed at repressing and prohibiting certain subjectivities—rather it is aimed at producing them as objects of knowledge and subjects of power. It is, for instance, naive to say, according to Foucault, that homosexuality is repressed and that one is challenging power by asserting one's homosexuality. By doing this, one is merely playing into the hands of power, further tying oneself to a subjectivity that power has created. Foucault calls his form of power "subjectification."[55] Stirner as well—while he does not analyze a specific notion of power like Foucault—talks about a similar process of subjectification carried out by the state. The state functions, as we have seen, through a strategy of tying individuals to a constructed subjectivity based on human essence. This is the basis of state power.[56] Thus, Stirner and Foucault argue that power produces identities which are politically useful and this subjectifying power is made possible by the humanist deification of man.

So Foucault argues that power produces subjectivities based on human essence, and it produces them in such a way that their liberation is really their continued domination. This is the cunning of power: it disguises itself in the language of repression, when it actually functions in a far more pervasive and insidious way. The repressive guise of power is essential to perpetuation of productive power, because it keeps alive the dream, the Apollonian illusion, that there is a world outside power—from which power can be resisted—when, in fact, there is not. Therefore, for Foucault, the anarchists' idea of there being an uncontaminated point of departure—in the form of human essence—would be nothing but a self-deluding fantasy, as power has already colonized this supposedly pure place. Political theory, then, can no longer rely on there being an essential point of departure outside power: politics must function within power's limits.

Resistance

While power is productive rather than repressive, this does not mean that power, for Foucault, is not oppressive. Repression refers to a human essence which power restricts. While power is not repressive in this way, it is still *oppressive* in the sense that it imposes limits upon individuals by tying them to a supposedly repressed human essence. Repression and oppression are often confused by those of Foucault's critics, such as Jurgen Habermas and Nancy Fraser, who argue that Foucault does not provide any reason why power should be resisted.[57] While Foucault questions moral and rational discourses, it is wrong to say that he does not provide ethical reasons for resistance. The fact that power is oppressive, that it imposes limits on the individual, that it imprisons him within a fixed subjectivity, would be reason enough to resist.

Moreover, Foucault does not want to impose strict moral and rational criteria upon resistance because this would be a limitation in itself. It would deny the *singularity* of resistance:

> One does not make the law for the person who risks his life before power. Is there or is there not a reason to revolt? Let's leave the question open. There are revolts and that is a fact. . . . For there to be a sense of listening to them and in searching for what they say, it is sufficient that they exist and that they have against them so much which is set up to silence them. A question of morality? Perhaps. A question of reality? Certainly.[58]

Resistance, then, does not necessarily need a reason: if it happens, then that is justification enough. Foucault sees resistance and power existing in a relationship of mutual antagonism and incitement—a relationship of *agonism*. This is a continuation of the war model according to which resistance is not necessarily sanctioned by moral and rational standards, or by the promise of a better world: resistance is an absolute refusal of domination—a desperate struggle, sometimes to the death, with a particular relation of power. It is similar to Stirner's notion of the insurrection as a spontaneous uprising. Foucault argues that one can study resistance from the starting point of power, just as power may be analyzed from the perspective of resistance.[59] Thus, resistance to power can be justified by the asymmetries and excesses of the power it confronts; by a regime's denial of further possibilities of a reversal in power relations. Foucault, therefore, would seem to have an ethic of resistance—permanent resistance, an ongoing struggle with power. As soon as power relations become blocked and hierarchical, as soon as resistance itself becomes aligned with power and creates the potential for further domination, this is when resistance is necessary.[60]

It is, therefore, mistaken to say that Foucault has no normative guidelines for resistance. Moreover, just because Foucault questions the rights discourse of the Enlightenment—and for this he has been criticized by Nancy Fraser—he does not discount the possibility that rights may be used in the struggle against power. In fact, he says: "Against power it is always necessary to oppose unbreakable law and unabridgeable rights."[61] Foucault argues that rights and values are ambiguous: they are not essentially on the side of power or essentially on the side of resistance. They are weapons to be used in struggle, and it is up to the individual to interpret them. This war analysis that I have employed does not cheapen or invalidate rights and values: it merely leaves them open to change and contingency. Foucault, like Stirner, then, does not oppose rights and values: he is only against their absolutization—when they are taken out of the grasp of the individual and serve the interests of power.

Therefore, the criticism that Foucault does not provide any reasons for resistance to power can be rejected. The second criticism—that Foucault does not allow any *possibility* for resistance—is perhaps more valid. Critics argue that because Foucault's notion of power is so pervasive, because it leaves no space uncontaminated by it, resistance to power is impossible: it has no ground, no place from which it can emanate. Even human essence, the point of departure for political theory since the Enlightenment, is not free from power. This criticism has been made so often and by so many people that it has become the standard criticism of Foucault. But the fact that it is clichéd does not make it invalid. Nancy Fraser is probably one of Foucault's most articulate critics: she argues that because the subject for Foucault is merely an effect of power relations, then "there is no foundation . . . for a critique oriented around the notions of autonomy, reciprocity, mutual recognition, dignity, and human rights."[62] Critics such as Fraser want to use human essence and the human values that emanate from this essence as a limit to power. However, because Foucault denies this limit, because he does not recognize a place outside power, they argue that this makes resistance impossible. Where does resistance come from?

This criticism of Foucault is possibly the most damaging one. Foucault can answer this criticism, but he cannot do so without revealing certain inconsistencies in his notions of power and resistance. These inconsistencies, however, do not point to the existence of a central contradiction in his work. Rather they reveal an attempt on the part of Foucault to leave the question of resistance open to further debate.

Foucault does not have, as the anarchists do, a point of departure outside power: he rejects human essence and the notion of a transcendental morality and truth. There is no eternal place or essence outside power from which resistance emanates: "there is no single locus of great Refusal, no soul of revolt, source of all rebellions, or pure law of the revolutionary."[63] However, for Foucault, this does not negate the possibility of resistance or freedom: "To say that one can never be 'outside' power does not mean that one is trapped."[64] Power creates resistance; resistance is the flipside of power. Foucault says then: "Where there is power there is resistance, and yet, or rather consequently, this resistance is never in a position of exteriority to power."[65] Power incites resistance: power is always checked by the potential for resistance that it creates. Foucault, then, can account for resistance. However, this would appear to be a rather impoverished notion of resistance: always dependent on power—purely reactive. It would seem that Foucault has a deterministic notion of resistance akin to a determinist Marxist who argues that revolution will only unfold according to the logic of capitalism. Foucault is aware of this possible interpretation, and tries to counter it by arguing that although there is no place outside power, there are certain elements which escape it, if only momentarily, and these elements give rise to resistance, a certain "plebeian quality."[66]

Foucault takes pains to ensure us that this is not some kind of essence that stands outside power. If this were the case, Foucault would be no different from the anarchists who insisted on a revolutionary human essence unpolluted by power. Foucault tells us that "plebs" is not a subjectivity or essence, but rather an energy, a discharge. However, Foucault does, on occasion, fall into the essentialist trap on this question. He argues for instance that "the rallying point for the counterattack against the deployment of sexuality ought not be sex-desire, but bodies and pleasures."[67] For Foucault, sex and sexuality cannot be a basis for resistance because, as he has shown, they are effects of power. However, he does not say why "bodies and pleasures" should be any different from sexuality. Foucault cannot possibly exempt bodies from his argument that everything is constructed discursively and through power relations; that there is no outside to power. This would, to some extent, go against his genealogical project, which was aimed, in part, at undermining the idea of the body as a stable essence outside history.[68] As Nancy Fraser rightly argues, Foucault gives us no reason why "bodies and pleasures" is a better basis for resistance than sex.[69]

Foucault's notion, then, of "bodies and pleasures" as a place of resistance is highly questionable. However, there is another way of thinking about resistance that avoids essentialism. Resistance may perhaps be seen as an excess which, while provoked by power, is not necessarily confined or determined by it: it is something which escapes, however temporarily, the grasp of power. Foucault argues that revolt, for instance, is produced by conditions of power, but it is not captured by it. Revolt is a dislocation, with unpredictable consequences.[70] This displacement is probably what Foucault was hinting at in his notion of "plebs": "This measure of plebs is not so much what stands outside relations of power as their limit, their underside, that which responds to every advance of power by a movement of disengagement."[71]

For instance, life is the target of power; yet life is also an underside of power, which resists power by exposing its limits. Life is, according to Foucault, the limit of power: when people are prepared to die to resist, "when life will no longer barter itself," then power has reached its limit.[72] Perhaps this limit is a kind of outside in terms of its pure openness and possibility.

Transgressing the Self

For Foucault, the death of God signified the death of infinitude and limitlessness. In other words, it meant the reign of the Limit.[73] Man was now limited by power, but power itself also had limits. The limits created by power are themselves limited. There is an excess, Foucault argues, which both transgresses and affirms power's limits. Transgression and limit depend on one another. Transgression exposes the limit of the limit.[74] Thus, the purpose of transgression is not to overcome the limits of power—as the anarchist revolution proclaimed—because these limits can never be totally overcome, because the overcoming of one set of limits will ultimately mean the construction of another. Transgression can only be ephemeral: it burns itself up once it has passed the limit and only exists insofar as the limit itself exists. Therefore, transgression can only be a critique conducted upon limits: it can only expose the limits which give rise to it and *limit* it, "like a flash of lightning in the night, which . . . gives a dense and black intensity to the night it denies."[75] In other words, transgression, for Foucault, is a constant overcoming, a transgression of transgression, and the politics of resistance must be humbled by this.

This notion of transgression runs counter to revolutionary philosophies, such as anarchism, which foresee the final overcoming of power and the eternal reign of freedom. For the proponent of the war model, however, power is here to stay. It can never be entirely overcome because every overcoming is itself the imposition of a new kind of power. Foucault has taken the anarchist logic of place to its ultimate conclusion. He has shown that there is no overcoming of the logic of place; that there is no promise of freedom taking the place of power, because freedom itself is another kind of power. This is close to Stirner, who argues that freedom is always based on power, and that one's idea of freedom may be another's domination. Foucault and Stirner, however, do not reject the idea of freedom: they merely argue that it is based on struggle and open to reinterpretation. For Foucault, freedom is not a final state that can be reached, but rather a constant relationship of struggle and renegotiation with power. Freedom cannot transcend power because, according to Foucault, freedom is the condition for the exercise of power.[76] Therefore, the relationship between power and freedom is not one of mutual exclusion as anarchists contended. There is rather a constant interplay, an agonistic struggle between them in which each is pitted at the other but, at the same time, depends upon the other. Freedom, then, cannot be seen as overcoming of power, or even existing outside the world of power. The two are fundamentally intertwined. However, this does not mean we are doomed to perpetual domination and that one, therefore, should no longer bother resisting power. On the contrary, while there is no ending power— because power is involved in almost every social relationship—there are certain arrangements of power which allow greater possibilities of freedom than others. The aim of resistance is to maximize these possibilities of freedom.

Freedom is always possible, even within the most oppressive conditions: it is a freedom which, while conditioned by power, is never completely limited by it, and which always has unpredictable effects. The point is to invent one's own forms of freedom; to not be seduced, as Stirner argues, by mankind's eternal dream of freedom, because this always results in another domination.[77] Stirner, as we have seen, calls this ownness—power over oneself, the personal autonomy that is denied under humanism, which grants all sorts of freedoms apart from this one.[78] Ownness, then, perhaps approaches a posthumanist, or poststructuralist, form of freedom: one that is dependent on power and antagonism and which is, nevertheless, an affirmation of this. Foucault also talks about various ethical and aesthetic strategies of existence and work on oneself—"askesis"—which increase the power that one exercises over oneself. This does not mean that freedom is limited to having power over oneself, to ownness—but this surely must be one of the fundamental conditions of freedom.

This notion of ownness is remarkably close to Foucault's idea that one should, as a way of combating subjectifying power, reject one's "essential" identity and invent for oneself new identities. Like Stirner, Foucault believes that because subjectification is made possible only by our willingly submitting to it, liberation should therefore start with ourselves: "Maybe the target nowadays is not to discover who we are, but to refuse who we are. . . . The political, ethical, social, philosophical problem of our days is not to liberate the individual from the State and its institutions, but to liberate ourselves from the State and the type of individualization linked to it."[79] If power works by confining us to an essential identity that it has produced, then we should reject political strategies, such as those of classical anarchism for instance, which are based on the liberation of one's essence.[80] In order to remain one step ahead of power we can perhaps engage in aesthetic and ethical practices which involve the constant reinvention of identity. While this is a strategy that promises no final liberation from power and is engaged in within the confines of power, it can still offer new possibilities of personal freedom. Foucault suggests that individuals refuse who they are—refuse to be limited by essence—and become something that they are not. The emphasis is on becoming and flux, rather than on the achievement of an identity. The individual might engage in an anarchism of subjectivity—rather than an anarchism based on subjectivity, on essence: the anarchism of Bakunin, Proudhon, and Kropotkin. Perhaps Foucault is only an anarchist who takes the idea of anarchism beyond the limits set down for it by humanism. He has extended the rejection of authority to the level of subjectivity, seeing human essence itself as a place of authority and calling for its destruction. As Reiner Schurmann argues, Foucault calls for us to constitute ourselves as anarchist subjects.[81] This may be seen as a subjectivity emptied of essence and based on antagonism and difference—a subjectivity founded on the model of war.

The war model is a rejection of all totalities and essences. Foucault argues, like Stirner, that unities must be broken down because the threads that tie them together are not based on a consensus of values, but on the domination of one kind of value over another. The war model, then, rejects the humanist idea of an essential common ground, a shared social reality.[82] For Foucault the struggles around values and interpretations are "anarchistic struggles."[83] However they are anarchistic not in the sense that they transcend power, but rather in the sense that they realize that power can never be transcended. Foucault's ethics seeks out lines of flight or escape from power, coupled with the realization that power can never really be escaped, only momentarily eluded. Foucault is on thin ground here, however, and this paradox—the paradox of the transgression of transgression, the limit of the limit, freedom within confinement—while being essential to his work, presents him, as we have seen, with various problems in theorizing resistance.

Foucault's use of the war model has *displaced* the notion of place: it has not only undermined the place of power, but also the place of resistance. By seeing human essence as an effect of power, Foucault has denied political theory the notion of the uncontaminated point of departure, the place upon which anarchism is founded. But has Foucault gone too far in this last respect? His anarchism has transgressed the limits of human subjectivity set down by Bakunin, Proudhon, and Kropotkin. But in following Stirner, in seeing the world in terms of difference and antagonism, has Foucault not created for himself his own set of limits which he cannot really transcend without being, to some extent, inconsistent? The dream of escape, the line of flight, the "nonplace" of resistance—while these are not sleights of hand, they are notions which need further explanation. This is the paradox of Foucault. However, it is not a paradox that cannot be solved dialectically. Rather, it is a paradox that continues to generate possibility at the limits of impossibility, openness at the limits of closure. Foucault has fundamentally altered the parameters and conditions of political theory, defining its limits but also showing us its exhilarating limitlessness. The problem left unanswered by Foucault, however—that of finding a positive non-essentialist figure of resistance—will be further explored, through Deleuze and Guattari, in the next chapter.

Notes

1. Foucault condemns those on the left who refuse to question the Gulag "on the basis of the texts of Marx or Lenin or to ask oneself how, through what error, deviation, misunderstanding or distortion of speculation or practice, their theory could have been betrayed to such a degree." See "Powers and Strategies," 135.

2. Quoted from Callinicos, *Is There a Future for Marxism?*, 108.

3. Michel Foucault, "Truth and Power," in *Power/Knowledge*, 109-133.

4. For instance, the Marxist explanation of the repression of masturbation in children might go as follows: onanism was suppressed by the bourgeoisie because it did not contribute to the production of the labour force required by capitalism. Foucault argues, on the other hand, that if a labor force were needed, might not the bourgeoisie have encouraged, rather than repressed, onanism in order to inculcate reproductive training in children? The argument works both ways.

5. Foucault, "Revolutionary Action," 231.

6. Foucault, "Revolutionary Action," 232.

7. Foucault: "one can perfectly well conceive of revolutions which leave essentially untouched the power relations which form the basis for the functioning of the State." See "Truth and Power," 123.

8. Michel Foucault, "The Politics of Crime," trans. M. Horowitz, *Partisan Review* 43, no. 3 (1976): 453-466.

9. Foucault, "Truth and Power," 121.

10. Michel Foucault, *The History of Sexuality VI: Introduction,* trans. R. Hunter (New York: Vintage Books, 1978), 93.

11. Michel Foucault, "The Ethic of Care for the Self as a Practice of Freedom: Interview with Michel Foucault," in *The Final Foucault*, ed. James Bernauer and David Rasmussen (Cambridge, Mass.: MIT Press, 1988), 1-20.

12. Michel Foucault, "The Subject and Power," in *Michel Foucault: Beyond Structuralism and Hermeneutics*, Hubert L. Dreyfus and Paul Rabinow (Chicago: University of Chicago Press, 1982), 208-226.

13. Colin Gordon, "Governmental Rationality: an introduction," in *The Foucault Effect: Studies in Governmentality*, ed. Colin Gordon et al. (Chicago: University of Chicago Press, 1991), 1-51.

14. Michel Foucault, "Governmentality," in *The Foucault Effect*, 87-104.

15. Foucault, "Governmentality," 103.

16. Foucault, "Governmentality," 103.

17. Foucault, "Governmentality," 103.

18. Foucault, *The History of Sexuality*, 94.

19. Foucault, *The History of Sexuality*, 93.

20. Foucault, *The History of Sexuality*, 96.

21. Foucault: "if power is properly speaking the way in which relations of forces are deployed and given concrete expression, rather than analysing it in terms of cession, contract or alienation, or functionally in terms of its maintenance of the relations of production, should we not analyse it primarily in terms of *struggle, conflict, war?*" See Michel Foucault, "Lecture One: 7 January 1976," in *Power/Knowledge*, 90.

22. Michel Foucault, "War in the Filigree of Peace: Course Summary," trans. I. Mcleod, in *Oxford Literary Review* 4, no. 2 (1976): 15-19.

23. Foucault, "Nietzsche, Genealogy, History," 91.

24. Foucault, "Lecture One," 90.

25. Foucault, "War in the Filigree of Peace," 17-18.

26. Foucault, "Nietzsche, Genealogy, History," 83.

27. Friedrich Nietzsche, *Beyond Good and Evil*, trans. R. J. Hollingdale (London: Penguin Books, 1990), 201.

28. Foucault, "Nietzsche, Genealogy, History," 78.

29. Foucault, "Nietzsche, Genealogy, History," 85.

30. Foucault, "Nietzsche, Genealogy, History," 85.

31. Foucault, "Nietzsche, Genealogy, History," 85.

32. Foucault, *The History of Sexuality*, 102.

33. Foucault: "we must cease once and for all to describe the effects of power in negative terms: it 'excludes', it 'represses', it 'censors', it 'abstracts', it 'masks', it 'conceals.' In fact, power produces; it produces reality; it produces domains of objects and rituals of truth." See Michel Foucault, *Discipline and Punish: the Birth of the Prison*, trans. A. Sheridan (London: Penguin Books, 1991), 194.

34. Bakunin saw science and knowledge as tools with which to unmask a power which works through religious obfuscation. The masses are oppressed because they are kept in ignorance—they are denied knowledge. See *Political Philosophy*, 83.

35. Foucault: "power and knowledge directly imply one another; there is no power relation without a correlative constitution of a field of knowledge, nor any knowledge that does not presuppose and constitute at the same time, power relations." See *Discipline and Punish*, 27.

36. Foucault, "Truth and Power," 133.

37. According to Stirner, "truth has never won a victory, but was always my *means* to the victory, like the sword" See *The Ego*, 354.

38. Kropotkin, *In Russian and French Prisons*, 338.

39. Foucault sees the domination of the prison as "cynical and at the same pure and entirely justified because its practices can be totally formulated within the framework of morality. Its brutal tyranny appears as the serene domination of Good over Evil, of order over disorder." See "Intellectual and Power: A conversation between Michel Foucault and Gilles Deleuze," in *Language, Counter-Memory, Practice*, 204-217.

40. The ultimate purpose of the GIP (Information Group on Prisons), in which Foucault was involved, was "to question the social and moral distinction between the innocent and the guilty." See "Revolutionary Action," 227.

41. Stirner, *The Ego*, 81.

42. Foucault: "it seems to me that the idea of justice in itself is an idea which in effect has been invented and put to work in different types of societies as a weapon of a certain political and economic power." See debate between Michel Foucault and Noam Chomsky, "Human Nature: Justice versus Power," in *Reflexive Water: The Basic Concerns of Mankind*, ed. Fons Elders, et al. (Canada: Condor Books, 1974), 133-197.

43. Foucault, "Power and Strategies," 141.

44. Foucault, *Discipline and Punish*, 30.

45. Foucault, *Discipline and Punish*, 200-201.

46. Stirner also sees selfsubjection as a mode of power. For Stirner, like Foucault, the state is an empty place of power, with no essence of its own: its unity is an illusion. What is important is its perceived unity and power, and our attachment to it. Thus the domination of the state depends on the domination of ourselves. Stirner then has forced political theory to address the problem of selfsubjection—how we participate in our own domination—and Foucault, through his analysis of sexuality, the asylum, and the prison, has continued this path of questioning.

47. Kropotkin: "The same has to be done with the great social phenomenon which has been called Crime until now, but will be called Social Disease by our children. Prevention of disease is the best of cures." See *In Russian and French Prisons*, 339.

48. Foucault, *Discipline and Punish*, 183.

49. Foucault, *Discipline and Punish*, 22.

50. Stirner, *The Ego*, 240.

51. See Tifft and Stevenson, "Humanistic Criminology." See also Larry L. Tifft, "The Coming Redefinitions of Crime: An Anarchist Perspective," in *Social Problems* 24, no. 4 (April 1979): 392-402.

52. Foucault, "Revolutionary Action," 221.

53. Foucault, "Revolutionary Action," 221.

54. Stirner, *The Ego*, 345.

55. Foucault: "This form of power applies itself to immediate everyday life which categorises the individual, marks him by his own individuality, attaches him to his own identity, imposes a law of truth on him which he must and which others must recognise in him. It is a form of power which makes individuals subjects." See "The Subject and Power," 212.

56. Stirner, *The Ego*, 180.

57. See Nancy Fraser, "Foucault on Modern Power; Empirical Insights and Normative Confusions," *Praxis International* 1, no. 3 (1981): 272-287.

58. Michel Foucault, "Is it Useless to Revolt?" *Philosophy and Social Criticism* 8, no.1 (1981): 1-9.

59. Foucault, "The Subject and Power," 211.

60. Foucault says: "My point is not that everything is bad, but that everything is dangerous. . . . If everything is dangerous, then we always have something to do. So my position leads not to apathy but to a hyper- and pessimistic activism." See Michel

Foucault, "On the Genealogy of Ethics: An Overview of Work in Progress," in *The Foucault Reader*, 340-372.

61. Foucault, "Is it Useless to Revolt?" 8.
This emphasis on rights—particularly individual rights—has some similarities with libertarian discourse. Indeed, there is much in Foucault's work which would suggest that if one were forced to find a political label for him, and for that matter perhaps, poststructuralist philosophy generally, it would be libertarianism, or at least left libertarianism. However, one must be careful about reading too much into this because Foucault and Stirner reject the liberal categories of the essential individual and rationality which libertarianism is based on. But if one were to look at some of the political implications of Foucault's and Stirner's ideas—their ethic of maximizing personal freedom and autonomy for instance—one could make a tenuous connection with libertarianism.

62. Nancy Fraser, *Unruly Practices: Power, Discourse and Gender* (Cambridge, U.K.: Polity Press, 1989), 56.

63. Foucault, *The History of Sexuality*, 95-96.

64. Foucault, "Power and Strategies," 141.

65. Foucault, *The History of Sexuality*, 95.

66. Foucault: "there is indeed always something in the social body, in classes, groups and individuals themselves which in some sense escapes relations of power, something which is by no means a more or less docile or reactive primal matter, but rather an inverse energy . . . a certain plebeian quality." See "Power and Strategies," 138.

67. Foucault, *The History of Sexuality*, 151.

68. Foucault, "Nietzsche, Genealogy, History," 87.

69. Fraser, *Unruly Practices*, 60.

70. Foucault, "Is it Useless to Revolt?" 5.

71. Foucault, "Power and Strategies," 138.

72. Foucault, "Is it Useless to Revolt?" 5.

73. Michel Foucault, "A Preface to Transgression," in *Language, Counter-Memory, Practice*, 29-52.

74. Foucault, "A Preface to Transgression," 34.

75. Foucault, "A Preface to Transgression," 35.

76. Foucault, "The Subject and Power," 221.
Foucault believes that power is only exercised upon free subjects. Power is action on action, and for power to operate there must be a certain freedom with regard to the possibilities of action open to us. For Foucault, then, slavery is not a power relationship "when the man is in chains." "The Subject and Power," 221.

77. Stirner says about the French Revolution: "The craving for a particular freedom always includes the purpose of a new dominion." See *The Ego*, 160.
Perhaps as Stirner argues, the idea of freedom should give way to ownness: ownness is based on a war model of relations, in which it is recognized that all freedom is based on power and must therefore be seized by the individual. Ownness allows one to invent one's own forms of freedom through resistance.

78. For Stirner, ownness is the strategy of inventing one's own forms of freedom. His notion of rebellion, discussed in the previous chapter, is based on this strategy of freeing oneself from subjectification, from a power which ties individuals to a fixed identity, and of reinventing one's personal autonomy: "insurrection leads us no longer to *let* ourselves be arranged, but to arrange ourselves." See *The Ego*, 316.

79. Foucault, "The Subject and Power," 216.

80. For example the politics of gay liberation would be no longer radical because homosexuality has been colonized by power and becomes a limit placed on the

individual. This would account for Foucault's interest in S/M as a transgressive practice and subjectivity: it was a strategy that attempted to turn the tables on power by eroticizing it and by freeing the body from the limits of sex. See Jon Simons, *Foucault and the Political* (London: Routledge, 1995), 99-100.

81. See Reiner Schurmann, "On Constituting Oneself as an Anarchist Subject," in *Praxis International* 6, no. 3 (October 1986): 294-310.

82. Foucault: "'The whole of society' is precisely that which should not be considered except as something to be destroyed." See "Revolutionary Action," 233.

83. Foucault, "The Subject and Power," 211.

Chapter Five

The War-Machine: Deleuze and Guattari

It was argued in the last chapter that Foucault tries to explain the phenomenon of resistance, yet cannot do so without revealing certain ambiguities in his thinking. Following in Stirner's wake, Foucault *deterritorializes* political thought, showing that resistance to power must take place within power's limits, and that there is no point of departure outside power. In doing this, Foucault comes close to defining a non-essentialist politics of resistance. However, in trying to provide a positive figure for resistance—"plebs," "bodies and pleasures"—Foucault falls victim to the very essentialism and foundationalism he was trying to escape. Moreover, it was suggested that resistance to power cannot be conceptualized without thinking in terms of an outside to power. However, the notion of an outside is, as we have seen, problematic for Foucault. While his notion of plebs could be seen as an excess produced by power, but momentarily eluding and resisting it, Foucault is unclear on this point. And while he chooses to leave the question of resistance open, the reader may be forgiven for taking this gesture of theoretical openness as a poor excuse for leaving the question unanswered. If, for Foucault, the study of resistance is vital for the study of power itself, then it is too important a problem to be left unattended.

Gilles Deleuze and Felix Guattari take up the question of resistance from where Foucault left it. They seek to give more content to Foucault's ambiguous idea of plebs, conceiving it in terms of either *desire*, or a *war-machine* that resists state "capture." These figures of resistance are made possible by theorizing an outside to state power, an outside formulated through the image of war. Deleuze and Guattari resume the assault on the notion of place through an analysis that emphasizes production and power over essence; flux and becoming over stasis; difference, pluralism, and nondialectical antagonism over place. Therefore, Deleuze and Guattari may be seen to be applying the war model of relations that I have perversely appropriated from Hobbes and expanded through Stirner and Foucault. This chapter will examine Deleuze and Guattari's contribution to the question of place—the place of power and the place of resistance. It will also consider their notion of desire as a figure of resistance: whether their idea of desire as constituting a revolutionary outside to power is a reaffirmation of the essentialist politics that Deleuze and Guattari claim to reject. Does desire fall victim to the logic of power, or is it the figure of resistance that has hitherto eluded us?

The Abstract State

Deleuze and Guattari's work provides us with a curious point of comparison with anarchism, particularly with regard to the question of the state. Unlike Foucault, they do not shy away from macropolitical analyses. Rather they collapse the distinction between the micro and macropolitical spheres, seeing one as always referring to the other—seeing a transformation in one area as always having implications in others. They argue that: "politics is simultaneously a *macropolitics* and a *micropolitics*."[1] Like the anarchists then, Deleuze and Guattari are inclined to make the state their target of critique, seeing it as an abstract form which gives rise to minor dominations, giving them meaning and form. The state provides "general models of realization" for the various dominations within society: "the apparatus of the State is a concrete assemblage which realizes the machine of overcoding of a society."[2] For Deleuze and Guattari, then, the state is an abstract form or model rather than a concrete institution, which essentially rules through more minute institutions and practices of domination. The state "overcodes" these dominations, stamping them with its imprint. Therefore, the state has no essence itself, but is rather an "assemblage," or even a process of "capture."[3]

Deleuze and Guattari's notion of the "state-form" is similar to the anarchist's idea of the "ruling principle" of the state: the state is a generic form, an abstraction, an idea which actualizes itself in different forms throughout history. Like the anarchists, Deleuze and Guattari see the state as an "abstract machine" that manifests itself in different forms and different regimes of signs. However, what is important about this abstract machine is not the form in which it appears, but rather its function. In the same way, anarchists criticized Marxists for paying too much attention to the form of state power—the liberal state, the workers' state—while neglecting its fundamental operation and function.[4]

For Deleuze and Guattari, moreover, there has always been a state—the *Urstaat*, the eternal state—which comes into existence fully formed.[5] Deleuze and Guattari are inspired here by Nietzsche's discussion of the origins of the state: a terrible, oppressive apparatus, imposed from without by a "master race" who "appear as lightning appears, too terrible, too sudden, too convincing, too 'different' even to be hated."[6] Moreover, they claim that this archaic state did not rise as a result of an agrarian mode of production, as Marx argued, but, in fact, predates, and is presupposed, by this mode of production: "It is not the State that presupposes a mode of production; quite the opposite, it is the State that makes productions a 'mode.'"[7] They see the state as an apparatus or machine, a model of thought and organization that *overcodes* economic flows, flows of production, organizing them into a mode. On this point, then, Deleuze and Guattari's notion of the state is close to anarchism: the origins of the state cannot be attributed to the mode of production, as Marxists argue. Rather it may work the other way around: the mode of production may in fact be derived from the state.

The modern state, for Deleuze and Guattari, however, is infinitely bound up with capitalism: it provides the models of realization for the capitalist axiomatic, reterritorializing the decoded flows released by capitalism.[8] The state is seen, therefore, as part of the capitalist machine: capital and the state form a system of signifiers and axioms that become internalized within individuals as infinite debt.[9] Thus, the "holy State" and "God-capital" become almost religious signifiers which individuals are subordinated to.[10] The state, however, is continually displaced by capitalist flows that reduce all social relations to commodity relations. Capital, while it "deterritorializes" desire by overthrowing traditional state-coded structures, simultaneously "reterritorializes" through the state, these flows of desire which, if unrestricted, present a threat to it. The state, they argue, plays a fundamentally repressive role, holding in check the free flow of forces, thereby dissipating the potential for revolution.[11]

For this reason, Deleuze and Guattari, like the anarchists, see the state as something to be resisted.[12] However this resistance must involve a rejection of state philosophies—discourses such as the social contract theory, which attempt to legitimize the state, making it appear necessary and inevitable.[13] Certain forms of thought, for instance, have complicity in the state, providing it with a legitimate ground and consensus: "Only thought is capable of inventing the fiction of a State that it is universal by right, of elevating the State to de jure universality."[14] Thus, Deleuze and Guattari, as well as the anarchists, discuss the way in which thought has complicity in state domination. However, Deleuze and Guattari take this analysis further than anarchism, looking at the way that the state has penetrated and "coded" thought, in particular rational thought. Rationality does not provide, as it did with the anarchists, a point of departure for resisting the state: the state actually depends upon rational discourses for its legitimization and functioning while, in turn, making these discourses possible. It is not just that these discourses seek to provide a rational justification for the state—they are manifestations of the state form in thought. Rational thought is state philosophy: "Common sense, the unity of all the faculties at the center of the Cogito, is the State consensus raised to the absolute."[15] The state is immanent in thought, giving it ground, logos, providing it with a model that defines its "goal, paths, conduits, channels, organs."[16] According to this analysis, most political philosophy—including even anarchism—based on a rational critique of the state and a Manichean division between "rational" society and "irrational" power, would be considered state philosophy. It leaves the place of state power intact by subjecting revolutionary action to rational injunctions that channel it into state forms. For Deleuze and Guattari, if the state is to be overcome one must invent new lines of political action, new *lines of flight* that do not allow themselves to be reterritorialized by rationality: "politics is active experimentation since we do not know in advance which way a line is going to turn."[17] It is clear that while anarchism constructed a theory of the state that was much broader than that of Marxism, Deleuze and Guattari go beyond even this. In a sense they turn their theory of the state back on anarchism itself. They continue Stirner's and Foucault's reinscribing of the political, seeing as the state precisely the same discourses that the anarchists saw as opposed to the state. They have expanded the argument by further rendering, through their expansive idea of power and the state, anarchism's uncontaminated point of departure impossible.

Desire and Oedipus

If anarchism took little account of the complicity of rationality in state domination, it also failed to recognize the link between desire and state power. For Deleuze and Guattari, desire is not necessarily suppressed by the state but, rather, *used* by it. This is similar, in many ways, to Stirner's idea of the state: an abstraction with no real essence, whose domination is made possible through our complicity—through our desire for the state, for authority.[18] Deleuze and Guattari argue that individuals can desire their own domination, just as they can desire freedom.[19] When we desire our own repression we are not necessarily falling victim to an ideological trap, we are not suffering from false consciousness. Rather, domination and repression are part of desire: "To the question 'How can desire desire its own repression, how can it desire its slavery?', we reply that the powers which crush desire, or which subjugate it, themselves already form part of the assemblages of desire."[20] Therefore political action against the state must take place at the level of desire: we must rid ourselves of the desire for the state, the desire for our own domination. If we do not do this, then the figure of the state will always haunt anti-authoritarian theory: resistance will always reinvent the state—it will always reaffirm the place of power. The political investment at the level of desire was a problem the anarchists never counted on. For anarchists there was always a division between the state and the desiring subject.[21]

Moreover, Deleuze and Guattari argue, like Foucault, that the subject itself is a fabrication, and that it is constructed in such a way that its desire becomes the desire for the state, the desire for its own domination. This has important implications for radical political theory: if power operates at the level of individual and collective desire, then perhaps the Enlightenment-humanist project should be questioned. The state, according to Deleuze and Guattari, where it once operated through a massive repressive apparatus, now no longer needs this—it functions through the self-domination of the subject. The subject becomes his own legislator: "the more you obey the statements of dominant reality, the more you command as speaking subject within mental reality, for finally you only obey yourself. . . . A new form of slavery has been invented, that of being a slave to oneself."[22]

Modern power has become individualized: it functions in a similar manner to Foucault's Panopticon, and Stirner's subjectifying state. We have already seen this in the way in which the idea of self-subjection as the modern operation of power has jeopardized the place of power: power no longer has a centralized place to which individuals are subordinated. Rather we subordinate ourselves to signifying regimes all around us. While Deleuze and Guattari argue that these local sites of power are still overcoded by the state's abstract machine, their analysis of modern power as self-subjection undermines the classical division—

which formed the basis of anarchism—between the place of power and the place of resistance. For Deleuze and Guattari there can be no distinct place of power because power, like desire, is involved in a multitude of instances, at every level of society. Nor can there be a distinct place of resistance because we voluntarily submit to, and often desire, domination: thus the "place" of resistance is essentially unstable, and is always in danger of becoming part of the assemblage of power. Resistance, then, must be a "long labor which is aimed not merely against the State and the powers that be, but directly at ourselves."[23]

In this modern signifying regime, desire is channeled to the state through our willing submission to oedipal representation and psychoanalysis. Oedipus has become the new image of thought, the abstract machine of the state.[24] It is a discourse that provides a justification for the modern state, and the knowledge which allows it to function, in the same way that classical philosophies, such as those based on the social contract theory, provided the abstract machine for the state and church. In fact Deleuze and Guattari see psychoanalysis as the new church, the altar upon which we sacrifice and subject ourselves, no longer to God but to Oedipus; psychoanalysts are "the last priests."[25] Psychoanalysis poisons the modern consciousness, confining desire within the discourse of Oedipus.

Oedipal representation does not repress desire as such, but rather constructs it in such a way that it believes itself to be repressed, to be based on a negativity, lack, and guilt. According to Deleuze and Guattari, "Oedipal desires are not at all repressed . . . Oedipal desires are the bait, the disfigured image by means of which repression catches desire in the trap."[26] Thus, oedipal repression is simply the mask for the real domination of desire. Desire is "repressed" in this way because unfettered it is a threat to state society. In this way, Deleuze and Guattari continue the poststructuralist critique of human essence constituting a place of departure outside power. Certainly for Deleuze and Guattari, desire is repressed, and this puts them at odds with Foucault who would argue that there is no desire as such to repress. However, the desire which they claim is repressed is not the desire of humanist discourses. It is not human oedipal desire which is repressed; on the contrary, they argue that this is actually a representation of this very repression. Psychoanalysis is a discourse that "speaks" for the individual, for the unconscious, representing its desires within the theater of Oedipus, thereby turning desire against itself.[27] Desires are interpreted as signifiers of the Oedipal unconscious, and it is through this process that desire is pulled into line, made safe, channeled into the state. In psychoanalysis, then, according to Deleuze: "All real desire has already disappeared: a code is put in its place, a symbolic overcoding of utterances, a fictitious subject of enunciation who doesn't give the patients a chance."[28] This critique of representation in psychoanalysis is similar to Foucault's attack on various discourses—political, medical, psychiatric, etc.—which attempt to speak for the individual, explaining away and marginalizing his wayward utterances, thereby controlling their subversive, unpredictable effects.[29]

Critique of Representation

This attack on representation has implications for anarchism, which was, as Todd May argues, essentially a critique of political representation.[30] For anarchists, political representation—the relegation of power from the masses to a few who purport to speak for them—is a relationship of domination. This was what the anarchists condemned in Marxism: the vanguardism of the party that purports to speak in the name of the masses; the privileging of the industrial working class over other identities on the basis that it is the most "class conscious" and is, therefore, representative of the rest of society. For anarchists, as we have seen, this politics of representation led only to further domination and the perpetuation of the place of power. Perhaps Deleuze and Guattari's critique of Oedipus may be seen as an extension of this anarchist critique of representation into the realm of subjectivity itself. For Deleuze and Guattari, subjectivity, constructed through oedipal desire, claims to represent desire, when in fact it imprisons it. As we have seen with Foucault and Stirner, the human subject is a fabrication constructed through the domination of the individual, through tying the individual to a fixed discursive identity that speaks for him. Thus, anarchism's rejection of the politics of representation may be turned back upon itself: the human subject, the essential figure of anarchist discourse, is itself a representative figure based on a dialectical negation of difference. Its claim to represent wants, aspirations, and desires, is in fact a subjection of these. Therefore, the poststructuralist interventions of Deleuze and Guattari, as well as Stirner and Foucault, have taken the anarchist critique of the politics of representation beyond its ontological limits.

Desire, for Deleuze and Guattari, is not about lack.[31] Like Foucault's conception of power, desire, for Deleuze and Guattari, is productive and positive. Rather than desire being an effect of lack [of a lost object of desire] as Lacan would argue, lack is an effect of desire. This positivity of desire, even in its negativity, goes back to Nietzsche's injunction of affirmation: it is better to will nothing than to not will at all. It could also refer to Stirner's idea of the ego as a *creative nothingness*. The refusal to see the world in terms of negativity and lack is perhaps one of the central tenets of the poststructuralist critique of place I have been discussing. The language of negativity, they argue, is part of a dialectical analysis that seeks to efface difference and plurality by defining it in terms of lack of the Same. Thus, madness is seen as a lack of rationality; criminality is seen as a deviation from, perversion of, lack of, normality.[32] Desire, then, for Deleuze and Guattari must be seen in terms of production—indeed, they call it "desiring-production." Desire produces the social, it produces the flows of capital, it even produces the signifiers and forces that repress it. It is a system of "a-signifying signs with which fluxes of the unconscious are produced in a social field."[33] The productivity of desire has an enemy in the state and its forces which, Deleuze and Guattari argue, "form a gigantic enterprise of anti production."[34]

The oedipal psychoanalytic structure is the main weapon of "anti-production": its function is to channel the plural, polyvalent flows of productive desire into the repressive schema of the state. Desire is profoundly social: it is about flows and becomings, and forming connections and assemblages with other desires, with the social. This is why it is essentially and fundamentally revolutionary: "because it always wants more connections and assemblages."[35] Therefore, according to Deleuze and Guattari: "it is of vital importance for a society to repress desire, and even to find something more efficient than repression, so that repression, hierarchy, exploitation, and servitude are themselves desired."[36] However, Oedipus individualizes this desire, cutting it off from its possible connections, imprisoning it within the individual subject. In the same way, Stirner argues that the essential human subject is a figure that imprisons the ego, trying to capture its pluralities and fluxes within a single concept. The Oedipal subject, then, according to Deleuze and Guattari, is a figure constructed in order to contain desire, and represent it in a way that contains and stultifies its threat to state society. Its liberation is desire's domination, in the same way that the emancipation of man, for Stirner, is concomitant with the further domination of the ego. This may be seen as part of the poststructuralist attack on the unity and the essentialism of Enlightenment subjectivity, central to anarchist philosophy.

Machinic Subjectivity

So for Deleuze and Guattari, the essential human subject is an effect of repression, as well as a place of authority inextricably linked to the authority of the state. They therefore try to disperse the subject through a nomenology of machines, *desiring machines*: "Everywhere it is machines—real ones, not figurative ones: machines driving other machines, machines being driven by other machines, with all the necessary couplings and connections."[37] The supposed essential unity of the subject is thus broken down. It becomes a series of flows, connections, and assemblages of heterogeneous parts of social and natural machines.[38] This breakdown is achieved through an association of organic and non-organic components. As individuals we plug into various social machines and, in doing so, we become components of larger machines. One cannot even think of the body as unified: we are composed of different parts that may function quite independently. This is the schizophrenic experience of the body. What is important is not the subject or the various components themselves, but rather what happens between components—connections and flows. The "subject" is part of, or secondary to, these flows—flows of desire.

Subjectivity, for Deleuze and Guattari, is not a place, a stale point of departure, but rather a process or a *becoming*.[39] Becoming is a process of evolution of two or more separate entities—a process of assemblage and connection. Subjects are linked to the state through a series of lines, and if we are to resist this subjectification we must refuse who we are and become other. This injunction to refuse one's essential identity has been a leitmotif running throughout this poststructuralist critique of place: Stirner and Foucault, as well as Deleuze and Guattari argue that becoming is a way of escaping subjectification.

Deleuze and Guattari's notion of subjectivity as becoming is similar to Stirner's idea of the ego as, not an essence but, on the contrary, a flux that denies essence. The ego, for Stirner, is a radical emptiness continually engaged in a process of change. It is not an identifiable unity or place, but rather a process, a multiplicity, a nonplace. Deleuze and Guattari have a similar notion which they refer to at various times as the "Body without Organs" [BwO].[40] The BwO is an anarchic dispersal of unity and organization. It is a smooth surface, a radical emptiness, a nonplace, like Stirner's ego. It is a process of immanence and sheer movement, which produces "lines of flight"—lines that refer to an outside. Lines of flight may be understood through Foucault's notion of transgression—an excess that escapes power only temporarily through its communication with an unstable outside. The BwO is a field of intensity and multiplicity in which essences and unities are broken down into flows. Becoming is the constant shifting of identities and assemblages with other identities, to the point where the concept of identity is no longer adequate to describe it. The BwO, like the ego, is a concept that allows one to escape, if only temporarily, state thought—thought imprisoned by unities, essences, and representation. It is a nonplace that allows thought and subjectivity to be freed from the imprisonment of place.

This machinic analysis of subjectivity implies a rejection of the notion of the place of resistance. Place, whether it be the place of power or the place of resistance, is characterized by an essential unity or fixity, and this is precisely what is being challenged by Deleuze and Guattari's analysis. There can be no essential ground or place of resistance, as the anarchists believed, because it is fundamentally unstable and may just as easily give rise to domination, as to resistance. There is no strict Manichean division, as there was in anarchist discourse, between the place of resistance and the state as the place of power. The subject, for Deleuze and Guattari, is already implicated in state domination, and the machinic flows that make up subjectivity can easily form connections with assemblages of power. The essential human subject, or even the human body itself, cannot serve as a ground for the critique of power because it has no unity, but is rather a volatile aggregate of different flows and forces. It could be argued that Deleuze and Guattari take the anarchist critique of authority and apply it to the body itself, thus producing an anarchism of the body. For Deleuze and Guattari, authoritarianism lies not only in the state, but also in the organized, unified conception of the human body and human subjectivity which is a product of state coding. The body, whose organic unity founded by natural laws was so central to anarchist discourse, is now a disorganized, anarchic arrangement of parts and flows.

Non-Authoritarian Thought

Deleuze and Guattari's work is an exercise in nonstate, non-authoritarian thought—thought "without a General" as they call it. They argue, like Stirner, that state authority exists as much in our thoughts and desires as it does in reality. Therefore, it is only by freeing thought from its state coding that we can free ourselves from the state. If we continue to think along authoritarian lines then the state will be perpetuated. Authoritarian thought is the place of power that must be resisted. What must be attacked are these discourses and norms of knowledge and rationality that imprison thought: "it is the image of knowledge—as place of truth, and truth as sanctioning answers or solutions for questions and problems which are supposedly 'given.'"[41]

Thought must also resist metaphor and representation, which posit a deeper truth or presence. As Deleuze and Guattari have argued, the representative logic of psychoanalysis is a way of suppressing, rather than expressing, desire. Representative thinking is a domination of thought, in the same way that the anarchists argued that representative politics was a domination of the individual. Deleuze and Guattari have simply deepened the anarchist critique of representation by attacking the norms of truth and rationality, the very discourses that the anarchists mobilized against political representation. In other words, the anarchists saw representation as an ideological distortion of truth and rationality, while Deleuze and Guattari see representation as functioning precisely through these discourses. Representation is grounded in essentialist, foundational thought—it signifies an essential truth, a unity or place. This foundationalist logic, Deleuze and Guattari call "arborescent thought."[42] It imprisons thought by tying it to a place, a central unity, truth or essence that determines its growth and direction. It is dialectical: thought must always unfold according to its binary logic and it is thus trapped within binary divisions— true/false, normal/abnormal, black/white, male/female, reason/unreason.[43] For Deleuze and Guattari, these are oppressive hierarchies in which the false is subordinated to the true, in which unreason is subordinated to reason, etc. Stirner and Foucault also engage in this attack on binary, dialectical thinking. They argue that binary logic constructs norms that judge and condemn difference. For Deleuze and Guattari, moreover, to see the world in terms of binary oppositions is an example of "reactive" thinking: it is a way of suppressing difference.

The Rhizome

So instead of this arborescent model of thought, Deleuze and Guattari propose a "rhizomatic" model of thought, a model that eschews essences, unities, and binary logic, and embraces multiplicity, plurality, and becoming. It may be seen as an anarchic model of thought. Again by *anarchic* I do not mean anything pertaining to the essentialist and rationalist anarchism of Bakunin and Kropotkin but, rather, something that disrupts this very essentialism and rationalism. Indeed, the *rhizome* is a model of thought that defies the very idea of a model: it is an endless, haphazard multiplicity of connections not dominated by a single center or place, but rather decentralized and plural. It is thought characterized by a radical openness to an outside. It embraces four characteristics: connection, heterogeneity, multiplicity, and rupture.[44] The purpose of the rhizome is to allow thought "to shake off its model, make its grass grow—even locally at the margins, imperceptibly."[45] It is a form of thought that rejects binary divisions and hierarchies, does not privilege one thing over another, and is not governed by a single unfolding logic. It thus questions abstractions which govern thought, which form the basis of various discourses of knowledge and rationality. In other words, it is thought which defies the state.[46] Like Stirner, Deleuze and Guattari look for multiplicities and individual differences, rather than abstractions and unities. Abstract generalities like truth, rationality, and human essence are images which, according to Deleuze and Guattari, as well as Stirner, deny plurality and mutilate difference into sameness. Rhizomatic thought allows these differences and multiplicities to function in a way that is unpredictable and volatile. It releases molecular lines which make "fluxes of deterritorialization shoot between the segments, fluxes which no longer belong to one or to the other, but which constitute an asymmetrical becoming of the two."[47] It is in this way that the binarization of thought, which is the basis of essential identities, is disrupted.

The differences, ruptures, and multiple connections that characterize rhizomatic thought have important implications for political philosophy. The political arena can no longer be drawn up according to the old battle lines of the state and the human subject. The Manichean division between the place of power and the place of resistance that characterized revolutionary philosophies, particularly anarchism, can no longer operate here. This is because, according to rhizomatic thinking, the line of revolution is capable of forming a multitude of connections, including connections with the very power that it is presumed to oppose. Deleuze and Guattari argue that: "These lines tie back to one another. That is why one can never posit a dualism or a dichotomy, even in the rudimentary form of the good and the bad."[48] The rhizome makes any kind of political action extremely unpredictable and volatile, capable of rupturing into lines of flight or lines of authority, or both: "You may make a rupture, draw a line of flight, yet there is still a danger that you will restratify everything, formations that restore power to a signifier."[49]

To restore power to the signifier is precisely what Deleuze and Guattari suggest we avoid. They try to free thought and language, through rhizomatic thinking, from the dominance of the signifier, from the rational linguistic schema that they see as authoritarian. For Deleuze and Guattari, linguistics participates in authoritarian or state thought and, therefore, in practices of domination. It does this by establishing a rational truth or essence of language, and this perpetuates the idea, the image, of a natural order of things that must be adhered to. Deleuze and Guattari show, then, that authority and domination exist not only in the apparatus of the state and centralized political institutions; they are also prevalent in thought, in images of thought, in linguistic structures, in words themselves. So it is not only the content of language that has political implications, it is the structure—the place—of language itself. Like the anarchists who were concerned not so much with the form of state power, but rather its very structure, Deleuze and Guattari are interested in the structure of thought and language.

Language, then, is political, and while it can participate in political domination, it can also be used as a tool against it. The political domination involved in linguistics is masked, operating through representation and signification. To counter this, Deleuze and Guattari posit a "pragmatics" that places language within a field where its relation to power is clear. According to the pragmatic analysis of language, utterances only have meaning in the context of power relations, so that language becomes part of a political assemblage, not something abstracted from it. For Deleuze and Guattari, "politics works language from within."[50] It is by making this connection between language and politics, and thereby making language a field of political contestations, that one can free language from essentialist structures and rational unities where the real domination lies. Linguistics has thus been deterritorialized by the political; it can turn upon itself and allow its dominant place of unity and rationality to be challenged politically. For Deleuze and Guattari, linguistics must become rhizomatic: it must be allowed to form multiple connections with fields traditionally viewed as being external to it. By seeing language as part of a political assemblage, it releases lines of flight which deterritorialize it, displace it, and challenge the authoritarian concepts and images which have captured it.

The attempt to use thought and language against itself in order to displace it has been a feature of the poststructuralist critique of place. Stirner for instance, contaminates and displaces the Hegelian dialectical structure by turning it upon itself. He uses the affirmation-negation logic of the dialectic when describing the development of man, but he cunningly subverts this by placing at the "end" of the dialectical process, not rationality, but an arational openness or egoism, thus offering the possibility of further contestation, rather than a culmination. Foucault uses a genealogical analysis of various discourses to make these discourses shudder with horror at their own perniciousness: the injustices committed in the name of justice, the immoralities perpetrated in the name of morality. He does not condemn these discourses from a place of higher morality or justice; he merely uses these discourses to condemn themselves. Moreover, he finds within various discourses certain muted voices of rupture which form lines of flight and excess, produced by the dominant discourse but, at the same time, displacing and resisting it. With Foucault there is always the possibility of escape, without there being an outside to escape to.

A Figure of Resistance

The "War-Machine"

Deleuze and Guattari, on the other hand, do have a notion of an outside, an outside that Foucault only hinted at, but could not proclaim without being inconsistent. Foucault calls for resistance to power without providing a positive figure for this resistance. He realized this and suggested, halfheartedly, some notion of "plebs," which, I suggested, is inadequate. For Deleuze and Guattari, this unwillingness or inability to positively define resistance leaves open a gap that could be filled by reactive or even fascist figures.[51] Their notion of the "war-machine" may be seen as an attempt to fill in this conceptual gap. The *war-machine* constitutes an outside to the state. While the state is characterized by interiority, the war-machine is characterized by absolute exteriority. However, it must be understood that this notion of the outside is not essentialist like the anarchist notion of natural laws. Rather, the war-machine is purely conceptual: it is an image of thought, an idea without an object, a plane of consistency that allows one to conceive lines of flight from the state. Thought, language, political action, and desire can all be "assemblages" of the war-machine.

Deleuze and Guattari's war-machine could be seen as a more positive application of the war model of analysis that has been used against the notion of place. The war model allows one to tear away the veil of essences and unities to reveal the struggle and antagonism behind identity: it is a nonplace formed by the absence of essence. The war-machine is a positive realization of this model of analysis. It is a nonplace, a space characterized by pluralities, multiplicities, difference, and becoming, which escapes state coding because it eschews the binary structures of the state. The state is a conceptual place that is coded and striated: it confines flows and thought within arborescent, binary structures. It claims universality, and it subjectifies those within its domain. The war-machine, on the other hand, is sheer nomadic movement, smooth, non-striated, and uncoded; a place characterized by its very inability to become a place. According to Deleuze: "State power does not rest on a war-machine, but on the exercise of binary machines which run through us and the abstract machine which overcodes us. . . . The war-machine, on the other hand, is run though with woman-becomings, animal becomings, the becomings imperceptible of the warrior."[52] The war-machine is, therefore, a social and conceptual mode that wards off the state.[53] In the same way, I am employing "war" as a conceptual tool that wards off place.

The origins of the war-machine are different from those of the state: "As for the war-machine itself, it seems to be irreducible to the State apparatus, to be outside its sovereignty and prior to its law: it comes from elsewhere."[54] The state and the war-machine are always opposed, but not in a binary, dialectical sense. Rather the war-machine is the state's exteriority: whatever escapes the state's capture. While certain functions of the war-machine can be appropriated by the state in order to make war, the war-machine itself is always fundamentally different, fundamentally exterior.[55] The war-machine is a nonplace, an absence of essence and central authority. The nonplace of war is essentially hostile to place, to the unity and authority upon which the state rests: "just as Hobbes saw clearly that the State was against war, so war is against the State and makes it impossible."[56]

Therefore Deleuze and Guattari, as well as Foucault, and indeed Stirner, use a war model that emphasizes antagonism and struggle, to dismantle the notion of place, which is the arrest and culmination of struggle. It is a tool of resistance against power and authority. However, it is not a place of resistance, like the anarchist notion of a natural human essence. War, for Deleuze and Guattari, is not a state of nature: it is not essential. Rather, it is a formation or assemblage, a mode that undermines essence. It is a conceptual mode, a way of thinking which, by its rhizomatic nature, is always open to reinterpretation and is therefore fundamentally precarious: it can always form connections with power. War can always be appropriated by the state. Resistance, for Foucault as well as Deleuze and Guattari, is a dangerous enterprise: it can always be colonized by the power it opposes. Resistance is no longer to be conceived in the anarchists' Manichean sense, as a revolution—an overthrow of power from a point uncontaminated by it. Rather resistance is seen in terms of war: a field of multiple struggles, strategies, localized tactics, temporary setbacks, and betrayals—ongoing antagonism without the promise of a final victory. As Deleuze argues: "the world and its States are no more masters of their plane than revolutionaries are condemned to a deformation of theirs. Everything is played in uncertain games."[57] The war-machine, then, with its shunning of essence and universalities, and its embracing of multiplicity, plurality, and openness, has become the figure of resistance for this poststructuralist assault on the place.

Desire

However, this notion of the war-machine is at odds with Deleuze and Guattari's other figure of resistance—desire. While the war-machine rejects essence, desire appears to have essentialist and metaphysical connotations. Deleuze and Guattari see desire as a universal notion that has always existed. They deny that desire is anthropomorphic and natural: they argue that it is *constructivist* rather than spontaneist.[58] They also argue that desire can desire its own repression. However, they still employ an essentialist notion of desire by claiming that it is fundamentally revolutionary.[59] This lapses into the Manichean logic of emancipation familiar to anarchism: on the one hand there is desire which is, in essence, revolutionary and life-affirming, and on the other hand there is state-coded society or the "socius," which attempts to capture desire, restricting its flows and corrupting it by representing it as oedipal desire. Unlike Foucault, Deleuze and Guattari argue that desire is actually repressed, only that this repression is masked by the construction of oedipal repression. They thus oppose constructed oedipal desire, in an ideological sense, to "real" desire which forms a revolutionary outside to power. Foucault would argue, on the other hand, that there is no notion of desire that escapes regimes of power. One might argue that Deleuze and Guattari's notion of desire is no more universal and essentialist than Foucault's idea of power. The difference is, however, that, for Foucault, power does not exist outside the signifying regimes that give rise to it. The notion of power that Foucault explores has not always existed, while the notion of desire propounded by Deleuze and Guattari is universal and outside history. Desire, for Deleuze and Guattari, is an emancipative force that can rend the chains of history and destroy the regimes that try to repress it. Their notion of desire, then, while not necessarily grounded in human essence, is nevertheless metaphysical. As Best and Kellner argue: "They [Deleuze and Guattari] are committed to a metaphysical concept of desire, claiming that desire is 'inherently revolutionary', that it has a fundamental nature, essence, or intentionality which is to be creative and productive, rather than manipulated and repressed."[60] While one can accept that Deleuze and Guattari's notion of desire is not anthropomorphic, it does, however, invoke essentialist ideas. Perhaps, then, this notion of desire has succumbed, after all, to the logic of place. Maybe by positing a notion of desire that is outside power and inherently revolutionary, Deleuze and Guattari have only ended up invoking an essential place of resistance, the very notion which they sought to dispel through rhizomatic thought.

So have Deleuze and Guattari fallen into the trap of place? Has their universal notion of desire only reaffirmed the very authoritarian unities and essences that they sought to overthrow? It may be argued that there are two lines in Deleuze and Guattari's thought. One is traced by the notion of desire, with its pitfalls, which can only lead to the essentialist thinking that it has been the purpose of this analysis to try to escape. The other line is traced by the war-machine, by rhizomatic thought, by the rejection of essences and generalities. The latter line—the line of war—is the one most productive for this analysis: it is the line of thought that attacks the logic of place. If, as Deleuze and Guattari argue, we are to free ourselves from authoritarian structures, if we are to think beyond the state, then we must reject the binary, essentialist, and representative, structures which imprison thought. We must free thought from the logic of place. The goal of political thinking, then, is to discover forms of resistance and thought which do not end up perpetuating the place of power: "is an organization possible which is not modeled on the apparatus of the State, even to prefigure the State to come?"[61] It is here that Deleuze and Guattari's concepts of the rhizome and the war-machine can be applied.

What is valuable, then, about Deleuze and Guattari's philosophy is not the unwieldy notion of desire, but rather the new non-authoritarian ways of thinking they introduce. Their work, like that of Foucault and Stirner, is there to be used: it is a toolbox of ideas and concepts that can be used politically. Rhizomatic thought and the war-machine can be used to criticize existing political categories, to expand the field of politics beyond its present limits. Deleuze and Guattari's critique of representation and metaphor in thought, particularly with regard to Oedipal thinking, can be applied, for instance, to a critique of political representation. Rhizomatic thought gives one an awareness of the possible connections that can be formed between resistance and the power being resisted. It has allowed one to escape the Manichean logic of revolutionary political theory, and to expand our thinking beyond these categories.

The task of philosophy, according to Deleuze and Guattari, is to free thought from the authoritarian categories of the state, which it had hitherto been in the service of. One must be able to think beyond the authoritarian logic of place— beyond the question of what is to replace the power one intends to overthrow. Rhizomatic thought can provide us with the conceptual armory to free politics from the blackmail of this eternal question. The rejection of metaphor, essentialism, and oppositional logic for multiplicity, plurality, and connection allows us to rethink politics in a way that avoids place. Resistance against domination begins with the rejection of authoritarian thought, and this is where Deleuze and Guattari's ideas have value. What must be eschewed is their essentialist conception of desire. This does not mean, though, that the notion of desire must be discarded altogether. Desire still plays a role in this analysis, and it is important to recognize the link between desire and domination. However, desire itself must be subjected to a rhizomatic, war analysis that would free it from the essentialism it is grounded in. The division, in other words, between "real," revolutionary, life-affirming desire, and the oedipal desire which represses it, must be abandoned, otherwise one remains trapped within the logic of place.

The discussion so far has tried to find a non-essentialist figure of resistance, and it is suggested that, paradoxically, that this cannot be theorized without referring to an exteriority that somehow eludes power. Stirner, Foucault, and now Deleuze and Guattari have all referred to it in some way. Thus the shadowy figure of the Outside continues to haunt this analysis, presenting us with a question that has not, and perhaps cannot, be answered adequately within the poststructuralist argument: is a notion of an outside necessary for resistance and, if so, how can a notion of an outside to power be formulated in a way which avoids reaffirming place? This question of exteriority is explored further in the next chapter, on Derrida.

Notes

1. Gilles Deleuze and Felix Guattari, *A Thousand Plateaus: Capitalism and Schizophrenia*, trans. B. Massumi (London: Althone Press, 1988), 213.

2. Gilles Deleuze, "Many Politics," in *Dialogues*, eds. Gilles Deleuze and Claire Parnet, trans. Hugh Tomlinson (New York: Columbia University Press, 1987), 124-153.

3. Deleuze and Guattari, *A Thousand Plateaus*, 436-437.

4. Bakunin, *Political Philosophy*, 221.

5. Deleuze and Guattari, *A Thousand Plateaus*, 437.

6. Nietzsche, *On the Genealogy of Morals*, 86.

7. Deleuze and Guattari, *A Thousand Plateaus*, 429.

8. Deleuze, "Many Politics," 129.

9. Ronald Bogue, *Deleuze and Guattari* (London: Routledge, 1989), 101.

10. Bogue, *Deleuze and Guattari*, 101.

11. Deleuze and Guattari, *A Thousand Plateaus*, 386.

12. Given the proximity of Deleuze and Guattari to the anarchists on the question of the State, it is somewhat surprising that they do not mention anarchism. There is, however, a work that refers to anarchism in the context of Deleuze and Guattari's ideas. See Rolando Perez, *On (An)archy and Schizoanalysis* (New York: Autonomedia, 1990).

13. Anarchists reject the justifications for the state put forward by Rousseau and Hobbes, as well as Hegel, who saw the state as the culmination of the development of Rationality. Bakunin, for instance, rejected the theory of the social contract as an ideology of the state: "According to this theory human society began only with the conclusion of the contract. But what then is this society? It is the pure and logical realisation of the contract . . . it is the State." See *Political Philosophy*, 209.

14. Deleuze and Guattari, *A Thousand Plateaus*, 375.

15. Deleuze and Guattari, *A Thousand Plateaus*, 376.

16. Deleuze and Guattari, *A Thousand Plateaus*, 434.

17. Deleuze, "Many Politics," 137.

18. Stirner, *The Ego*, 312.

19. As Foucault says in his introduction to *Anti-Oedipus*, Deleuze and Guattari have made us aware of the "fascism in us all, in our heads and in our everyday behaviour, the fascism that causes us to love power, to desire the very thing that dominates and exploits us." See Michel Foucault, "Preface" to Gilles Deleuze and Felix Guattari, *Anti-Oedipus: Capitalism and Schizophrenia* (New York: Viking Press, 1972).

20. Deleuze, "Many Politics," 133.

21. The transgression of this division was hinted at by Bakunin when he spoke of the "power principle" as the lust for power.

22. Deleuze and Guattari, *A Thousand Plateaus*, 162.

23. Deleuze, "Many Politics," 138. Stirner's idea of insurrection also called for strategies of resistance against ourselves: he argued that insurrection starts from "men's discontent with themselves," and he saw insurrection as a way of freeing the self from the internalised authoritarianism that is concomitant with essential identities. See *The Ego*, 316.

24. Gilles Deleuze, "Dead Psychoanalysis: Analyse," in *Dialogues*, 77-123, 88.

25. Deleuze, "Dead Psychoanalysis," 81.

26. Deleuze and Guattari, *Anti-Oedipus*, 116.

27. Deleuze, for example, speaks of "little Hans," a patient of Freud's whose "animal-becoming" as a line of flight or escape becomes reterritorialized through the Oedipal representative schema into a desire for the father. See Deleuze, "Dead Psychoanalysis," 80.

28. Deleuze, "Dead Psychoanalysis," 80.

29. Indeed, as Deleuze once said in an interview with Foucault, "You were the first . . . to teach us something absolutely fundamental: the indignity of speaking for others." See "Intellectuals and Power," 209.

30. May, *The Political Philosophy of Poststructuralist Anarchism*, 50.

31. "Lack" is a term in Lacanian psychoanalysis, which refers to the gap between the individual and the object of his desire, a gap that nevertheless defines the identity of the subject. Deleuze and Guattari argue that because Lacanian logic founds desire on this lack of the object, this constructs desire as negative and reactive, whereas, in fact, it is productive. Lacan's logic of the lack will become crucial for my argument and will be discussed in subsequent chapters.

32. Foucault says in his guide on how to live a "non-fascist" life: "Withdraw allegiance from the old categories of the Negative (law, limit, castration, lack, lacuna), which Western thought has so long held sacred as a form of power and an access to reality. Prefer what is positive and multiple, difference over uniformity, flows over unities, mobile arrangements over systems. Believe that what is productive is not sedentary but nomadic." See preface to *Anti-Oedipus*.

33. Deleuze, "Dead Psychoanalysis," 78.

34. Deleuze and Guattari, *Anti-Oedipus*, 235.

35. Deleuze, "Dead Psychoanalysis," 79.

36. Deleuze and Guattari, *Anti-Oedipus*, 116.

37. Deleuze and Guattari, *Anti-Oedipus*, 1.

38. Bogue, *Deleuze and Guattari*, 94.

39. Deleuze's example of the orchid and the wasp explains becoming. See Gilles Deleuze and Claire Parnet, "A Conversation: What is it? What is it for?," in *Dialogues*, 1-33.

40. Deleuze and Guattari, *Anti-Oedipus*, 58.

41. Deleuze, "A Conversation," 24.

42. Its image of thought is the root and tree system: "trees are not a metaphor at all but an image of thought, a functioning, a whole apparatus that is planted in thought to make it go in a straight line and produce famous correct ideas. There are all kinds of

characteristics in the tree: there is a point of origin, seed or centre; it is a binary machine or principle of dichotomy, which is perpetually divided and reproduced branchings, its points of aborescence; . . . it has a future and a past, roots and a peak, a whole history, an evolution, a development. . . . Now there is no doubt that trees are planted in our heads: the tree of life, the tree of knowledge, etc. The whole world demands roots. Power is always arborescent." See Deleuze and Parnet, "A Conversation," 25.

43. Deleuze, "Many Politics," 128.
44. Deleuze and Guattari, *A Thousand Plateaus*, 7.
45. Deleuze and Parnet, "A Conversation," *Dialogues*, 24.
46. Deleuze and Guattari argue that it is a thought which: "would be defined in the movement of learning and not in the result of knowledge, and which would not leave it to anyone, to any Power, to 'pose' questions or to 'set' problems." See *A Thousand Plateaus*, 24.
47. Deleuze, "Many Politics," 131.
48. Deleuze and Guattari, *A Thousand Plateaus*, 9.
49. Deleuze and Guattari, *A Thousand Plateaus*, 9.
50. Deleuze and Guattari, *A Thousand Plateaus*, 83.
51. Paul Patton, "Conceptual Politics and the War-Machine in *Mille Plateaux*," *Substance* 44/45 (1984): 61-79.
52. Deleuze, "Many Politics," 141.
53. Deleuze and Guattari argue that primitive societies employed war as a mechanism for preventing the formation of distinct, centralized organs of power—in other words, the state. See Deleuze and Guattari, *A Thousand Plateaus*, 357.
54. Deleuze and Guattari, *A Thousand Plateaus*, 353.
55. Deleuze and Guattari, *A Thousand Plateaus*, 353.
56. Deleuze and Guattari, *A Thousand Plateaus*, 353.
57. Deleuze, "Many Politics," 147.
58. Deleuze, "Dead Psychoanalysis," 96.
59. Deleuze, "Dead Psychoanalysis," 78.
60. Steven Best and Douglas Kellner, *Postmodern Theory: Critical Interrogations* (London: Macmillan, 1991), 106.
61. Deleuze, "Many Politics," 145.

Chapter Six

Derrida and the Deconstruction of Authority

The last chapter showed the way in which Deleuze and Guattari located the place of power in language and in the philosophical structures which condition our reality. They unmasked a hidden authoritarianism in metaphysical notions such as essence and truth, which ground language and thought. They tried to free philosophy from these injunctions by developing a non-essentialist, rhizomatic model of thought. It is a nonplace characterized by difference, plurality, flux, and even antagonism; a model of resistance to the authority of state governed thought, developed through a war model or machine. It was found, however, that although the rhizome and the war-machine are useful tools of anti-authoritarian thought, they are still ultimately insufficient in themselves for conceptualizing resistance. This is because they do not adequately conceptualize the outside to which they refer. While more positive, perhaps, than Foucault's bodies and pleasures and plebs, they still remain, in a sense, "trapped" within a paradigm and a language of difference which renders them nothing more than lines of flight and escape, without an outside to escape to.

Jacques Derrida also tries to undermine structures of authority and hierarchy in philosophy. He employs a war model of writing to expose the suppressed antagonisms and differences within the western philosophical discourse whose claims to universality, wholeness, and lucid self-reflection have been sounded since the time of Plato. His critique has important implications for political theory: his questioning of the claims of philosophy may be applied to the claims of political institutions and discourses that are founded upon them. Moreover, Derrida's discussion of the relation between metaphysical structures of essence and presence, and the hierarchies and dominations they make possible, as well as his critique of oppositional and binary thinking, allows his work to be read, along with that of Stirner, Foucault, and Deleuze and Guattari, as an assault on the place of power. However, I will argue that the logic of deconstruction operates in a somewhat different way to the poststructuralist logic of dispersal. This difference in approach is crucial: it exposes the limits of poststructuralism argument from within those limits themselves, and in doing so, opens the way for the logic of anti-authoritarianism to advance beyond its self-imposed confines. Derrida helps us to explore, through the logic of deconstruction, the possibility of strategies of resistance that refer to an exteriority, an outside to power—a possibility which points to the limits of the poststructuralist argument.

Deconstruction

"Deconstruction" is the term most commonly associated with Derrida and, while it is a widely misunderstood and misused term, it will nevertheless be used here to describe the general direction of Derrida's work. Christopher Norris defines deconstruction as a series of moves that include: the dismantling of conceptual oppositions and hierarchical systems of thought; and an unmasking of *aporias* and moments of self-contradiction in philosophy.[1] It might be said, then, that deconstruction is a way of *reading* texts—philosophical texts—with the intention of making these texts question themselves, forcing them to take account of their own contradictions, and exposing the antagonisms which they have ignored or repressed. What deconstruction is not, however, is a philosophical system. Derrida does not question one kind of philosophy from the standpoint of another, more complete, less contradictory system. This would be to fall into the trap of place, to merely substitute one kind of authority for another—just as the anarchists substituted the authority of man for the authority of the state. Derrida, therefore, does not come from a point of departure outside philosophy. There is no essential place of resistance outside the system. Rather, Derrida works within the discourse of western philosophy itself, looking for hidden antagonisms that jeopardize it. Moreover, his aim, as we will see, is not to destroy philosophy, as has often been claimed. On the contrary, Derrida's critique of philosophy is itself fundamentally philosophical. By opening philosophical discourse to this questioning, Derrida is being faithful to the spirit of philosophy: unquestioning and slavish adulation of philosophy ultimately makes a mockery of it. Deconstruction is therefore a strategy of questioning philosophy's claims to reflexive self-identity. This is what makes it important for our analysis: it forces us to question the purity of any identity of resistance.

Deconstruction may be seen as a critique of the authoritarian structures in philosophy, in particular *logocentrism*—that is philosophy's subordination, throughout its history, of writing to speech. This is an example of what Derrida calls the "metaphysics of presence" in western philosophy. It is an indication of how much philosophy is still grounded in the metaphysical, and therefore, authoritarian, concepts which it claims to have transcended. Derrida points to Plato's *Phaedrus,* in which writing is rejected as a medium for conveying and recording truth: it is seen as an artifice, an invention which cannot be a substitute for the authenticity and the immediate presence of meaning associated with speech. Where speech is seen as a means of approaching the truth because of its immediacy, writing is seen as a dangerous corruption of speech—a lesser form of speech that is destructive of memory, and susceptible to deceit, to the perversion of truth.[2] Derrida attacks this "logocentric" thinking by pointing out certain contradictions within it. Derrida shows that Plato cannot represent speech except through the metaphor of writing, while at the same time denying that writing has any real efficacy as a medium at all.[3] Speech is, therefore, dependent on the writing it excludes. Writing is a *supplement* to speech—it is excluded by presence, but is, at the same time, necessary for the formation of its identity.

The unmasking of this logic of "supplementarity" is one of the deconstructive moves employed by Derrida to resist the logocentrism in philosophy. It is important from the perspective of our argument to understand this logic: it will be used later on against the idea of an essential revolutionary identity. Speech claims to be a self-presence immediate and authentic to itself, whereas writing is seen as a diminishing of this presence. However, Derrida shows that this authenticity and purity of self-identity is always questionable: it is always contaminated by what it tries to exclude. According to this logic, then, no identity is ever complete or pure: it is constituted by that which threatens it. Derrida does not want to deny self-identity or presence. He merely wants to indicate that this presence is never as pure as it claims to be. It is always open to the other, and contaminated by it.

This logic may be applied to the question of essence, and the place of resistance in anarchist discourse. I have already shown the way that Bakunin was forced to concede that human essence was not a complete identity: the desire for power, which was the principle threat to human subjectivity, formed an essential part of this identity. Moreover, the poststructuralist thinkers discussed in the previous chapters have argued that discourses and practices of power are actually implicated in the construction of human subjectivity—in the construction of the very identity which power is said to be an enemy of. Might it be said, then, that power is the supplement to human subjectivity, in the same way that writing is the supplement to speech? Perhaps power is something that both threatens, and is necessary for the constitution of, human identity. The identity of resistance is made highly problematic if it is, in part, constituted by the very forces it professes to oppose. This undermines, then, the idea of the uncontaminated point of departure, the place of resistance to power.

Critique of Essential Identities

Derrida's critique throws into doubt the question of human essence and whether it can continue to be the foundation for resistance to power. Like the previous poststructuralist arguments, Derrida's critique of self-identity forces us to confront the fact that power itself cannot be contained in stable identities— like the state, for instance. Rather, power is an identity that is always unstable, contingent, and diffuse. So not only does this deconstructive logic make the identity of the revolutionary subject problematic, it also undermines the identity of the power it is said to oppose.

Furthermore, Derrida continues this critique of essential identity by showing that not only is its purity questionable, but also that it constitutes an authoritarian identity. It establishes a series of hierarchical binary relationships, in which one term is subordinated to another—Derrida sees these as "violent hierarchies." Logocentrism, as we have seen, establishes the hierarchical binary of speech/writing in which writing is subordinated to speech, representation to presence. Presence constitutes a form of textual authority that attempts to dominate and exclude its supplement. However, this authority is shown to be continually jeopardized by the excluded supplement because it is essential to the formation of the dominant term's identity. Stirner, in the same way, saw the un-man as a sort of excess or supplement which jeopardizes the identity of man. These binary structures form a place of power in philosophical discourse. Moreover, as we have seen, they provide the foundations for political domination. Foucault argues, for instance, that philosophy's binary separation of reason/unreason is the basis for the domination and incarceration of the mad. Binary structures in philosophy perpetuate practices and discourses of domination. So Derrida may be seen as expanding the poststructuralist critique of essential identity and the oppositional thinking.

However, Derrida does not simply want to invert the terms of these binaries so that the subordinated term becomes the privileged term. For instance, he does not want to put writing in the place of speech. Inverting the terms of the binary leaves intact the hierarchical structure of the binary division. Such a strategy of revolution or inversion only reaffirms the place of power in the very attempt to overthrow it. We have seen the way in which Marxism fell victim to this logic of place by replacing the bourgeois state with the equally authoritarian workers' state. We have also seen the anarchists, in their attack on state power, merely replace it with a new logic of power and authority, this time based on human essence. This logic of place has haunted political philosophy. Derrida recognizes the dangers of this trap: "What must occur then is not merely a suppression of all hierarchy, for an-archy only consolidates just as surely the established order of a metaphysical hierarchy; nor is it a simple change or reversal in the terms of any given hierarchy. Rather the *Umdrehung* must be a transformation of the hierarchical structure itself."[4] In other words, in order avoid the lure of place, one must go beyond both the anarchic desire to destroy hierarchy, as well as the mere reversal of terms. This only reinscribes hierarchy in a different guise: in the case of anarchism, a humanist guise. Rather, as Derrida suggests, if one wants to avoid this trap, then the hierarchical structure itself, its place, must be transformed.

Textual Anarchism

It could be argued, then, that Derrida has an anarchism of his own, if by *anarchism* one means a questioning of all authority, including textual and philosophical authority, as well as a desire to avoid the trap of reproducing authority and hierarchy in one's attempt to criticize it. It is also clear that his critique of metaphysical authority and hierarchy has great implications for classical anarchism. First, it undermines the essentialist categories on which anarchism is based, questioning the purity and stability of these identities. Second, it shows that any critique of power, hierarchy, and authority cannot simply be an outright rejection of these terms. This sort of oppositional thinking merely reaffirms the original terms. Rather, as Derrida might argue, political action must invoke a rethinking of resistance and authority in a way that traces a path between these two terms, so that one does not merely reinvent the place of power. Derrida may be used in this argument as a supplement to anarchism. His critique both challenges it, and yet, if anarchism were to take account of this very critique, then it could perhaps be greatly advanced. By showing that the identity of the anarchist subject is actually constituted through its subordinated other—the power that it claims to eschew—then anarchism would be forced to reflect on the authoritarian possibilities within its own discourse, and develop appropriate strategies of resistance to this.

This deconstructive attempt to transform the very structure of hierarchy and authority, to go beyond the binary opposition, is also found in Stirner. He argues, as we have seen, that the sacred cannot simply be transgressed by affirming the sacrilegious, because this is to remain caught within the framework of the binary opposition: even though it is a form of resistance, it is resistance according to the terms of the dominant position.[5] Sacrilege therefore only reinscribes the sacred. The idea, then, is not to replace one term with another—but to displace both terms of the hierarchy—to *displace* place.[6] This strategy of displacement, rather than replacement, adopted by Derrida, provides certain clues to developing a non-essentialist theory of resistance. Rather than reversing the terms of the binary opposition, one should perhaps question, and make problematic, its very structure.

The End(s) of Man: the Problem of Humanism

The prevalence of these binary structures indicates, according to Derrida, how much philosophy is still tied to metaphysics: it is still dominated, in other words, by the place of metaphysics. In the same way, one might argue that political theory is still dominated by the need for a place, for some sort of essence that it has never had, and yet continually tries to reinvent. The demand for a self-identical essence in politics and philosophy would be, according to Derrida, the residue of the category of the divine. God has not been completely usurped from philosophy, as it has always been claimed. God has only been reinvented in the form of essence.[7] As much as we may claim the contrary, we have not ousted God from philosophy. The place, the authority of the category of the divine remains intact, only reinscribed in the demand for presence. A connection can be made here with Stirner who believes, as we have seen, that the humanist insurrection against theology was merely an inversion of terms, leaving the actual place of the divine intact: man merely became the new God, the new form of authority. So for Derrida, and indeed for Stirner, the man of humanist discourse has been reinscribed in the place of God.[8] This specter of God-Man has yet to be exorcised from our midst.[9] Derrida's analysis is important here because it exposes the authoritarianism that still inhabits structures in thought. Moreover, it shows that any kind of political resistance must first be aware of its own latent metaphysical structures and, therefore, its own potential for domination.

Derrida argues, then, that it is necessary to think the end of man, without thinking essence: a project that, I have already suggested, is extremely difficult. In other words, one must try to approach the problem of the end of man in a way that avoids the perilous trap of place. The Enlightenment humanist proclamation of the death of God did not resound at all confidently for Stirner. In the same way, philosophy's proclamation of the death of man does not entirely convince Derrida. Perhaps, then, Foucault's sounding of the death knell of man—when he predicted that the figure of man would disappear like a face drawn in the sand at the edge of the sea—should be taken with a grain of salt. There is still, at least for Derrida, the intransigent specter of God-Man-Essence that refuses to be exorcised: it remains as firmly entrenched in philosophy, and indeed in politics, as ever.[10] Moreover, as Derrida has argued, it is not possible to destroy this place. Heidegger, by positing a pre-ontological Being to overcome metaphysics, has remained only more faithful to the metaphysical tradition.[11] This strategy of absolute rejection never works: it merely reinvents it in another form. It constructs the dubious binary of authority-power/revolution, in which revolution is potentially the new form of power. This was found to be the case with anarchism.

However, have Foucault, and Deleuze and Guattari, fallen into the same trap? While they have not constructed absolute oppositions between resistance and power (they are very emphatic about this), they have perhaps attacked humanism a little too violently, and, in doing so, have been forced into positing an essentialist or metaphysical figures of resistance which, in the context of their work, is problematic. It could be argued that Foucault's dispersal of the subject into sites of power and discourse, and Deleuze and Guattari's fragmentation of the subject into an anarchic and haphazard language of machines, parts, and flows, are operations which deny radical politics of a point of departure. This has left a theoretical void which, as we have seen, could only be filled by essentialist concepts, such as desire and bodies and pleasures. So maybe, in other words, in their rejection humanism, perhaps Foucault, and Deleuze and Guattari have, paradoxically, denied themselves the possibility of non-essentialist forms of resistance.

In this way, Derrida points to the limits of the poststructuralist argument. He forces us to ask why we have not been able to develop, through the logic of poststructuralism, non-essentialist theories of resistance, seeing that poststructuralism may itself be seen as a form of resistance against essentialism. Perhaps we have been too hasty in rejoicing at the end of man—has it forced us into a theoretical void, a political dead-end? It is here, then, that Derrida can be seen as departing from the poststructuralist rejection of the problematic of man.

The Two Temptations of Anti-Authoritarian Politics

Derrida allows us to reevaluate the problem of humanism. He describes two possible ways dealing with the problem of place in philosophy—the two temptations of deconstruction. The first strategy:

> To attempt an exit and a deconstruction without changing terrain, by repeating what is implicit in the founding concepts and the original problematic, by using against the edifice the instruments or stones available in the house, that is,

equally, in language. Here, one risks ceaselessly confirming, consolidating, *relifting (relever)*, at an always more certain depth, that which one allegedly deconstructs. The continuous process of making explicit, moving toward an opening, risks sinking into the autism of the closure.[12]

So this strategy of working within the discourse of Enlightenment humanist metaphysics, using its terms and language, risks reaffirming and consolidating the structure, the place, that one is trying to oppose. Derrida is talking here about Heidegger's critique of humanism, which, he argues, involved a replacement of man with the equally essentialist and metaphysical Being. However, in terms of my argument, perhaps we could say that, in a perverse kind of way, this is also the strategy adopted by the anarchists. Anarchism tried to present a critique of political power using the language of Enlightenment humanism. It was found, however, that this was ultimately self-defeating. As Stirner showed, power and authority are tied to the very humanist discourses and essentialist categories that were used by the anarchists to criticize it. By remaining within the epistemological and ontological framework of Enlightenment humanism, anarchism trapped itself within the confines of its own critique. As it accused Marxism of doing, anarchism itself merely challenged the form of authority, but not its place. In other words, due to the logic of this strategy, anarchism only reaffirmed the place of power.

The second strategy, according to Derrida, is:

> To decide to change terrain, in a discontinuous and irruptive fashion, by brutally placing oneself outside, and by affirming an absolute break or difference. Without mentioning all the other forms of *trompe-l'oeil* perspective in which such a displacement can be caught, thereby inhabiting more naively and strictly than ever the inside one declares one has deserted, the simple practice of language ceaselessly reinstates the new terrain on the oldest ground.[13]

This alternative move of making an absolute break with the discourse of humanist metaphysics, of seeking an outside to which one can escape, and from which one can resist authority, may be seen to represent the logic of poststructuralism.[14] As I suggested before, Foucault, and Deleuze and Guattari may be seen to be making an absolute break with humanism—smashing the subject into fragments and effects of discourses, machines, desires, and practices, etc. Up until now the anti-authoritarian program has followed this logic, but if we take into account Derrida's argument here, perhaps we should at least question it. Paradoxically, it has the same effect as the first strategy: by attempting a complete change of terrain—through lines of flight, for instance— one only reaffirms one's place within the old terrain. The more one tries to escape the dominant paradigm, the more one finds oneself frustratingly within it. As we have seen, Foucault, and Deleuze and Guattari have often ended up resorting to essentialist categories to explain resistance. This is because, in its overhasty rejection of humanism and the subject, poststructuralism has denied

itself a point of departure for theorizing resistance. It has left itself a theoretical
vacuum, an empty place, which can be filled only by essentialist concepts. In
other words, as Derrida would argue, this strategy also risks reaffirming place.
Derrida argues that deconstruction—and for that matter, any form of resistance
against authority—is always caught between the Scylla and Charybdis of these
two possible strategies, and must therefore navigate a course between them.
These two strategies of deconstruction skewer political theory: they are the two
possible paths confronting anti-authoritarian thought and action. They are both
dominated by the threat of place.

Beyond Poststructuralism?

Derrida can perhaps show us a way out of this theoretical abyss. There may
be a way of combining these two seemingly irreconcilable paths in a way that
allows anti-authoritarian thought to advance. Rather than choosing one strategy
over another, Derrida believes that we must follow the two paths
simultaneously.[15] We must find a way of combining or "weaving" these two
possible moves, thereby transcending them. For instance, as Alan Schrift
argues, Derrida does not completely dispense with the category of the subject—
rather he seeks to displace and reevaluate it.[16] Rather than think in terms of the
end of man, as Foucault does, Derrida refers to the "closure" of man in
metaphysics.[17] The difference is that, for Derrida, man will not be completely
transcended but, rather, reevaluated, perhaps in terms of Nietzsche's "higher
man."[18] For Derrida, the authority, the place, of man will be decentered within
language, but the subject will not be discarded altogether. It is not clear that
there is an enormous difference between the two positions. However, Derrida's
refusal to dispense with the subject does point to a number of interesting
possibilities for anti-authoritarian thought: perhaps the category of the subject
can be retained as a decentered, non-essentialist category, existing as its own
limit, thus providing a point a departure for theorizing resistance. This idea will
be developed further when I discuss Lacan in the next chapter. However it is
clear already that Derrida is exposing certain limitations with the
poststructuralist argument: by dispensing with the subject altogether, and by not
being able to provide adequate figures of resistance in its place, Foucault and
Deleuze and Guattari have, despite their contribution to the critique of
essentialist discourse, perhaps only reaffirmed essentialist categories in their
very attempt to dismiss them. By discarding man so hastily, they have perhaps
neglected the possibility of his reemergence in another form. So Derrida's
critique goes to the heart of the anti-authoritarian problematic: it goes beyond
the limits, or at least, works at the limits of the poststructuralist argument—
thereby pointing to a beyond. He suggests, for instance, that the motif of
difference is inadequate—while it claims to eschew essence, perhaps it only
allows another essence to be formed in its place.

Differance

Deconstruction tries to account for the suppressed, hidden differences and heterogeneities in philosophical discourse: the muffled, half-stifled murmurs of disunity and antagonism. It might be argued that Derrida employs a war model as a mode of analysis that breaks down unities and essences, unmasking the suppressed heterogeneities, antagonisms, and absences, behind the facade of totality. Derrida calls this strategy "differance"—*difference* spelled with an "a"—in order to signify that it is not an absolute, essential difference. It is rather a difference, or movement of differences whose identity is always unstable, never absolute.[19] Because *differance* does not constitute itself as an essential identity of difference, because it remains open to contingency, thereby undermining fixed identities, it may be seen as a tool of anti-authoritarian thought: "It governs nothing, reigns over nothing, and nowhere exercises any authority . . . Not only is there no kingdom of differance, but differance instigates the subversion of every kingdom."[20]

This warlike series of differences has a "structure" or, as Rodolphe Gasché says, an "infrastructure."[21] The infrastructure is a *weave*, an unordered combination of differences and antagonisms. It is, as Derrida says, a "combat zone between philosophy and its other."[22] It is a system, moreover, whose very nature is that of a nonsystem: the differences that constitute it are not dissolved by the infrastructure, nor are they ordered into a dialectical framework in which their differences become only a binary relation of opposites.[23] This is a "system" of nondialectical, nonbinary differences: it threads together differences and antagonisms in a way that does not order or efface them. Infrastructures are not essentialist: their very essence is that of a non-essence.[24] It does not have a stable or autonomous identity, nor is it governed by an ordering principle or authority. It is a "place" that eschews essence, authority, and centrality. Its structural inability to establish a stable identity—is a threat to place, to the authority of identity. As Derrida argues then: "There is no essence of the differance; not only can it not allow itself to be taken up into the *as such* of its name or its appearing, but it threatens the authority of the *as such* in general, the thing's presence in its essence."[25]

It is here also perhaps that Derrida goes beyond the poststructuralist argument. While he employs a war model of difference, like Foucault, and like Deleuze and Guattari, he uses it in a slightly different way: differance refers back to some sort of "structure" or *infrastructure*, some sort of unity constructed on the basis of its own disunity, constituted through its own limits. Now because poststructuralism lacks this idea of an "infrastructure" of difference which remains structurally open—even to the possibilities of the Same—it could be seen as essentializing difference. So, paradoxically, maybe it is precisely because poststructuralism lacks a structure or "place," in the way that Derrida provides, that it falls back into a place—a place constituted by essentialist ideas. Derrida's argument is pointing to the need for some kind of point of departure—not the uncontaminated point of departure of anarchist discourse—but rather a point of departure constructed through the logic of supplementarity, and based on its own "contaminatedness."

The infrastructure, then, may be used as a tool of anti-authoritarian thought: it is a model which, by its own structural absence of place, by its own lack of essence, undermines from within various structures of textual authority. At its center is an absence, a lack. It is "governed" by a principle of *undecidability*: it neither affirms identity or nonidentity, but remains in a state of undecidability between the two. The infrastructure is a way of theorizing difference—the difference, or series of differences which makes the formation of stable, unified identities in philosophy impossible. It is also a model that allows thinking to transcend the binary structures that limit it. So the aim of this strategy is not to destroy identity or presence. It is not to affirm difference over identity, absence over presence. This would be, as I have suggested, falling once again into the trap of place: it would be to reverse the established order, only to establish a new order. Difference would become a new identity, and absence a new presence. The aim of war—my notion of war, at any rate—is not to seek the founding of a new order, but rather the displacement of all orders—including its own. Moreover, the undecidable nature of this war model derived from Derrida—its state of undecidability between difference and the same, essence and non-essence, presence and absence, authority and anarchy, etc.—traces the general path of deconstruction. The war model of deconstruction refuses to be circumscribed by these oppositional structures which inform much radical political theory, including anarchism: it affirms neither one side nor the other, but combines and, therefore, transcends them. For instance, it affirms neither essence nor non-essence, but goes beyond these opposing terms and, in doing so, reevaluates them: it does not reject essence, but rather constructs its essence as a non-essence.

The Undecidable Outside

Derrida argues that the strategy of deconstruction cannot work entirely within the structures of logocentric philosophy; nor can it work completely outside it. Rather, it traces a path of undecidability between the two positions or "terrains." In this way it might be argued that deconstruction avoids the trap of place: it establishes neither a place of power, nor a place of resistance—which, as I have suggested, are two sides of the same logic of domination—but, rather, constructs a path between them, disrupting the identity of both terms. It works from within the discourse and metaphysical structures of philosophy to find an outside. It is neither inside nor outside philosophy, but rather operates at the limits of philosophical discourse.[26] Deconstruction cannot attempt an immediate neutralization of philosophy's authoritarian structures. Rather, it must proceed through a strategy of displacement—what Derrida calls a "double writing," which is a form of critique neither strictly inside, nor strictly outside, philosophy. It is a strategy of continually interrogating the self-proclaimed closure of this discourse. It does this by forcing it to account for the excess that always escapes and, thus, makes problematic, this closure. For Derrida, this excess has nowhere to escape to: it does not constitute a place of resistance and, once it escapes, it disintegrates. This excess, moreover, is produced by the structures it threatens: it is a supplement, a necessary but, at the same time, dangerous and wayward part of the dominant structure. This excess which deconstruction tries to identify, confronts philosophy with a limit to its limitlessness, a limit to its closure. This proclaimed totality of philosophy, this limitlessness, is, at the same time, a limit itself. However, its complete closure to what threatens it is impossible because, as deconstruction has shown, the thing that it attempts to exclude is essential to its identity. There is a strange logic at work here, a logic which continually impedes philosophy's aspiration to be a closed, complete system. Deconstruction unmasks this logic, this limit of the limit.

The limits that Derrida identifies are produced within the tradition of philosophy—they are not imposed from a nihilistic, irrational outside. As Derrida says: "The movements of deconstruction do not destroy structures from outside. They are not possible and effective, nor can they take accurate aim, except by inhabiting those structures."[27] This positioning of limits is important here because it points, perhaps, to the possibility of an outside—an outside of resistance—*on the inside*. To position oneself entirely on the outside of any structure as a form of resistance is only to reaffirm, in a reversed way, what one resists. This idea, however, of an outside created by the limits of the inside may allow us to conceive of a politics of resistance which does not restore the place of power. So not only does Derrida suggest a way of theorizing difference without falling back into essentialism—something which points to the limits of the poststructuralism—he also points to the possibility of an outside—something that poststructuralist argument could not do convincingly.

So this limit, this impossibility of closure is perhaps, at the same time, the constitution of a possible outside—an outside constructed from the limitations and contradictions of the inside. These contradictions make closure impossible; they open philosophical discourse to an other. This is a *radical* outside; it is not part of the binary structure of inside/outside. Unlike the anarchist place of resistance located in essential human subjectivity, the outside located by deconstruction has no stable identity. It is not clearly divided from the Inside by an inexorable line: its "line" is continually reinterpreted, jeopardized, and constructed, as we shall see, by relations of antagonism. It is a finite and temporary outside. Moreover, it is an outside that obeys a strange logic: it exists only in relation to the inside it threatens, while the inside exists only in relation to it. Each is necessary for the constitution of the identity of the other, while at the same time threatening the identity of the other. It is therefore an outside that avoids the two temptations of deconstruction: on the one hand, it is an outside that threatens the inside; on the other hand, it is an outside formulated from the inside. Derrida makes it clear that it cannot be seen as an absolute outside, as this would only reconsolidate the inside that it opposes. The more one tries to escape to an absolute outside, the more one finds oneself obstinately on the "inside." As Derrida says: "the 'logic' of every relation to the outside is very complex and surprising. It is precisely the force and the efficiency of the system that regularly changes transgressions into 'false exits.'"[28]

Using Derrida's argument here, we can perhaps say that the poststructuralists discussed have found only "false exits"—because they have not, and perhaps cannot within the confines of their argument, adequately theorize the outside to which they implicitly refer. Without this, as I suggested, they leave a theoretical void, which can only be filled by essentialist ideas, which are problematic within the limits of their argument. Their transgression of essence, unity, and place has led only to the possibility of their reemergence. An absolute break, such as that made within poststructuralism, is only a reaffirmation of the "system" one wishes to escape. Transgression, as Derrida argues then, can only be finite, and it cannot establish a permanent outside: "by means of the work done on one side and the other of the limit the field inside is modified, and a transgression is produced that consequently is nowhere present as a *fait accompli*. One is never installed within transgression, one never lives elsewhere."[29]

Deconstruction may be seen as a form of transgression that, in transgressing the limits of metaphysics, also transgresses itself.[30] It affirms nothing, does not come from an oppositional outside, and dissipates upon crossing this limit. It exposes the limits of a text by tracing the repressed absences and discontinuities within the text—the excess that the text fails to contain.[31] In this sense it is transgressive. However, it is also a self-effacing movement—a transgression that cancels itself out. Deconstruction neither affirms, nor destroys, the limit it "crosses": rather it reevaluates it, reinscribing it as a problem, a *question*. This uncertainty as to the limits of transgression is the closest Derrida comes to the outside. It remains to be seen whether it has been adequately theorized.

An Ethics of Impurity

This undecidable outside is, for Derrida, ethical. Philosophy has been opened to what it excludes, to its other. This forcing of philosophy to confront its own structures of exclusion and repression, is a thoroughly ethical gesture. Derrida is influenced here by Emmanuel Levinas, who tries to think the limits of the Hegelian tradition by showing the point at which it encounters the violence of an outside, of an *alterity* that is ethical in its exclusion and singularity.[32] Deconstruction may be seen, therefore, as an ethical strategy that opens philosophy to the other: like Foucault's notion of resistance, deconstruction tries to step, if only for an instant, beyond the confines of reason and historical necessity. This "stepping beyond" constitutes an ethical dimension—*an ethics of alterity*. Derrida writes:

> To 'deconstruct' philosophy, thus, would be to think—in a most faithful, interior way—the structured genealogy of philosophy's concepts, but at the same time to determine—from a certain exterior that is unqualifiable or unnameable by philosophy—what this history has been able to dissimulate or

forbid, making itself into a history by means of this somewhere motivated repression.[33]

This questioning of philosophy does not lead to the moral nihilism that deconstruction has often been accused of promoting. As John Caputo argues, deconstruction is a strategy of responsibility to the excluded other. Unlike hermeneutics, which tries to assimilate difference into the order of the same, of Being, deconstruction tries to open a space for difference. Derrida's is, therefore, a *responsible anarchy*, not an irresponsible anarchy as some have claimed.[34] Deconstruction, then, is by no means a rejection of ethics, even when it questions moral philosophy: rather, it is a reevaluation of ethics.[35] It shows us that moral principles cannot be absolute or pure: they are always contaminated by what they try to exclude. Good is always contaminated by evil, reason by unreason. What Derrida questions, like Stirner and Foucault, is the *ethics of morality:* if morality becomes an absolute discourse, then can it still be considered moral or ethical? Deconstruction allows us to open the realm of ethics to reinterpretation and difference, and this opening is itself ethical. It is an ethics of impurity. If morality is always contaminated by its other—if it is never pure—then every moral judgment or decision is necessarily undecidable. Moral judgment must always be self-questioning and cautious because its foundations are not absolute. Unlike anarchist moral philosophy, grounded upon the firm foundations of human essence, deconstructive anti-authoritarian ethics has no such privileged place and, therefore, enjoys no such self-assurance.

Law, Authority, and Justice

This undecidability of decision and judgment, which is the necessary outcome of a deconstructive critique, has implications for political discourses and institutions, particularly the institution of law. Derrida argues that the authority of law is questionable and, to a certain extent, illegitimate. This is because the authority that supposedly grounds law, is only legitimized once the law is instituted. That means that the authority upon which law is established is, strictly speaking, nonlegal, because it had to exist prior to law. Therefore, the originary act of instituting law is an illegitimacy, a violence.[36]

Anarchism would employ a similar critique of law, arguing that it has no moral authority. However, unlike the anarchists who criticize "artificial" law from the perspective of what they consider to be a morally superior "natural" system of law, Derrida allows no such privileged standpoint. Using a deconstructive logic, then, one could argue that the so-called natural law that anarchists use as a pure point of departure, is, in actual fact, not so pure: its identity is contaminated by the political authority it is juxtaposed to. So, in the same way that writing is the supplement to speech in Derrida's analysis, perhaps the artificial law that anarchists oppose to natural law, can be seen as a supplement to this natural law—that which contaminates its identity by making the constitution of this identity possible.

A deconstructive interrogation of law reveals the absence, the empty place at the base of the edifice of law, the violence at the root of institutional authority. The authority of law can, therefore, be questioned: it can never reign absolute because it is contaminated by its own foundational violence. This critique can allow one to question any institutional discourse that claims to rest on law, and this makes it an invaluable tool of resistance to power and authority.[37]

However, if one is to avoid reestablishing the authority of law, then law must be distinguished from justice. Law, for Derrida, is merely the general application of a rule, while justice is an opening of law to the other, to the singularity which law cannot account for. Justice exists in a relation of alterity to law: it opens the discourse of law to an outside. For Derrida, justice, unlike law, cannot be deconstructed: "Justice in itself, if such a thing exists, outside or beyond law, is not deconstructible. No more than deconstruction itself, if such a thing exists."[38] One could ask, though, if justice [and indeed, deconstruction] is not deconstructible, then is this not positing some sort of essence that sits a little uncomfortably with the antiessentialist logic of deconstruction itself? Without an adequate conception of the outside, justice cannot be conceptualized as Derrida intends it, and inevitably falls back into essentialist terminology. It would seem, then, that while Derrida has expanded the anti-authoritarian argument by exposing its possible pitfalls and limits, he falls back into the same trap: without an adequate conceptualization of the outside, he is forced to resort to essentialist concepts.

In any case, for Derrida, justice performs a deconstructive displacing of law. For a decision to be just, Derrida argues, for it to account for the singularity denied by law, it must be different each time. It cannot be the mere application of the rule—it must continually reinvent the rule. Therefore, justice conserves the law because it operates in the name of the law; but, at the same time, suspends the law because it is being continually reinterpreted.[39]

Justice, moreover, exists in an ethical realm because it implies a freedom and a responsibility for one's own actions.[40] Justice is the experience of the impossible because it always exists in a state of suspension and undecidability. It is always incalculable: the promise of something yet to come, which must never be completely grasped because then it would cease to be justice and become law. As Derrida says: "There is an avenir for justice and there is no justice except to the degree that some event is possible which, as an event, exceeds calculation, rules, programs, anticipations."[41] Justice is an "event" that opens itself to the other, to the impossible: its effects are always unpredictable because it cannot be determined, as law can and is, by an a priori discourse. It is an excess that overflows from law and cannot be grasped by it. Justice functions as an open, empty signifier: its meaning or content is not predetermined.

So justice occupies an ethical ground that cannot be reduced to law or political institutions, and it is for this reason that justice opens up the possibility for a transformation of law and politics.[42] My critique of the place of power in political philosophy has been aimed at precisely this: a transformation of politics, particularly the politics of resistance. This transformation, though, is not an absolute destruction, but rather a refounding of political and legal discourse in a way that unmasks their lack of legitimate ground and, thus, leaves them open to continual and unpredictable reinterpretation. The classical political discourse of emancipation, for instance, should not be rejected but, rather, reformulated in this manner. While the Enlightenment ideal of emancipation has the potential for becoming a discourse of humanist domination—we have seen this in the experience of anarchism—it can also become a discourse of liberation if it can be un-moored from its humanist foundations and refounded as a nonplace. As Derrida says:

> Nothing seems to me less outdated than the classical emancipatory ideal. We cannot attempt to disqualify it today, whether crudely or with sophistication, at least not without treating it too lightly and forming the worst complicities. But beyond these identified territories of juridico-politicization on the grand political scale, beyond all self-serving interpretations . . . other areas must constantly open up that at first seem like secondary or marginal areas.[43]

One could argue that because poststructuralism abandons the humanist project, it denies itself the possibility of using the ethical-political content of this discourse for resistance against domination. In other words, it has thrown the baby out with the bath water. Because Derrida, on the other hand, does not rule out the Enlightenment-humanist project, he does not deny himself the emancipative possibilities contained in its discourses. Nor should the anti-authoritarian project deny itself these possibilities. Perhaps, as we shall see later on, the ethical-political content of anarchism itself, which is derived from Enlightenment-humanism, can be adopted by the anti-authoritarian argument— that is, if it can be freed from the humanist foundations which limit it to certain forms of subjectivity. Derrida suggests that we can do precisely this: we can free the discourse of emancipation from its essentialist foundations, thereby expanding it to include other political identities and struggles hitherto regarded as of little importance. In other words, the discourse of emancipation can be left structurally open, so that its content would no longer be limited or determined by its foundations. The *Declaration of the Rights of Man*, for instance, may be expanded to encompass the rights of women and even animals.[44] The logic of emancipation is still at work today, although in different forms and represented by different struggles.

The question of rights reflects upon the differences between deconstructive politics and the revolutionary political logic of anarchism. Both strategies have a notion of political rights and a form of emancipatory struggle on the basis of these rights. The difference is, though, that anarchism sees these rights as essential and founded in natural law, while the politics of deconstruction would see these rights as radically founded: in other words, these rights are without stable foundations and, therefore, their content is not prefixed. This leaves them open to a plurality of different political articulations. This logic of a radical refounding based on a lack will become clearer later. As we have seen, however, the anarchist discourse of rights is founded upon a stable human essence. We have also seen the way in which these rights are strictly determined by this human essence: they remain rights limited by the figure of man and are denied to any form of subjectivity outside this conception. Stirner's notion of the un-man, as a subjectivity excluded by man, was a reaction to this oppressive humanist logic. A deconstructive analysis questions this idea of natural, inalienable rights. Derrida, for instance, in his critique of liberal social contract theory, suggests that these "natural" rights are actually constituted discursively through the social contract and that, therefore, they cannot claim to be natural.[45] These rights, then, are displaced from the social to the natural realm, and the social is subordinated to the natural, just as writing is subordinated to speech. As Derrida argues in his critique of Rousseau, the social is the supplement that threatens, and at the same time is necessary for, the identity of the natural: the idea of natural rights can only be formulated discursively through the contract. There is no pure natural foundation for rights, then, and this leaves them open to change and reinterpretation. They can no longer remain inscribed within human essence and, therefore, can no longer be taken for granted. If they are without firm foundations, we cannot always assume that they will continue to exist: they must be fought for, and in the process they will be reformulated by these struggles.

Deconstructive An-archy

It is through this deconstructive logic that political action becomes an-archic. An-archic action is distinguished here from anarchist action, which is, as we have seen, political action governed by an original principle such as human essence or rationality. While it is conditioned by certain principles, an-anarchic action is not necessarily determined or limited by them. An-archic action is the possible outcome of a deconstructive strategy aimed at undermining the metaphysical authority of various political and philosophical discourses. Reiner Schurmann defines an-archic action as action without a "why?"[46] However, my deconstructive notion of *an-archy* might be somewhat different: it may be defined as action with a "why?"—action that is forced to account for itself and question itself, not necessarily in the name of a founding principle, but in the name of the deconstructive enterprise it has embarked upon. In other words, an-archic action is forced to account for itself, just as it forces authority to account for itself. It is this self-questioning that allows political action to resist place, to avoid becoming what it opposes. So this notion of an-archism may be a way of advancing the anti-authoritarian political project embarked upon by the classical anarchists. An-archism seeks to make this anti-authoritarian project account for itself, making it aware of the essentialist and potentially dominating categories within its own discourse. Moreover, it seeks, through the logic of deconstruction, to free the anti-authoritarian project from these categories that inevitably limit it. It therefore expands the anarchist critique of authority by pushing it beyond its own limits, and allowing it to reinvent itself. Derrida's unmasking of the authority and hierarchy which continues to inhabit western thought, as well as his outlining of various strategies to counter it, have made this an-archist intervention possible.

Derrida occupies a number of crucial terrains, then, in the anti-authoritarian argument. His unmasking and deconstruction of the textual authority of logocentric philosophy has allows us to criticize, using the same logic, the political institutions and discourses which are based on this authority. The logic that he employs here is important for the perspective of our argument: it questions the purity and closure of any identity. A pure identity of resistance, an uncontaminated point of departure is denied because it is always contaminated by the identity it excludes. Using this logic, then, the identity of the human subject in anarchist discourse is contaminated by the identity of power. Derrida also forces anti-authoritarian thought to resist oppositional thinking, to operate outside the binary structures which have hitherto imprisoned it within the pernicious logic of place.

More importantly, however, Derrida suggests a way of resisting this oppositional, binary thinking: he allows us to develop a strategy of deconstruction which traces a path of critique, displacing, and thereby transcending the two poles of anti-authoritarian thought—the complete affirmation, and the complete destruction, of authority. It is in this way that Derrida allows to understand and reflect on the limits of the poststructuralist argument, and in this way, the limits of our own argument. He forces us to question our abandonment of the humanist subject. By dispensing with the category of the subject, poststructuralism has opened up a theoretical void it cannot fill within the confines of its own argument. Derrida has argued that by seeking an absolute break, one reaffirms one's place in the terrain one seeks to escape. In the same way, I have argued that poststructuralism, in its attempt to seek lines of flight and escape, to seek an absolute break with man and the terrain of essentialist humanism, has only reaffirmed it, because it has left itself without a point of departure, and it can only fill this void with essentialist figures of resistance. Not only does Derrida expose the limits of this argument, he also allows us to develop ways of breaking out of the dead-end the poststructuralist argument has left us in. Rather than dispersing the subject in a universe of difference, perhaps, following Derrida, the subject may be retained as its own limit, an identity that is structurally open. Moreover, instead of the poststructuralist model of difference, which only becomes, according to this argument, an essentialist category, Derrida proposes an infrastructure—a unity constructed through disunity and difference. This allows the identity of difference to be left structurally open. In doing this, Derrida hints at the possibility of an outside generated from the inside, an important development from the perspective of our argument. He unmasks this "line" of undecidability between the inside and the outside, and works at the limits of the inside to find an outside, just as he works at the limits of the poststructuralist argument in order to find a "beyond."

It is becoming apparent that the anti-authoritarian project can no longer be sustained within the framework of difference, and that the argument, in a perverse way, is "returning"—in the Lacanian sense—to the need for some sort of radical point of departure—some sort non-essentialist outside. Derrida's argument, by pointing to these limitations within the logic of poststructuralism, emphasizes more than ever the need for a radical exteriority. It is on this question, however, that Derrida exposes his own limitations: while he tries to formulate a notion of the outside in terms of the ethical "realm" of justice, it still remains radically undertheorized. I have argued that this idea of justice is meaningless without a better defined concept of the exteriority to which it refers. By Derrida's own admission, a notion of an outside is necessary for a critique of the dominant order: "A radical trembling can only come from the outside," he says.[47] If this is the case, it is a concept and a reality that we must now confront, and it is becoming clear that we cannot do this within the confines of the poststructuralist argument. And while Derrida makes significant advances in this direction, he does not go far enough. A theory of the outside is necessary for a critique of power and authority, and perhaps it requires going beyond the limits of the poststructuralist argument in order to do so. What, then, is this enigmatic outside that has been lurking in the shadows of the critique of authority? How is it constituted and why is it necessary, structurally, for a critique of power? More importantly, how can it be constructed without bringing in the essentialist and foundationalist terms and logic that we have been trying to shed? These are the questions that will be explored in the next chapter when I discuss the contribution of Lacan.

Notes

1. Christopher Norris, *Derrida* (London: Fontana Press, 1987), 19.

2. Moreover, speech is associated with the authority of the teacher, while writing is seen by Plato as a threat to this authority because it allows the pupil to learn without the teacher's guidance. Norris, *Derrida,* 31.

3. As Derrida points out: "it is not any less remarkable here that the so-called living discourse should suddenly be described by a metaphor borrowed from the order of the very thing one is trying to exclude from it." See Jacques Derrida, *Dissemination,* trans. B. Johnson (Chicago: University of Chicago Press, 1981), 148.

4. Jacques Derrida, *Spurs: Nietzsche's Styles* (Chicago: University of Chicago Press, 1978), 81.

5. For instance, Stirner has argued that crime only reaffirms the law that it transgresses. See *The Ego,* 202.

6. Nietzsche too, believes that one cannot merely oppose authority by affirming its opposite: this is only to react to and, thereby, affirm the domination that one is supposedly resisting. Nietzsche believes that one must transcend oppositional thinking altogether—to go beyond truth and error, beyond being and becoming, beyond good and evil. He argues, for instance, that it is simply a moral prejudice to privilege truth over error. However, he does not try to counter this by privileging error over truth, because this leaves the opposition intact. Rather he refuses to confine his view of the world to this opposition. Nietzsche *displaces,* rather than replaces, these oppositional and authoritarian structures of thought—he displaces place. He says: "Indeed what compels us to assume that there exists any essential antithesis between 'true' and 'false'? Is it not enough to suppose grades of apparentness and as it were lighter and darker shades and tones of appearance?" See Friedrich Nietzcshe, *Beyond Good and Evil,* 65.

7. Derrida is influenced here by Nietzsche, who argues that as long as we continue to believe absolutely in grammar, in essence, in the metaphysical presuppositions of

language, we continue to believe in God. See Alan D. Schrift, "Nietzsche and the Critique of Oppositional Thinking," *History of European Ideas* 11 (1989): 783-790, 786.

8. Derrida: "What was named in this way . . . was nothing other than the metaphysical unity of Man and God, the relation of man to God, the project of becoming God as the project of constituting human-reality. Atheism changes nothing in this fundamental structure." See Jacques Derrida, *Margins of Philosophy,* trans. A. Bass (Brighton: Harvester Press, 1982), 116.

9. According to Derrida, for instance, Heidegger's notion of Being does not displace the category of God-Man-Essence as it claims to have done: on the contrary, Being merely reaffirms this place. The notion of Being is only a re-inscription of humanist essence, just as man was, according to Stirner, only a re-inscription of God. The authority of religion, of metaphysics, remains intact. See Derrida, *Margins of Philosophy,* 128.

10. Derrida plays upon this idea of specter or "spirit." He reflects on Marx's dismissal of Stirner's terminology of ghosts or "spooks." See Jacques Derrida, *Specters of Marx: The State of Debt, the Work of Mourning and the New International,* trans. P. Kamuf (New York: Routledge, 1994), 120-121. I have argued in the chapter on Stirner, that Marx's ridicule of Stirner exposes his own desire to exorcise the demons of ideology that Stirner unmasks. There is a certain conjunction of concepts here between Stirner and Derrida: they both have a hauntology, which seeks to expose certain specters, such as the specter of religion (God) and metaphysics, that continue to haunt structures and ideas that claim to have exorcised and transcended them.

11. Rodolphe Gasché, *The Tain of the Mirror: Derrida and the Philosophy of Reflection* (Cambridge, Mass.: Harvard University Press, 1986), 119.

12. Derrida, *Margins of Philosophy,* 135.

13. Derrida, *Margins of Philosophy,* 135.

14. Derrida says that this style of deconstruction is the one that "dominates France today." See *Margins of Philosophy,* 135.
Also Schrift sees this strategy in Foucault's *The Order of Things.* See Alan D. Schrift, "Foucault and Derrida on Nietzsche and the End(s) of 'Man,' " in *Exceedingly Nietzsche: Aspects of Contemporary Nietzsche-Interpretation,* eds. David Farrell Krell and David Wood (London: Routledge, 1988), 131-149, 137.

15. Schrift, "Foucault and Derrida," 138.

16. Schrift, "Foucault and Derrida," 138.

17. Schrift, "Foucault and Derrida," 145.

18. Schrift, "Foucault and Derrida," 145.

19. As Derrida says: "differance is the name we might give to the 'active', moving discord of different forces, and of differences of forces . . . against the entire system of metaphysical grammar." See *Margins of Philosophy,* 18.

20. Derrida, *Margins of Philosophy,* 22.

21. See Gasché, *Tain of the Mirror,* 147-154.

22. Derrida, *Dissemination,* 138.

23. Gasché, *Tain of the Mirror,* 152.

24. Gasché, *Tain of the Mirror,* 150.

25. Jacques Derrida, *Speech and Phenomena, and Other Essays on Husserl's Theory of Signs,* trans., D. Allison (Evanston: Northwestern University Press, 1973), 158.

26. Rodolphe Gasché, *Inventions of Difference: On Jacques Derrida* (Cambridge, Mass.: Harvard University Press, 1994), 28.

27. Jacques Derrida, *Of Grammatology,* trans. G. C Spivak (Baltimore: Johns Hopkins University Press, 1976), 24.

28. Derrida, *Of Grammatology,* 135.

29. Jacques Derrida, *Positions,* trans. A. Bass (London: Athlone Press, 1981), 12.

30. See Michael R. Clifford, "Crossing (out) the Boundary: Foucault and Derrida on Transgressing Transgression," *Philosophy Today* 31 (fall 1987): 223-233.

31. Clifford, "Crossing (out) the Boundary," 230.

32. Norris, *Derrida*, 231.

Levinas tries to transcend western philosophy, to rupture it by confronting it with the other, the point of irreducibility which will not fit into its structures. See John Lechte, *Fifty Contemporary Thinkers: from structuralism to postmodernity* (London: Routledge, London, 1994), 117.

33. Derrida, *Positions*, 6.

34. See John Caputo's "Beyond Aestheticism: Derrida's Responsible Anarchy," *Research in Phenomenology* 19 (1988): 59-73.

Derrida talks about the ethical responsibility of texts: he argues that philosophical texts must bear some responsibility for the way they are interpreted, suggesting that Nietzsche's texts contained certain themes which lent themselves to Nazism. See Norris, *Derrida*, 204-205. As I suggested in the first chapter, there is a similar connection that can be made between Marx's texts and the authoritarianism that ensued after the Bolshevik revolution. See Norris, *Derrida*, 204-205.

35. Richard Kearney, "Derrida's Ethical Re-Turn," in *Working Through Derrida*, ed. Gary B. Madison (Illinois: Northwestern University Press, 1993), 28-50.

36. Derrida: "Since the origin of authority, the foundation or ground, the position of the law can't by definition rest on anything but themselves, they are themselves a violence without ground." See Jacques Derrida, "Force of Law: The Mystical Foundation of Authority," in *Deconstruction and the Possibility of Justice*, ed. Drucilla Cornell et al. (New York: Routledge, 1992), 3-67.

37. However, as Derrida argues, deconstruction cannot have as its aim the complete destruction of all authority: this only succumbs, as we have seen, to the logic of place. As Derrida says, the two temptations of deconstruction, can be likened to Walter Benjamin's notion of the alternate paths of the general strike—to replace the state or to abolish it: "For there is something of the general strike, and thus of the revolutionary situation in every reading that founds something new and that remains unreadable in regard to established canons and norms of reading, that is to say the present state of reading or what figures the State, with a capital S, in the state of possible reading." See Derrida, "Force of Law," 37. In this sense, deconstruction may be seen as a strategy of resistance against the authority of meaning—the state—in the text of philosophy, just as other struggles like anarchism might resist the state in the "text" of politics. Indeed, there is no point separating the deconstruction of philosophical texts with the deconstruction of power: the two "realms" of struggle are inextricable because political authority is dependent upon its sanctioning by various texts, such as those by Hobbes, for instance, and by the logocentric discourse of reason. I have explored this connection through Deleuze and Guattari. Anarchism may be seen in this way, as a kind of deconstructive writing aimed at the overthrow of the state. The deconstructive moment is a revolutionary moment, and it is therefore susceptible to the political trap of place—to the reaffirmation of the power it opposes. If such struggles against domination are to avoid this trap they must pursue a path between reaffirmation and complete destruction, which, as anarchism, and as I suggested, poststructuralism, have unconsciously demonstrated, come to the same thing. Derrida's deconstruction of law has furnished antiauthoritarian thought with a unique strategy. However, this strategy, Derrida argues, is continually haunted by the lure of place, a seduction which antiauthoritarian thought and action must avoid.

38. Derrida, "Force of Law," 14-15.

39. As Derrida says: "for a decision to be just and responsible, it must . . . be both regulated and without regulation: it must conserve the law and also destroy it or suspend it enough to have to reinvent it in each case, rejustify it." See "Force of Law," 23.

40. Derrida, "Force of Law," 22-23.

41. Derrida, "Force of Law," 27.

42. Derrida, "Force of Law," 27.

43. Derrida, "Force of Law," 28.

44. Derrida, "Force of Law," 28.

45. Michael Ryan, "Deconstruction and Social Theory: The Case of Liberalism," in *Displacement: Derrida and After*, ed. Mark Krupnick (Bloomington: Indiana University Press, 1983), 154-168.

46. Reiner Schurmann, *Heidegger on Being and Acting: From Principles to Anarchy,* trans. C. M. Gros (Bloomington: Indiana University Press, 1987), 10.

47. Derrida, *Margins of Philosophy,* 134.

Chapter Seven

Lack of the Outside/Outside of the Lack: (Mis)Reading Lacan

The last chapter showed the way in which Derrida advanced the anti-authoritarian argument by exposing the limits of the poststructuralist "model" of difference—a model which had up until now determined the logic of this argument. In doing this, Derrida has pointed to the possibility of a new way of theorizing the subject—one that retains the subject as its own limit, rather than dispensing with it. His argument also points to the need and possibility for an outside [to philosophy, discourse, power] constructed, paradoxically, from the inside. While it was found that Derrida cannot adequately theorize this outside, he nevertheless laid the theoretical groundwork for it. I will try in this chapter, using the ideas of the psychoanalytic thinker Jacques Lacan, to construct a notion of the outside through this radical retention of the subject.

Lacan wrote about the "obsessive" and the "hysteric" subject. The obsessive never quite catches up with the object of his desire, while the hysteric, in his desperate pursuit of the object of desire, overtakes it and goes beyond it. Therefore, neither attains the object of his desire, one going too far and the other not going far enough. The object of desire eludes them both. Perhaps we can say that in *our* analysis, the slippery and elusive object of desire is the Outside—a notion that sits most uncomfortably with a non-essentialist politics of resistance and yet, paradoxically, remains absolutely crucial to it. Perhaps we can also say that Foucault is like the obsessive neurotic, who hints at and desires an outside to power, but never goes far enough in defining it. And maybe Deleuze can be likened to the hysteric who, in his mad dash after the Outside, after a figure of resistance, ends up missing it altogether by defining it in terms of a metaphysical notion of desire. Derrida possibly comes closest to an outside in his notion of differance, but it still remains somewhat ambiguous. So it seems that while a notion of an outside is necessary for a politics of resistance, it remains so far in this analysis, sufficiently opaque and abstract as to be without much value.

The figure of the Outside lives amongst the shadows of radical political theory, only half hinted at and obscurely alluded to, but without any real attempt made at defining or exploring it. It remains, paradoxically, on the limits of this work, yet at the center of the discussion. The question central to this discussion is *how can we formulate a notion of resistance to domination that does not reaffirm the place of power by succumbing to essentialist temptations?* Stirner, Foucault, Deleuze and Guattari, and Derrida have, in their own ways, hinted at the need for an outside. However, they have been unable to formulate it clearly. It seems that the closer one gets to the outside, the more elusive and indefinable it becomes. The rigors of the poststructuralist argument do not allow for an outside to power and discourse: an outside that was posited by the anarchists, yet remained trapped within the logic of place. Perhaps, like Lacan's impossible object of desire, the outside remains unapproachable. And yet some notion of an outside is necessary if the argument is to proceed. This chapter will attempt, then, to explore the possibility of an outside which is not essentialist and which does not reproduce place.

The Subject of the "Lack"

While the outside appears to be an impossible and indefinable "object," perhaps, paradoxically, the only way that it can be grasped is precisely by recognizing its fundamental impossibility. Lacan's idea of the lack at the basis of subjectivity may be used here to explore the radical impossibility that structures the notion of the outside.

Lacan's notion of subjectivity would seem at first glance to coincide with the poststructuralist argument.[1] He rejects the Cartesian subject, the subject of autonomous self-knowledge, the self-transparent subject. The autonomous subject of the Cogito is subverted within language: the consciousness is an *effect* of signification. Moreover, the preeminence placed on consciousness neglects the role of the unconscious which "is structured like a language."[2] It is a "chain of signifiers."[3] Contrary to the cogito, then, the subject is given meaning by an external world of signifiers, by the symbolic order—the Other. The subject is seen as secondary to the signifier and constituted only in relation to the signifier; the subject is written as $S(s)$—the small (s) representing the subject, the big S representing the signifier.[4] Lacan's analysis subverts the Enlightenment idea, which informs anarchist theory, of an autonomous essential subjectivity: Lacan's subject has no independent identity outside the order of the signifier. This notion of subjectivity appears to fit quite neatly into the logic of poststructuralism, which sees the subject as an effect of discursive and power arrangements.

There is, however, an important difference between Lacan's analysis and that of the poststructuralists. The difference here is the notion of a radical gap or lack between the subject and the signifier—a lack that actually constitutes the subject. The subject is subverted in Lacan's analysis, not because it is entirely determined by signifiers, as the logic of poststructuralism would suggest, but because its determination by signifiers is fundamentally *flawed*.

According to Lacan, the individual enters the symbolic network, the order of signifiers where he is represented for another signifier. However, this representation ultimately fails: there is a lack or gap between the subject and its representation. The subject fails to recognize himself in the symbolic order and is thus alienated. He is pinned to a signifier (s1) which represents him for another signifier. The subject is incapable of fulfilling this symbolic identity and so there is an excess or surplus of meaning produced by this failed interpellation—a radical gap or absence between the subject and meaning. This is what Lacan calls "object *a*," and it is this that actually constitutes the subject. The subject is, then, the failed "place" of signification; the "empty place of the structure" of symbolization.[5] The subject is the *subject of the lack*: it is the name given to this gap or void in the symbolic structure, this fundamental misrepresentation.

There is always something in language that cannot be signified, a gap or blockage of some sort—but it is precisely this failure of signification that allows signification.[6] The lack, then, is always part of the process of signification. The signifier can never wholly account for what it is supposed to signify: "When we speak or read a word, we do not stop at the mere sound or drops of ink. . . . We see through the word to another that is absent."[7] There is, therefore, a lack between the signifier and what it signifies—an excess of meaning that eludes signification, and yet enables it to take place. Subjectivity is constituted by this gap, by this failure of signification. The subject exists, then, as its own limit—as the limit of its own full realization in the symbolic order. The subject is s(O)—with the O crossed out or barred. This symbolizes the failure of the signifier to represent the subject, the "cut" in the signifying chain that represents the subject: "we must bring everything back to the function of the cut in discourse, the strongest being that which acts as a bar between the signifier and signified . . . . This cut in the signifying chain alone verifies the structure of the subject as discontinuity in the real."[8]

The subject is, therefore, constitutively split: its alienation within the symbolic order of language cannot be overcome. This split is, Lacan argues, the result of a primary repression of oedipal desires. This original prohibition constructs the subject's desire as continually blocked and frustrated by the signifier that eludes it. The subject is, thus, constituted through this prohibition of desire, a desire for the impossible object—its representation in the Other which can never be attained.[9] So the subject is constituted through its fundamental inability to recognize itself in the symbolic order. It is represented precisely by its failure of representation. Whereas poststructuralism would see the subject as fully determined by its representation, Lacan sees the subject as only partially determined. There is always an excess of meaning that disrupts symbolization, which blocks the signifying circuit by eluding representation.[10] This gap, this surplus of meaning that cannot be signified, is a void in the symbolic structure—the "Real." The Real resists being subsumed in the symbolic order and therefore blocks the formation of a full identity. The Real is the traumatic kernel of identity: something which never actually existed but whose effects are nevertheless felt.

Beyond Poststructuralism

This lack or void which constitutes the subject is not, however, a fullness or essence. It is, on the contrary, an absence, an emptiness—a radical lack. In other words, it is a nonplace that resists essence because it does not allow a stable identity to arise. The subject can never form a complete or full identity because the lack can never be filled. This notion of absent fullness allows Lacan to go beyond the paradigm of poststructuralism. While the subject is subverted in the order of signifiers, as poststructuralists would argue, it is not wholly determined: the process of signification is blocked by the void that defies representation. The leftover, surplus meaning escapes signification, and it is this that constitutes subjectivity. For Lacan, then, the subject is split: subjectivity is not just an effect of the Symbolic Other, of discourse, law, power, etc.—it is also the Real, the *leftover* from this failed signification. The subject is defined through the failure of self-recognition. Therefore, poststructuralist motifs of nonself-representation and difference do not necessarily undermine subjectivity: rather, they *are* the structure of subjectivity.[11] Poststructuralism would see the subject as dispersed by a plurality of signifiers. Lacan, on the other hand, would see this plurality and nonrepresentation as actually constitutive of the subject. So, whereas the logic of poststructuralism proposes the transgression of identity, Lacan's analysis points to an identity based on transgression—an identity constituted upon its own impossibility. As Slavoj Zizek argues, Lacan goes beyond the mere deconstruction of subjectivity: he posits a *reconstruction* of the subject based on the limits of its own impossibility.[12] Moreover, the subject is represented by one signifier—the Master Signifier—instead of a multitude of signifiers; only this representation is, as we have said, flawed. The subject is not dispersed in Lacan's analysis: it is not entirely determined by multiple signifying regimes [discourses] as it is for poststructuralists. Rather, it is constitutively split between signification and the meaning that eludes it. There is always a lack between the subject and signification—a void that disrupts signification—which can never be overcome. This is why the identity of the subject is always failed. This constitutive lack—the gap between meaning and signification, between the subject and representation—perhaps points to the possibility of the radical outside and may enable us to go beyond the limits of the poststructuralism.

Both Stirner and Lacan's arguments are used as points of intervention in this discussion. Stirner's critique of essence allowed us to break out of the Enlightenment-humanist logic of anarchism and, thus, anticipate poststructuralism. Lacan ideas are used here in a similar way, to transcend the parameters of the poststructuralism—a logic that has reached its conceptual limits and, therefore, no longer advances the argument. It may be useful, in this case, to look at the similarities between Stirner and Lacan's notions of subjectivity. Perhaps Stirner's notion of the ego can help us to see Lacan's lack in terms of a radical absence or emptiness, but an emptiness that is nevertheless creative. Stirner has often been seen as affirming a new essential subjectivity, one that is supremely individualistic, selfish, and egotistical. Indeed, this was how Marx saw him—as an ideologue of the bourgeoisie. However, as I have argued, Stirner can be read in another way: rather than seeing the ego as an essential identity, it may be seen as a radical emptiness, a nonplace which rejects essence, affirming instead flux, contingency, and becoming. The ego, for Stirner, is an emptiness or void that, precisely because it is a nothingness, is fundamentally creative. Once this emptiness at the base of identity is accepted, the subject is no longer limited by essence and is allowed to recreate himself, to explore new identities. These identities are never essential, though, because they in themselves are based on nothing. So, like Lacan, Stirner does not necessarily reject subjectivity; rather, he sees it as founded on a fundamental emptiness or lack, and so it is always partly fragmented and incomplete. It can never become a closed, whole identity.

So there is a surprising convergence here between Stirner and Lacan. For Stirner, the subject is alienated by various signifiers—man, human essence—and there is always a gap between the subject and the way it is represented: "They say of God 'Names name thee not'. That holds good of me: no concept *expresses* me, nothing that is designated as my essence exhausts me; they are only names."[13] Stirner's subject is alienated by the names and signifiers that are imposed upon it in the Symbolic Order. Stirner's subject, like the Lacanian subject, is somehow misrepresented, and the "names" or signifiers cannot adequately express or account for it. There is, for Stirner, like Lacan, always an excess of meaning produced by this alienation: the un-man may be seen as that surplus of meaning which eludes signification, which does not fit in with the symbolic order of "fixed ideas" and which always disrupts it. While this surplus is produced by signification, it somehow escapes it and counteracts it. Thus, the Stirnerian un-man may be compared with the Lacanian Real as a radical absence or excess which cannot be signified, and which blocks the complete subsumption of the subject into the symbolic order. Moreover, Stirner's ego may allow us to see Lacan's lack as creative and productive: a gap out of which new possibilities and desires may be produced. While Deleuze saw Lacan's idea of desire grounded in lack, as negative and reactive, it may, in another sense, be seen as positive and productive: if desire is grounded in lack, in emptiness and impossibility, it can never become a closed, essentialist identity and, therefore, remains open to other possibilities.

This notion of a creative lack, a productive emptiness, is crucial for my argument in two related ways. First, it allows one to retain a notion of the subject—effectively denied by poststructuralist logic—albeit a subject whose identity is fundamentally flawed and incomplete. It is a subjectivity that eschews the ground of essence. It is based rather on a war model of radical antagonism and lack—a nonground. It is a subjectivity based on its own impossibility, and it thus remains open to contingency and reinterpretation.

A Radical "Outside"

Second, it allows us to theorize a notion of the outside that has so far eluded us. Given the poststructuralist argument about the pervasive nature of power, language, and discursive structures, one cannot talk, as the anarchists did, about an actual place outside power and discourse from where the domination that it gives rise to can be opposed. There is, as we have said, no essential, uncontaminated point of departure outside power. However, what if the outside were to be seen as a "thing" which is inside the world of power and discourse, yet somehow missing from that structure? It may be seen as a kind of traumatic void, a kernel of emptiness which is within the structure of symbolization, yet which constitutes an outside because it resists symbolization. In other words, the Real or lack is not necessarily the outside of the symbolic order of Law but rather an "excluded interior"; a "thing" which is not exactly outside the structure but absent from it. Lacan talks of the Real as "excluded in the interior."[14] J.A. Miller sees the Real as a kind of Moebius strip, which confuses the line between the subject and the symbolic; the subject is the "cut" which allows the strip to be laid out flat.[15] This notion of the *excluded interior* or *intimate exterior* may be used to redefine the outside. Because it is an outside produced by the failed and incomplete "structure," it is not an essence or metaphysical presence. It does not transcend the world of the symbolic [or discourse or power] because it "exists" *within* this order. It is not a spatial outside, but rather a *radical* outside—an outside, paradoxically on the "inside." Therefore the gap between meaning and symbolization can be constituted as a radical outside, not because it is from a world outside the symbolic structure, not because it is a transcendental essence, but because it is a void which cannot be filled, a lack which cannot be represented.

This outside of the lack thus avoids the pitfalls of essentialism and place. It is not a presence but rather a creative and constitutive absence. This concept is useful in several respects. It can possibly provide a nonessential "ground" or nonplace for resistance; it opens the structure of subjectivity to change and contingency, allowing the invention of new political identities. If the subject is not wholly determined and interpellated, there is a "space" opened for a politics and an identity—albeit an unstable one—of resistance.

Power and Lack

Moreover, the logic of the lack can be applied to the question of power itself. It may be argued that the identity of power is ultimately a failed identity. As Ernesto Laclau and Lilian Zac argue, power can never become absolute, because when it does it loses its identity as power.[16] If power is ubiquitous, as Foucault argued, then it becomes indefinable and abstract; it can no longer really be seen as power. Perhaps this was the mistake that Foucault made in his analysis of power. For power to have an identity it cannot be absolute; there must be a gap between it and what it oppresses. Even Foucault conceded, although power is "everywhere," it exists in an agonistic relation to resistance, and this would indicate the need for some notion of a gap that defines power in opposition to itself. However, Foucault, as we have seen, is rather unclear on this point. This lack in the structure of power is what constitutes power's identity as "power" and it cannot function without it. It differentiates power from other signifiers. Yet, paradoxically, this lack makes resistance to power possible. Like Derrida's notion of the supplement, the lack is both necessary for the constitution of identity of power, while at the same time it destabilizes and allows it to be resisted. In other words, the lack is the limit of power: it is the limit that both defines it and threatens it. Perhaps this notion of a constitutive lack as the limit of power was what Foucault was driving at. This lack, however, is not an essential place of resistance: it is created by power itself, and is only the excess or surplus of meaning which escapes it. The Real of power is not outside the order of power, but rather operates on the inside: it is the void within power that both subverts its meaning and, through this subversion, gives it meaning. So, therefore, the Lacanian idea of a constitutive lack may be applied to power; it creates the possibility of a radical outside that both constitutes and resists power.

This notion of power as constituted by its fundamental lack can be contrasted with Foucault's idea of power as all pervasive. Foucault argued that although power is "everywhere," it masks itself through the juridico-discursive model, which leaves a gap between power and the society that it oppresses. For Foucault, power would not be tolerable if it did not mask itself partially, if there did not appear to be a "place" of resistance that it does not invade. So, for Foucault, while power disguises itself through the lack, this lack or gap between power and what it dominates does not actually exist. A Lacanian notion of power would be almost directly opposed to this: rather than power disguising itself through an ideological lack, it is actually constituted through a real lack. Power cannot be omnipresent because if it is, it loses its identity as "power." For power to exist, then, there must be some kind of gap limiting it. As I have argued, this gap is not a metaphysical or essentialist notion like the anarchist idea of human essence; it is itself a void in the symbolic structure of power, but it exists nevertheless, and while it exists it limits power. So this lack between power and the subject is not a deception, as Foucault suggested: it would, be according to Lacan, real and actually constitutive of power as an identity.

There is a parallel here with Stirner's conception of the state. Stirner argues that the power of the state is not absolute; in fact, it is very fragile and is based largely on the subject's obedience to it. Once the subject realizes this, then the state's power over him will be undermined. The state is, like God, an abstraction based on the individual's abdication of his own authority; it is merely an inverted image of the individual, based on his own lack. Stirner says: "So in State-life I am at best—I might as well say, at worst—a bondman of myself."[17] Using a similar, yet Lacanian-inspired, logic Zizek argues that everyone knows that the power of bureaucracy is not absolute, yet we behave as though it is and this is what perpetuates its power.[18] So one might say, then, that rather than power being ubiquitous and absolute, while claiming that it is not—as Foucault argues—power *is* actually limited and lacking, yet claims to be ubiquitous and absolute. For Foucault, in other words, the all-pervasiveness of power is masked by a lack; whereas for Lacan, the lack in power would be masked by its all-pervasiveness.

Law, Transgression, and Pleasure

This possible Lacanian conception of power as founded upon a lack is based on his analysis of law. Lacan argues that the Law functions only through its failure to function, through its essential incompleteness. In his reading of Kant and Sade, Lacan suggests that the Law produces its own transgression, and that it can only operate through this transgression.[19] The excess of Sade does not contradict the injunctions, laws, and categorical imperatives of Kant: rather, they are inextricably linked to it. Like Foucault's discussion of the "spirals" of power and pleasure, in which power produces the very pleasure which it is seen to repress, Lacan suggests that the very denial of enjoyment—embodied in law, in the categorical imperative—produces its own form of perverse enjoyment, or "jouissance" as a surplus. Kant has failed to recognize this reverse side of the Law, the obscene pleasure of the Law.[20] Sade exposes this obscene enjoyment by reversing the paradigm: he turns this perverse pleasure into a law itself, into a sort of Kantian universal principle or right. The right to pleasure is, for Sade, the necessary accompaniment and logical extension of the Rights of Man: "Let us say that the nerve of the diatribe is given in the maxim which proposes a rule for *jouissance*, bizarre in that it makes itself a right in the Kantian fashion, that of posing itself as a universal rule."[21] Sade unmasks, then, the perverse pleasure which permeates the Law based on the renunciation of this pleasure. He does this by turning this pleasure, denied yet affirmed by the Law, into the Law itself. So, the pleasure of the Law becomes the law of pleasure. The desire that transgresses and exceeds the Law is only the other side of the Law. This is why Sade is seen as the necessary counterpart to Kant.

This link between law [or, for our purposes, power] and the pleasure which both transgresses and affirms it, is also recognized by Kafka. The seemingly neutral, faceless, anonymous bureaucracies that are so much part of Kafka's writings, produce, through their very renunciation of pleasure, their own excess of perverse pleasure. This is often manifested in the sadistic enjoyment that Kafka unmasks in bureaucratic functioning. Take, for instance, the torture machine—the Harrow—in Kafka's *In the Penal Settlement.*[22] Its hideous workings are described by the executioner in mundane detail, in a voice of absolute bureaucratic neutrality. The effect is to produce an excess of punishment and suffering which palpitates at the limits of the Law. The Harrow is a machine which literally carves the law into the condemned man's body: the letter of the Law is inscribed only through the excess—the irrational excess of sadistic pleasure—which seems to transgress its limits. The renunciation of enjoyment—embodied in the neutral letter of the Law, in the anonymous functioning of the bureaucracy—produces its own perverse enjoyment, an enjoyment based on its own denial.

For Lacan, law does not prohibit or repress pleasure; on the contrary, it produces it, but produces it as "repressed": "But it is not the Law itself that bars the subject's access to *jouissance*—rather it creates out of an almost natural barrier a barred subject."[23] So rather than prohibition being grounded in law, law is actually grounded in prohibition, in the fundamental lack between the subject and his representation, the object of his desire.[24] The enjoyment which exceeds law, Lacan argues, is produced within the order of law: enjoyment is never a spontaneous transgression of the Law, but rather an injunction of the Law—an injunction to "Enjoy!" We are always being told to enjoy ourselves, to be happy, to not be depressed, and yet this enjoyment is seen in terms of a rebellion, a transgression of some sort. As Foucault argues, when we confess our deepest "secrets" and most perverse pleasures, when we affirm our "repressed sexuality," this gives us a certain pleasure, because we think we are flouting a repressive power or law. However, in doing this, we are playing right into the hands of the very power we believe we are transgressing. Similarly for Lacan, the Law does not prohibit or repress, but rather, incites its own transgression: "Indeed, the Law appears to be giving the order, 'Jouis !' "[25]

Therefore for Lacan, the Law generates a surplus or excess of pleasure that resists it. Moreover, the rule of law depends upon this excess. For Lacan, the function of the Law is precisely to *malfunction*: to produce an excess which both transgresses against it and which, *through this transgression*, allows it to operate.[26] For Lacan, an identity is constituted only through its distortion, its inability to be constituted. Similarly, it is only through its distortion that the Law has meaning. Kafka's bureaucratic machine seems to function, not despite but rather through, its chaotic workings, through its inability to function properly. This fundamental link between Law and its transgression is also suggested by Stirner, who argues that crime merely reaffirms the law that it transgresses against.[27] Foucault, too, recognizes this connection: he argues that the purpose of the prison, for instance, is precisely to fail: to continue to produce an excess of criminality which it is supposed to eliminate. It is only through the production of its transgression, of its failure, that the prison continues to operate. Is it not obvious that the prison system has a vested interest in perpetuating criminality: if there were no crime, there would be no need for prisons? So there is a fundamental and constitutive failing in the functioning of the Law—a lack in the structure of power.

The Imaginary State

For Stirner, moreover, power—embodied in the state—is based on this fundamental lack: it is founded upon the abstraction of the individual's own authority and power. In itself the state is nothing: it is based entirely upon the individual's obedience to it—to its signifier. The state is merely a hypostatized self, an ego. Like Lacan's subject who futilely seeks his own representation in the Symbolic Order—a representation which always eludes him—Stirner's individual recognizes the state, and through this recognition actually reproduces the state as an oppressive force over him. In seeking and obeying the state, the individual is merely seeking an abstracted version of himself: he is, in a sense, chasing after his own tail. The state, then, for Stirner, is an illusion, a fantasy-construction. This is not to say that it does not actually exist, but it only comes into existence when the individual starts seeking it and abdicates his authority to it. Kafka's *The Castle* also depicts the structure of power—the bureaucracy—as an "illusion," a fantasy: the more the protagonist seeks contact with the bureaucracy, the further it seems to recede into fantasy and the more elusive it becomes. The individual, in trying to approach the structure of power is only seeking his own recognition in the Symbolic Order.[28] However, as Lacan has shown, this recognition is structurally impossible; there is always something blocking it or lacking from it—namely, the Real.

So if power and authority are structured in this way—in terms of a fundamental impossibility—where does this leave us? First, it is necessary to see how this Lacanianized notion of power departs—if it does at all—from the poststructuralist idea of power. While only Foucault engaged the question of "power" directly, Deleuze and Guattari, and indeed Derrida, also dealt with power in, for instance, linguistic and philosophical structures. While, these notions of power are very different, it can be argued that for poststructuralists, the place of power is dispersed. For Foucault, power is multiform and "comes from everywhere;" for Deleuze and Derrida, power is implicated in a dispersed series of linguistic and discursive structures. Power, for poststructuralists, has perhaps little meaning as a concept in its own right: it is a thoroughly plural, dispersed notion. A Lacanian notion of power might differ from this in the following way: rather than power having no single identity, power would have an identity and a structure, but one which is fundamentally flawed—an identity constituted, as we have seen, through its own transgression. A Lacanian concept of power would be a form of power which did not work, which did not function properly, which allowed an excess to escape it, but which operated precisely through this failure. There is a constitutive lack, then, in the structure and identity of power: a lack which allows the possibility of an outside, from where it might be resisted. This resistance, however, would always be an undecidable: while it can threaten power, it also, according to this two-sided logic, allows power to achieve an identity. So while poststructuralists might argue that the diffuse, multiform character of power denies it any real identity, Lacan would argue that this is precisely why power has an identity. The identity of power is failed and based on a lack, but this does not rob it of an identity. On the contrary, this is precisely how its identity is formed. However, this notion of power does not necessarily conflict with the poststructuralist notion: difference and plurality are not denied, but rather form part of a flawed, open identity.

Politics of the Real

Moreover, perhaps the notion of the place of power can be seen in terms of the Lacanian Real—as that impossible object which eludes signification. The place of power is manifested in many forms. For anarchists, it was embodied in the state, and in statist revolutionary programs. For Stirner, it came in the form of human essence, which became just as dominating as religious essence. For Foucault, Deleuze and Guattari, and Derrida, the place of power realized itself in institutional and discursive practices, and linguistic regimes. Perhaps these were just different and ultimately unsuccessful attempts to symbolize the one thing: the place of power—the Real that cannot be symbolized. These symbolizations of power were somehow inadequate: there was always a surplus of meaning that resisted and eluded it. The Real of domination is the traumatic kernel that always returns in another form.[29] The poststructuralist notion of power—as diffuse as it is—is maybe just another attempt to symbolize the *unsymbolizable*. In the same way that the identity of the subject is constituted through a lack between it and its representation, perhaps the identity of power is also constituted through a similar lack—through its inability to be entirely represented.

Does this mean, though, that the place of power will always be with us; that our inability to completely come to terms with it will mean that we cannot engage or resist it? Has the logic of the Real left us, politically, at a dead end? One may, perhaps, look at it in another way: if a complete representation of the place of power eludes political theorizing, then it disrupts the self-assurance of any theory or politics of resistance that it has truly countered the logic of place. The Real of the place of power leaves every theory of resistance open to the question of whether it has really accounted for its own potential for domination. In other words, the logic of the Real leaves the notion of resistance open to doubt. Like Derrida's notion of difference, the Real forces the identity of resistance to account for itself. The logic of the Real, while presenting power with an outside which resists it, also confronts resistance itself with an outside—the place of power—which questions it.

The Lacanian Real—that traumatic kernel or surplus which escapes signification—is a logic, then, which may be applied to political thinking. First, the subject of politics is neither completely undermined, nor completely essentialized. Rather, according to this logic, the identity of the political subject is flawed and incomplete; its identity is never wholly constituted by signifiers, as the logic of poststructuralism suggested. This means that the identity of the subject is contingent: it is always open to the possibility of resistance against subjectification. In other words, the subject is inevitably political: its identity remains open to contestation. This also means that the subject of resistance is not an essential identity as the anarchists believed. The identity of resistance is never pure or stable. However, this does not mean that the subject can never form an identity of resistance. On the contrary, by freeing the subject from essence, it allows it to form new identities of resistance. The logic of the Real, when applied to the political subject, simply makes political identities undecidable, and open to contingency and contestation. In other words, it politicizes identities.

Second, the logic of the Real can be applied to the identity of society. For instance Ernesto Laclau and Chantal Mouffe see the social as series of signifiers founded, like the Lacanian subject, on a constitutive lack. There is always something missing from the social totality, something that escapes social signification—a gap upon which society is radically founded. There is an excess of meaning that escapes various social signifiers. This means that the identity of society is incomplete; it can never form a closed identity, because there is always a Real that remains unsymbolizable. Society is, therefore, an "impossibility."[30] The Real is the *empty signifier* that "the social" is structured around: it is not fixed by any essence and, thus, remains open to different political signifiers, which try to "fill" this symbolic empty place. Political projects have been attempts to "fill" or "suture" this fundamental lack in society, to overcome its fundamental antagonism. But this is an impossibility: the Real of antagonism, which eludes representation, can never be overcome.

Both Marxism and anarchism were political projects that attempted to overcome the fundamental antagonism and alienation that rent society apart. Marxism was an attempt to overcome the trauma of class antagonism and to transcend the logic of classical liberal economism that insisted on an isolation of the political sphere from the economic sphere, of the state from society. In other words, it sought to overcome the antagonism in society, which alienated the individual, and to reconcile society with itself. Anarchism was a rejection of the Marxist logic of economic determinism that, anarchists claimed, only produced a further alienation and antagonism between the individual and political power. Both theoretical interventions ultimately failed due to the logic of the Real: they tried to overcome the fundamental antagonism in society, which could not be overcome because this was the very condition of society. They were, in other words, ultimately failed attempts to approach and overcome the Real—that which can never be overcome. The Real cannot be suppressed: it only manifests itself somewhere else. Thus, we saw that the overcoming of the class antagonism only produced another antagonism, this time between the individual and the abstract political power of the state.

Antagonism and the Social

Theories of revolution such as Marxism and anarchism advocated the overthrow of the existing order in the desire to establish the fullness prevented by it. Both theories attempted to overcome domination, but in this very attempt, as we have seen, they ended up reaffirming it. This political logic of "filling" the unfillable gap in society, of overcoming the void that can never be overcome, is an example of *hegemonic* politics.[31] Because society can never form a closed identity, this leaves a gap open for different political articulations to "fill out" the social totality; although this is, as we have seen, only partially possible. Perhaps this logic of hegemony—of the constitutive openness of the social—can help us to explore the problem of the place. If the place of power is the Real that can never be completely overcome, then projects of resistance will be only partially successful in overcoming domination. Perhaps, then, the logic of the place of power can only be resisted through the realization that it can never be entirely transcended.

Society, according to this analysis, is founded upon a radical antagonism that constitutes it through its own impossibility. The antagonism is the Real that cannot be symbolized, the trauma which does not in itself exist, but whose effects are nevertheless felt. Antagonism prevents society from achieving a full identity: it is the fundamental outside—the limit of society. It is the excess of meaning which surrounds society and which limits it. The Real functions like the Derridean supplement. Antagonism is the constitutive outside of society. It both threatens the identity of society—because it leaves it open to different articulations—and, paradoxically, allows it to achieve an identity, albeit incomplete—because it is only through various political articulations which try to overcome this fundamental lack that society has an identity at all.

Antagonism, then, is a constitutive outside which subjects society to the logic of undecidability: society may be seen, rather than as an impossible object, as an undecidable object, caught between the Real of antagonism and signification. It is governed by this radical gap, this emptiness, in the same manner as the Lacanian subject.

Antagonism is not, however, the essence of society. Rather, it is precisely that which denies society an essence. As Laclau and Mouffe argue: " 'Society' is not a valid object of discourse. There is no single underlying principle fixing—and hence constituting—the whole field of differences."[32] Antagonism exists, therefore, as the excess of meaning that cannot be grasped by social signifiers, which surrounds "society" as its limit.[33] This idea of society as a field of differences founded on a radical antagonism, runs contrary to the anarchist notion of society as an essential identity governed by natural laws. Stirner, also, realized that society has no essence, that it is not a thing in itself: it has no ego. Antagonism may be compared, for instance, with Deleuze's notion of the war-machine, which is, as we have seen, a radical exteriority of fluxes, becomings, and differences that threatens the state form—the order of essence and fixed identity. Can we not say, then, that this notion of antagonism as a nonplace, a radical outside, is an extension of the war model of relations, a model that has appeared throughout this discussion? The war model has been used as a tool of analysis: it is a model of relations that embraces dislocation and antagonism, thus eschewing any idea of an essential identity. It is that which is in itself nothing, but which blocks the constitution of a complete identity. It may be seen in terms of the Lacanian idea of trauma. It has been applied in various ways, from Stirner to Derrida, to question and undermine the idea of essence or place. In other words, it has functioned as a nonplace that threatens the identity of place. The war machine, when used in this Lacanian sense, however, does not reject the idea of society. It does not seek to abolish society, devouring it in a conflagration of absolute difference and plurality. This would be another attempt to essentialize society—to impose the essence of difference on society. Rather, war is used as a motif to attack the idea of society as an essence, a closed identity. It merely leaves this identity open to political contingency. So rather than the war model entirely subverting the idea of society, it retains society as its own limit.

Trauma and Rational Communication

It may be useful, at this point, to compare this war model of politics, based on the Lacanian lack, to the Habermasian model of rational communication or "communicative action." This comparison is relevant because Jurgen Habermas' idea of communication and consensus, based on shared rational norms and understanding, is quite close to anarchism: it is perhaps the last bastion of the privileged subject of Enlightenment-humanist rationality, the logic which informs anarchism. It is also relevant to the question of resistance against domination, because Habermasians argue that without any notion of shared rational norms—which this Lacanian analysis would question—there can be no possibility of any coherent political or ethical action.[34]

Habermas tries to describe the requirements for an ideal speech situation in which consensus can be achieved without constraint. For Habermas, communicative action presupposes a universal intersubjective understanding that is latent within the *lifeworld*: "Yet these participants in communicative action must reach an understanding *about something in the world* if they hope to carry out their action plans on a consensual basis." [35] Thus, political subjects can reach a rational understanding about the world through speech acts referring to this context, and this points to the possibility of resolving disagreement and reaching consensus. It points, in other words, to a possibility of communication without power and constraint. The lifeworld is, then, the shared common ground upon which rational consensus is to be based. Anarchism, too, tried to achieve a unified identity in this way, through a perceived common essential ground of rationality and morality. Like Habermas, the anarchists dreamt of a form of communication that was transparent, rational, and entirely free from power. Habermas believes that there is "a universal core of moral intuition in all times and in all societies," and this derives from the "conditions of symmetry and reciprocal recognition which are unavoidable propositions of communicative action."[36] So while, for Habermas, this moral "core" does not necessarily naturally occur within the human subject, as it does in anarchist theory, it is still a transcendent ideal and a universal possibility.

However, it is this ideal of a universal ground which the war model rejects: it sees the trauma of antagonism behind consensus, the rift behind unity and cohesion. Lacan himself would reject this idea of a common ground, a shared symbolic world interpretation.[37] The Lacanian analysis tells us that at the base of every identity, social and political, there is a lack, which disrupts the complete constitution of this identity. I have argued that this lack is the Real of antagonism and power which, as Lacan would argue, always *returns*, although in different forms, despite attempts to repress it.[38] According to Lacan, it is this traumatic void in the symbolic structure of subjectivity that always disrupts its identity. The Real may even return in the form of the very forces that try to repress it. Thus, as Lacan has showed us, Sadeian pleasure returns as the excess produced by the Kantian law that tries to repress it. Habermas has tried to do precisely this: to repress this antagonism, the lack that is irrepressible. He tries to construct, or at least describe the circumstances that make possible, a speech situation free from constraint. However, one could argue, using this Lacanian logic, that this very attempt to exclude constraint and power from rational communication is itself the *return* of constraint and power. The Real of power has returned as the very conditions set up to exclude it, thus disrupting the identity of rational communication itself. Rational communication, which is supposedly free from power and constraint, is found, according to this Lacanian-inspired analysis, to be very much embroiled in power and constraint. For instance, what the Habermasian model does not recognize is that these rational norms, which it claims are universal, are not universal at all, but rather are grounded in a particular epistemological and cultural paradigm, and are, thus, inextricably related to power. How would the ideal speech situation deal with the mad, for example, who did not accept these rational norms? Habermas' model does not take account of its own groundedness in a specific epistemological form that restricts difference. So Habermas has only reinstalled power and constraint in the universal notion of intersubjective norms constructed to free communication from power and constraint. Power may be seen, then, as the excess produced by the very structures set up to exclude it. The war model would maintain that any consensus that saw itself as overcoming power, was actually a form of domination.

Habermas believes that the intersubjective understanding presupposed by communicative rationality can free communication from constraint. However, apart from the Lacanian Real that undermines this supposition, we have already seen from the poststructuralists discussed that rationality is already itself a form of constraint, or at least involved with practices of constraint. So I would argue, contrary to Habermas, that communicative rationality is itself a discourse of constraint and domination, if anything because it claims to be otherwise. This is not to say, of course, that there cannot be forms of communication that are not discourses of domination. But there cannot be a discourse of communication that does not involve power in some way. In the chapter on Foucault, I tried to distinguish between his notions of power and domination. However, as I have argued, domination comes from the same world as power. The idea is to try to invent forms of action and communication that minimize the potential for domination. We must resign ourselves, however, as Stirner's theory of ownness exhorts us to do, to the fact that we will never be free of relations of power. This is not so much a resignation, however, as an *affirmation* of this fact. So while the Habermasian perspective sees the possibility of a world free from power, the war model of trauma does not. Even the constitutive exterior to power that I have formulated is not a universe free from power, but rather a lack in the structure of power pointing to an empty, undefined possibility at the limits of power. I have argued, then, that any social reality, no matter how universal and consensual it claims to be, is disrupted by the Real which always returns to haunt it: the limits of power and antagonism which do not allow it to form a complete identity.

So the social is founded upon its own emptiness, then—upon an *empty place* of power. While social reality is constructed by power—this we know from the logic of poststructuralism—society cannot be completely determined by political signifiers. This is because, as I have said, society is an undecidable object—there is always an excess which eludes political articulation. The state, for instance, is a political signifier which, for Deleuze and Guattari, dominates or "codes" every social signifier. But even here there is a radical exterior—the war-machine—that resists the state form. This lack which eludes political domination cannot, however, be seen in terms of a natural essence which binds society. There is no uncontaminated point of departure that the anarchists dreamt of. Rather, this gap between society and its political representation exists in the flawed identity of the signifier of society. There is no essential place of resistance. The lack is, rather, a nonplace of resistance: it is not of a different order to power and, therefore, cannot become an absolute place. It must be understood through Lacan's idea of *trauma*: it is the traumatic kernel of power, the *outside on the inside*. This nonplace, because it is an outside, and because it cannot be fixed by political signifiers, can provide a "ground" for resistance to domination. Because it remains open to contingency and difference in the politics of resistance, it does not allow one politics of resistance to dominate others and, thus, reaffirm the place of power. Like Claude Lefort's notion of the *empty place of power*, which characterizes democracy, the idea of the nonplace provides structural resistance against the seductive logic of the place of power.[39] By seeing identity—political and social identity—as fractured and open, the logic of the lack has allowed us to think outside the paradigm of place.

The Lack and Democratic Politics

The constitutive openness in the structure of identity may allow one to resist the logic of political domination. The logic of political domination operates, as we have seen, through Man, through the image of "the People." The People is constituted as a symbol through which totalitarianism articulates itself. That is why Lefort sees democracy and totalitarianism as systems linked at the symbolic level. He argues that democracy is symbolized by the tension between the rule of "the People" and the "empty place of power" that cannot be filled. In other words, the *empty place* is the lack that constitutes democratic society. Totalitarianism, Lefort argues, is a political logic that tries to occupy this empty place of power by identifying itself with the image of the People.[40] The People functions as an organic metaphor: it allows society to represent itself as an organic whole, a Body constantly threatened from without by various contaminants and parasites which must be purged.[41] This idea of contamination and "elimination" is necessary if totalitarian society is to reproduce itself. Can we not see the same logic at work in anarchist discourse: the anarchist idea of natural society and the natural man that was part of it, as an organic whole whose identity and function is threatened by contamination and corruption from power? Stirner recognized the symbolic role of Man and the People in articulating political domination: "The kernel of the State is simply 'Man', this unreality, and it itself is only a 'society of men.'"[42] The People, then, is the symbolic identity of the place of power, a political unit which has been articulated in order to facilitate political domination. However, if one takes account of the lack in the structure of identity, then the People, or Man, can never be theorized as a unity or an organic whole: they are destroyed as the symbolic articulators of political domination. The unity of identity, upon which political domination relies, is thus fragmented and made contingent through this Lacanian logic. As Zizek says: "The Lacanian definition of democracy would then be: a sociopolitical order in which the People do not exist—do not exist as a unity, embodied in their unique representative."[43] Perhaps we should take this idea seriously and try to outline a political and ethical project which would not function through the symbolic unity of the People, and which did not rely on essentialist notions of humanity, morality, and rationality. This will be attempted in the next chapter.

Lacanian ideas have been used here to go beyond the poststructuralist project of deconstructing identity. The logic of the Real has not deconstructed identity, but has rather *reconstructed* identity on the basis of its own impossibility. While it is not clear that there is a great deal of difference between the two projects—deconstruction does not necessarily reject identity, but merely *questions* it—Lacan's notion of the lack allows one to look at the argument in a different way and, thus, advance it. (1) It has allowed us to construct a notion of an outside which is necessary for a politics of resistance but which has, thus far, eluded us. By seeing this outside, moreover, in terms of a lack—an impossible object lacking from the structure of signification—Lacan has enabled us to avoid turning this outside into an essentialist notion and thus falling into the trap of reaffirming place. (2) While the identity of this radical outside is itself incomplete and fractured—according to the Lacanian logic of signification—it can still provide a ground for resistance. The fact that it is not a fixed identity means that the politics of resistance, developed through this theoretical outside, is freed from an all-determining essence, like the anarchist notion of humanity. It thus remains open to an indefinite field of different articulations of resistance. It does not allow, as we have said, one form of resistance to dominate another. Therefore the fractured and non-essential identity of this outside is precisely its strength. (3) The subject itself—as constituted through a lack, a failure of signification—is open to different and contingent political identities, allowing it to resist a domination that operates through subjectification, through the fixing of identity. Resistance against one's fixed identity has always been a feature of the poststructuralist political project. Now the Lacanian radical outside has finally allowed this resistance to be theorized. (4) The notion of the constitutive outside has been applied to the idea of society itself: the social is seen as being founded on the Real of antagonism that limits it and prevents it forming a complete identity. This opens the social to different political articulations that can never overcome the lack in its own identity and, consequently, will never be able to become completely dominant. The politics of resistance will, therefore, be determined by this hegemonic logic: it will never be able to form a closed dominant identity because its identity is flawed. The politics of resistance is structurally open to difference and reinterpretation. (5) The identity of power, according to Lacanian logic, is also a failed identity, itself constituted through lack. As we have shown, the structure of power is flawed; it produces an excess which both resists it and allows it, at the same time, to be constituted. The identity of power is ultimately undecidable: what threatens it is also what allows its formation as an identity. The outside produced by power allows a space for resistance against it.

These five points are just different ways of talking about the Outside—a notion that has been developed through the Lacanian logic of the lack. The central question of this analysis has been: how can resistance to domination be theorized without falling into essentialist traps which, as we have seen, merely perpetuate this domination? Therefore, there must be some sort of structural outside to power from where it can be resisted, but which does not become essentialized. Because, on the one hand, this Lacanian outside of the lack is constituted by signification as an excess which escapes it, and because, on the other hand, it still allows an identity of resistance—albeit a fractured and undecidable one—it satisfies the two, seemingly contradictory requirements of the non-essentialist place of resistance that we are trying to theorize. Now that a theoretical space, or nonplace, has been opened up for this resistance, the question remains in this discussion: what are the ethical parameters of this resistance, or, how can this possibility of resistance be developed into an ethical project of resistance against domination? This will be the subject of the next, and last, chapter.

Notes

1. See Jan Marta, "Lacan and Post-Structuralism," *The American Journal of Psychoanalysis* 47, no. 1 (1987): 51-57.

2. Jacques Lacan, *The Four Fundamental Concepts of Psycho-Analysis*, 203.

3. Jacques Lacan, *Ecrits: A Selection,* trans. A. Sheridan (London: Tavistok, 1977), 297.

4. Lacan, *Ecrits,* 141.

5. Slavoj Zizek, "Beyond Discourse-Analysis," in *New Reflections on the Revolution of Our Time,* ed. Ernesto Laclau (London: Verso, 1990), 249-260.

6. Bice Benvenuto and Roger Kennedy, *The Works of Jacques Lacan: An Introduction* (London: Free Association Books, 1986), 176.

7. John P. Muller, "Language, Psychosis, and the Subject in Lacan," in *Interpreting Lacan,* eds. Joseph Smith and William Kerrigan (New Haven: Yale University Press, 1983), 21-32, 8.

8. Lacan, *Ecrits,* 299.

9. Lacan, *Four Fundamental Concepts of Psycho-Analysis,* 306.

10. Lacan, *Four Fundamental Concepts of Psycho-Analysis,* 306.

11. Peter Dews, "The Tremor of Reflection: Slavoj Zizek's Lacanian Dialectics," *Radical Philosophy* 72 (July/August 1995): 17-29.

12. Slavoj Zizek, *For They Know Not What They Do: Enjoyment as a Political Factor* (London: Verso, London, 1991), 39.

13. Stirner, *The Ego,* 366.

14. Charles Shepherdson, "The Intimate Alterity of the Real," *Post-Modern Culture* 6, no. 3 (1996) <http://jefferson.village.virginia.edu/pmc/contents.all.html> (11 July 2000).

15. Jacques-Alain Miller, "La Suture," Cahiers pour l'Analyse, nos. 1-2 (Jan.-Apr. 1996): 39-51. Quoted in Jacques Lacan, ed. *Language of the Self: the Function of Language in Psychoanalysis,* (Baltimore: John's Hopkins Press, 1968), 296.

16. Laclau and Zac, "Minding the Gap," 18.

17. Stirner, *The Ego,* 196.

18. Slavoj Zizek, *The Sublime Object of Ideology* (London: Verso, 1989), 36.

19. See Jacques Lacan, "Kant with Sade," *October* 51 (winter 1989): 55-95.

20. Zizek, *For They Know Not What They Do,* 232.

21. Lacan, "Kant with Sade," 58.

22. See Franz Kafka, "In the Penal Settlement," in *Metamorphosis and Other Stories,* trans. W. and E. Muir (London: Minerva, 1992), 7-64.

23. Lacan, *Ecrits,* 319.

24. Lacan, *Ecrits,* 319.

25. Lacan, *Ecrits,* 319.

26. Charles Shepherdson, "History of the Real." *Post-Modern Culture* 5, no. 2 (1995) <http://jefferson.village.virginia.edu/pmc/contents.all.html> (11 Jul. 2000)

27. Stirner, *The Ego,* 202.

28. Zizek mentions the subject's interpellation by the bureaucracy for Kafka: it is seen as a failed interpellation in which the subject cannot recognize himself or identify with anything. See Zizek, *Sublime Object of Ideology,* 44.

29. Zizek talks about concentration camps as the Real of twentieth century civilization: it is a traumatic kernel that has manifested itself in various forms—the Gulag for instance. See Zizek, *Sublime Object of Ideology,* 50.

30. Ernesto Laclau and Chantal Mouffe, *Hegemony and Socialist Strategy: Towards a Radical Democratic Politics* (London: Verso, 1985), 122.

31. Laclau and Mouffe, *Hegemony and Socialist Strategy,* 134.

32. Laclau and Mouffe, *Hegemony and Socialist Strategy,* 111.

33. Laclau, *New Reflections on the Revolution of Our Time,* 90.

34. This is the same criticism that, as we have seen, has been levelled against Foucault by Fraser.

35. Jurgen Habermas, *Moral Consciousness and Communicative Action.* Trans. C. Lenhardt (Cambridge, Mass.: MIT Press, 1990), 136.

36. Jurgen Habermas, *Autonomy and Solidarity: Interviews,* ed. Peter Dews (London: Verso, 1986), 228-9.

37. Peter Dews, "The Paradigm Shift to Communication and the Question of Subjectivity: Reflections on Habermas, Lacan and Mead," *Revue Internationale de Philosophie* 49 (1995): 483-519.

38. Lacan, *The Four Fundamental Concepts of Psycho-Analysis,* 49.

39. Claude Lefort, *The Political Forms of Modern Society: Bureaucracy, Democracy, Totalitarianism,* ed. John B. Thompson (Cambridge, U.K.: Polity Press 1986), 279.

40. Lefort, *The Political Forms of Modern Society,* 279.

41. Lefort, *The Political Forms of Modern Society,* 287.

42. Stirner, *The Ego,* 180.

43. Zizek, *Sublime Object of Ideology,* 147.

Chapter Eight

Towards a Politics of Postanarchism

The previous chapter attempted to construct a constitutive outside to power—a nonplace—which would make resistance to domination possible. It is a theoretical outside that tried to satisfy the two apparently opposed conditions of resistance: that it form a space outside power from which resistance can be formulated; and, at the same time, that it not fall into the trap of essentialism—that it does not, in other words, become a metaphysical or essential point of departure outside power. Through the Lacanian lack, one can satisfy these two demands or, at least, reformulate the terms of these demands in such a way that they are no longer in direct opposition. One can construct a path of undecidability between them which would allow for a genuinely non-essentialist politics of resistance to arise.

Now that theoretical space has been opened for a politics of resistance, it remains of this discussion to try to define this project of resistance, to describe its political parameters and ethical limits. These ethical and political contours will be provided by certain moral principles contained in the anarchist discourse. The idea of ethical limits, especially those of a philosophy like anarchism, whose foundations have been so soundly shaken by poststructuralism, may seem somewhat inappropriate for a non-essentialist theory of resistance against authority. After all, have we not argued that the moral and rational discourses of anarchism are based on an essentialist notion of man which was found to be not only constructed by the very power that it professed to oppose, but also an institution of authority and exclusion itself? The authoritarian implications of essentialist ideas of man and human nature have been exposed by Stirner through Derrida. However, the notion of ethical limits does not necessarily go against the anti-authoritarianism of the thinkers discussed. On the contrary, anti-authoritarianism implies its own ethical sensibility. Stirner, Foucault, Deleuze and Guattari, and Derrida, have all involved, whether they liked it or not, a moral strategy of some sort in their critique of authority. Their suspicion of morality and rationality has only been because of the way these discourses have been tied to various essentialist ideas and were, consequently, an oppressive burden placed upon the individual. However, if one can release these discourses from their indebtedness to human essence, if one can free them from their foundation in man, then perhaps they can be reconstituted in a way that makes them valid to political thinking today. Perhaps, by using the poststructuralist critique, one can theorize the possibility of political resistance without essentialist guarantees: a politics of *postanarchism*.

Indeed the conflict between anarchism and poststructuralism need not be something that puts obstacles in the way of radical political theorizing. On the contrary, the tension between these two political traditions provides us with the

157

impetus and the tools to rethink the very meaning of politics. Perhaps we can find a way of bridging the gap between anarchism and poststructuralism, without snuffing out the very productive flicker of conflict between them. By incorporating the moral principles of anarchism with the poststructuralist critique of essentialism, it may be possible to arrive at an ethically workable, politically valid, and genuinely democratic notion of resistance to domination— one which remains suspicious of all temptations of authority. In other words, through the theoretical interaction between anarchism and poststructuralism, it may be possible to formulate a notion politics that resists the logic of place.

The Critique of Authority

Poststructuralism may be seen as a broad critique of authority. Insofar as it can be said to have a political project, poststructuralism attempts to unmask the authoritarian assumptions and implications in various discourses and discursive structures. It exposed the domination latent in institutions and discourses which were seen as somehow innocent of power; which were seen as essential and, therefore, absolved from political analysis. Stirner's critique of morality; Foucault's rejection of the "essential" division between reason and madness; Deleuze and Guattari's attack on oedipal representation and state-centered thought; Derrida's questioning of philosophy's assumption about the importance of speech over writing, are all examples of this fundamental critique of authority. Therefore, anarchism and poststructuralism, although they function in different ways and in different arenas, and although they may be turned against one another, share, at least, a common thread which leads to a rejection of authority and domination, and a rejection of discourses which reproduce, in the name of liberation, this authority and domination.

Anarchism is a point of departure for this anti-authoritarian project because it was, and is, fundamentally, a critique of political and religious authority—in particular, the authority of the state. This rejection of authority is the very basis of anarchism, and the destruction of authority, through revolution, is its ultimate goal.[1] It was this fundamental condemnation of political authority that distinguished it from other revolutionary philosophies such as Marxism, which reduced political domination to economic domination, seeing the state as secondary to bourgeois economic arrangements. This led, as we have seen, to the neglect of political authority and the autonomy of the state, and consequently, the reaffirmation of state power.

While the importance of anarchism lay in its exposing the authoritarianism within Marxism, and the unmasking of the place of power within the state, it was found that anarchism itself contained authoritarian possibilities. Stirner's critique of Feuerbachian humanism was used to expose the authoritarianism within anarchism's essentialist notions of human nature, the natural order, and human morality and rationality. It was in this way that anarchism was pushed back upon itself, and the critique of authority opened up by anarchism, was taken beyond the limits laid down by it. The ideas that formed the basis of anarchism's project of resistance against authority were found by Foucault, Deleuze and Guattari, and Derrida, to be not only thoroughly questionable—in the sense that they were constituted by the very forms of power and authority that they were supposed to oppose—but were also, in themselves, structures and discourses which lent themselves to the perpetuation of political domination. One example of this is Derrida's contention that ideas such as essence form themselves into oppressive binary hierarchies. Another is Deleuze and Guattari's critique of rationality as a discourse and philosophy of the state. Foucault's idea that something as supposedly essential and natural as sexuality is actually constituted by discourses and practices which are fundamentally intertwined with power and domination, is further example of this poststructuralist extension of the critique of authority.

In other words, anarchism's pure place of resistance against power, its uncontaminated point of departure—the essential human subject and its related discourses of morality and rationality—was found to be somewhat impure, and contaminated by power.[2] The place of resistance was, on the contrary, a place of power and domination. The only trouble with this was that, while it exposed the authoritarian potential within anarchism and indeed any revolutionary philosophy which was based on essentialist ideas, it deprived the anti-authoritarian project of its own point of resistance. It denied it the possibility of an outside from which authority and power could be criticized: if power constituted the terms of resistance themselves, and if there was no getting away from power, as poststructuralism seemed to suggest, then upon what basis could resistance be established? While there were attempts to answer this question within the poststructuralist framework—Foucault's notion of "plebs" and permanent resistance, and Deleuze and Guattari's idea of revolutionary desire—these were found to be either too ambiguous, or too essentialist, for a clearly defined, non-essentialist project of resistance.

The Limits of Poststructuralism

This was the quandary, then, that the anti-authoritarian project found itself in. On the one hand, we have a revolutionary philosophy—anarchism—which offers an outside to power and a basis for resistance, but which is steeped in essentialist ideas, which are irrelevant to today's struggles and lend themselves to perpetuating new forms of domination. On the other hand, however, we have a diverse series of critical strategies—poststructuralism—which, while rejecting essentialism and the political ideas associated with it, offers no real outside to power or any foundation for resistance and, therefore, little possibility of a coherent theory of political action. This is not to say that poststructuralism amounts to nihilism, and that there is no possibility of a political or ethical, critique of power and authority within the framework of poststructuralism itself. Contrary to this prevailing criticism, poststructuralism is politically and ethically engaged and can offer certain possibilities for liberation. However, without some kind of notion of a constitutive outside to power, poststructuralism has difficulty offering a coherent and ethically viable theory of resistance. This is more or less evident in the case of Foucault, who struggled with the idea of resistance, and tried to construct a kind of outside which would make resistance possible. As we saw, though, Foucault could not do this within the limits that he laid down for himself. Poststructuralism, like any philosophy or critical strategy, has its limits. The whole point of poststructuralism is not that it should be taken as a coherent philosophy that can solve the problems of theory. Rather, perhaps poststructuralism should be taken merely as a series of limits—limits that can, nevertheless, be worked through, transcended, and built upon. While, then, poststructuralism does allow for various possibilities of resistance, it means going beyond these limits if one is to construct a theory and a politics of resistance demanded by the critique of authority.

The Lacanian Intervention

This is precisely why Lacan's arguments were applied: to break through the limits of poststructuralism, just as Stirner helped us go beyond the limits of anarchism. Lacan's notion of the lack as a gap, a radical emptiness produced by signification, yet escaping it, and which is, therefore, neither outside nor inside the structure of signification, was used here to theorize a non-essentialist outside to power. It seemed to satisfy the two contrary, yet necessary, terms of anti-authoritarian project: something which forms a constitutive outside to power and discourse, yet is not necessarily of a different order to power and discourse, but which is, rather, produced by them as a lack within their own structure. This pointed to the possibility of transcending the seemingly stifling contradiction in this anti-authoritarian project.

Ethical Limits

While the possibility has been created, then, for a non-essentialist politics of resistance to domination, it remains an empty possibility. If it is to have any political currency at all it must have contours and limits. It must have an ethical framework of some sort—some way of determining what sort of political action is defensible, and what is not. The idea of limits does not necessarily go against the anti-authoritarian project. On the contrary, limits are demanded by it. The very critique of authority is based on the idea of ethical limits: the principle that, for instance, domination, whatever form it takes, transgresses the limits of ethical acceptability and should, therefore, be resisted. This would be an ethical limit that both anarchists and poststructuralists would agree upon, and could become the basis for a broader ethical critique of authority. Moreover, this does not have to be an ethical limit imposed from a metaphysical place that transcends discourse. Rather, it is something generated *within* the discourse of anti-authoritarianism itself: by its definition alone, anti-authoritarianism implies an ethical limit.

However, there is a problem central to this question of ethical limits. For anarchists, ethical limits can only be based on an idea of humanity which power encroaches upon, whereas for poststructuralists, this idea of human essence, or the essential humanity of man, is itself a site of authority and power. Rather than human essence constituting an ethical limit opposed to domination, it is an idea that gives rise to, and perpetuates, domination by imposing limits upon the individual—limits that are *unethical*. In other words, for anarchists, human essence—and the morality based on this—is that which allows the individual to limit power and authority; while poststructuralists would argue that human essence—and the morality based on this—is what allows power and authority to limit the individual. It appears, then, that the whole question of ethics remains skewed on this seemingly irresolvable contradiction. Is it possible, for instance, to construct an ethical critique of authority without merely perpetuating the very authority we wish to oppose? In other words, is it possible to have an ethics not founded on essentialist notions of humanity and man? Is it possible to free ethics from these essentialist notions while retaining its critical value and political currency? This is the question that the anti-authoritarian program must now address. I will argue that such an articulation of ethics is possible, but that it must involve a radical reconstruction of the idea of ethics.

If one accepts that an ethical critique of authority can no longer be grounded in essentialist and universal conceptions of subjectivity, morality, and rationality, then does anarchism, which is based on these premises, still have a place in the politics of resistance? Perhaps, as Reiner Schurmann argues, we should be thinking in terms of *anarché* rather than anarchy. For Schurmann, anarché is an ontological anarchism; a rejection of metaphysical principles such as human essence, and an affirmation of action without universal guarantees and stable foundations. He distinguishes anarché from the anarchism of Kropotkin and Bakunin, seeing this as a reinvention of the place of power: "What these masters sought was to *displace* the origin, to substitute the 'rational' power, *principium*, for the power of authority, *princeps*—as metaphysical an operation as has ever been. They sought to replace one focal point with another."[3]

In other words, anarchism's rejection of political authority was based, nevertheless, in a new form of authority—that of rational and moral first principles. These metaphysical first principles merely provided a moral and rational justification for further domination: "The first philosophies furnish power with its formal structures."[4] As Stirner would argue, the acceptance of the universal authority of rational and moral first principles is a reaffirmation of religious authority. In light of this poststructuralist rejection of place, it is no longer realistic to talk about a stable, universally ethical or rational ground. As Heidegger would see it, we live in an age of metaphysical closure in which the notion of universal first principles is questionable.[5] This is the age of undecidability, of uncertainty, in which political action no longer has a firm ontological base, in which we can no longer rely on first principles to guide us. Political action in this sense becomes an-archic: a form of praxis that no longer refers to metaphysical first principles, to an authoritarian *arché*. Political action can no longer rely on such a priori notions and guarantees of foundations. As Schurmann argues, the form of anarchy relevant here, "is the name of a history affecting the ground or foundation of action, a history where the bedrock yields and where it becomes obvious that the principle of cohesion, be it authoritarian or 'rational', is no longer anything more than a blank space deprived of legislative, normative power."[6]

It is this age of uncertainty into which we are thrown, and we must make do as best we can.[7] This "blank space" that Schurmann speaks of is what we have referred to as the nonplace created by the war model of relations as well as the Lacanian lack. It is a "space" defined by its structural resistance to essential foundations and dialectical logics which try to determine it; it remains open to difference and plural discourses. It is a "space" which signifies the death of place, the death of essentialist foundations.

Politics in the Age of Uncertainty

Political theory must live in the age of the Death of God and the Death of Man. In other words, it must continue without the essential foundations that had hitherto determined its direction. This instills a sense of uncertainty and dislocation, and it is this fundamental dislocation that the war model of relations—a model of analysis used throughout the discussion—has tried to account for. The poststructuralists I have discussed were all prophets of this dislocation. Their work points to a fundamental breakdown of universal values and essentialist notions—an affirmation of rift and antagonism. Stirner talks about the all-consuming nothingness of the ego. Foucault bases his analysis of power itself on the model of war. Deleuze and Guattari, as we have seen, talk about a rhizomatic conceptual and linguistic model that eschews any sense of unity and continuity. Derrida's work is aimed at unmasking the plurality and antagonism hidden behind supposedly uniform and coherent philosophical and linguistic structures. Nietzsche was also aware of this fundamental sense of dislocation. Nietzsche's madman, on hearing of God's death—no, of his murder—cries:

> But how did we do this? How could we drink up the sea? Who gave us the sponge to wipe away the entire horizon? What were we doing when we unchained this earth form its sun? Whither is it moving now? Whither are we moving? Away from all suns? Are we not plunging continually? Backward, sideward, forward, in all directions? Is there still any up or down?[8]

Nietzsche is haunted by a sense of crisis, by a fundamental breakdown in the metaphysical and social order caused by the Death of God, by this loss of place. As Ernesto Laclau argues, God is no longer there to determine the social order, to legitimate power in society, to relegate between subject and object, identity and function. God provided the fundamental link between power and legitimacy.[9] However, with the death of God there is a gap left between them. Anarchism, as we have already suggested, may be seen as an attempt to fill this social lack. By describing an essential order, governed by natural laws and guided by moral and rational principles, anarchists tried to overcome the antagonism and ontological uncertainty—created by political and religious authority—which, as they saw it, rent society apart. In the words of the anarchist Proudhon: "Anarchy is order; (government is civil war)."[10] Thus, the place of power was reinvented.

There are two logics at work here: the logic of *antagonism*, characterized by the war model of poststructuralism, which rejects ontological certainty and social unity; and the logic of *incarnation*, which characterizes a revolutionary philosophy like anarchism, consisting of the movement to overcome this dislocation and fill out the lack in the social order. However, as Laclau has argued, any attempt to fill the social lack is ultimately doomed to failure because this lack cannot be overcome, and is constitutive of society itself. While these two logics are opposed, however, they are nevertheless related: there can be no logic of incarnation without first a notion of dislocation and antagonism to overcome. This relatedness makes the logic of incarnation always undecidable: while it claims to be essential and "already there," it is always based on the logic of dislocation. In this sense, anarchism, while it claimed to be based on an essential and universal natural order, is actually founded on the dislocation and antagonism it tries to dispel. In other words, any ontological or social order is always founded on a constitutive disorder, and this makes it ultimately undecidable.

This radical undecidability may be theorized in another way, using Laclau's logic of the empty signifier.[11] The model of empty signification can perhaps be applied to the question of morality and rationality and their role in the anti-authoritarian project. Perhaps morality and rationality could be conceived as empty signifiers which are no longer founded on a particular essence, or tied to a particular subjectivity, thus becoming open to a theoretically endless and contingent series of signifieds and identities. The poststructuralist critique of the discourses of rationality and morality has been on the basis that they are grounded in a certain subjectivity or way of life that excludes others. Stirner argues, for instance, that humanist morality is always tied to a particular conception of what constitutes human essence: it is always based on the figure of man, which excludes different identities and subjectivities—the un-man. He therefore says: "Morality is incompatible with egoism, because the former does not allow validity to *me*, but only to Man in me."[12] In other words, morality mutilates the individual because it always refers to a particular identity that the individual has to conform to: it excludes difference and otherness. Similarly, Foucault is suspicious of rationality because it is tied to a particular model and series of norms that exclude and dominate those who do not measure up to them; rationality is constituted through its exclusion of the irrational, the mad, the other. Deleuze and Guattari attack the morality and rationality which oedipalize the subject according to psychiatric norms, while Derrida questions the *ethics* of morality by unmasking the violent binary hierarchies upon which it is based. This attack on moral and rational norms does not mean that poststructuralism is not ethically engaged: poststructuralism is merely a critique of the way that these norms are grounded in a particular essence or identity that excludes others. It is a critique of the way that morality and rationality, because

they are essentialized, are used to justify the domination of those who do not
conform to this essential subjectivity.

This critique of the latent authoritarianism inhabiting discourses of morality
and rationality, applies to anarchism itself. While anarchism claims to espouse a
morality for everyone, a "truly human anarchist morality,"[13] it is bound,
nevertheless, to a particular essential identity—a certain picture of what
constitutes the "truly human." For instance, Bakunin bases anarchist morality
on the importance of work: "Human morality accords such rights only to those
who live by working."[14] Thus, the identity of the worker is privileged above
others; different identities and lifestyles—those that are not based on work—are
apparently excluded from this "human morality." Is there not a paradoxical
similarity here between the moral emphasis that Bakunin places on work, and
today's conservative radio talk-show hosts who endlessly glorify the "hard
worker" at the expense of "dole recipient?" So while Bakunin talks about a
"truly human morality," it seems that he has specific ideas of what "human"
means and, consequently, who this morality applies to. Kropotkin, too, founds
anarchist morality on a human essence and a natural identity, thus limiting it.
But what if one were to renounce this essential human identity, as Stirner's
egoist does, and become something other? According to anarchist morality, this
would be seen as immoral, or irrational, and would thus involve an exclusion of
some sort. Even some modern anarchists retain a notion of an essential human
identity upon which morality and rationality are based.[15] Morality in anarchist
discourse, then, is tied to particular identities that are supposed to be
representative, but which, for this reason, inevitably exclude and dominate other
identities and ways of life.

Ethics without Ground

However, does this essential grounding of morality and rationality that has
been so much part of Enlightenment humanist philosophies like anarchism,
mean that we should reject these discourses out of hand? No, on the contrary,
they have a necessary role to play in anti-authoritarian struggles. Without any
notion of morality and rationality it is impossible to develop a critique of
authority. Derrida talks about the continued importance of the ideals and ethics
of the Enlightenment notion of emancipation. But he argues that it must not be a
closed discourse—it must be available to other struggles and identities hitherto
considered of no importance. If these discourses are to have any relevance at all,
they must be freed from their grounding in essential identities: they must be
reconstituted, in other words, as empty signifiers whose fixedness to particular
signifieds is made theoretically impossible. Using the logic of empty
signification, anarchist morality and rationality no longer have to remain tied to
a certain conception of humanity or nature. They can be freed from such
essentialist grounds and become free-floating signifiers, structurally open to a
multitude of different struggles.

An example of this might be the intervention of feminism in anarchist discourse. Carol Erlich argues that radical feminism and anarchism share a rejection of all forms of institutional authority, male or female. She says: "what the socialists, and even some feminists, leave out is this: we must smash all forms of domination."[16] This link between feminist struggles and the anarchist struggle against authority had traditionally been ignored by anarchists.[17] However, using the logic of the empty signifier, there is no reason why the anarchist ethics of resistance to authority cannot signify other struggles, like feminism, or the struggles of the disabled, consumers, the unemployed, the young, the old, environmentalists, the mentally ill, welfare recipients, or indeed any individual or group of individuals resisting particular forms of domination and exploitation. As I have said, though, this will only be a partial signification—there will always be an excess of meaning that eludes this representation and destabilizes it. This excess of meaning keeps the empty signifier from becoming a closed one—it keeps it constitutively open to a plurality of political articulations and interpretations.

Anarchist morality must be freed, then, from its foundations in human essence in order to become a truly democratic morality, which would no longer be closed off to different struggles. Proudhon, the anarchist, once called for a humanist morality that was not grounded in God. In the same way the anti-authoritarian project calls for a humanist morality which is not grounded in man. It is only by freeing morality and rationality from their grounding in such signifieds, that the anti-authoritarian project can avoid reinventing the place of power. It is only through this process of an extension of meaning that anti-authoritarian politics can avoid new forms of domination and exclusion, and become truly democratic.

It is this process of extending signification that, Laclau argues, is fundamental to a radical democratic project. According to this logic, meaning is no longer imposed on political struggles from a metaphysical point outside. Their direction is no longer determined in advance, or dialectically mediated, by an essential foundation. This was the case, as we have seen, in anarchist discourse where the struggle for liberation was ontologically determined, and thus limited, by the dialectical unfolding of human essence and the development of man.[18] Now, however, the foundations of these discourses have been rejected, and their ontological certainty has been thrown into doubt. Laclau sees this as a positive development: "Humankind, having always bowed to external forces—God, Nature, the necessary laws of History—can now, at the threshold of post-modernity; consider itself for the first time the creator and constructor of its own history."[19]

While this ontological uncertainty and constitutive openness in meaning is no doubt positive and indeed necessary, it poses certain problems. For instance, if the project of resistance to authority is open to a plurality of interpretations and struggles, then it would seem that there is no way of determining what form these struggles might take. Obviously the definition of anti-authoritarianism provides limits of its own. For instance, it would be (hopefully) theoretically impossible for an overtly authoritarian political logic such as fascism to be constituted as an anti-authoritarian project. However, theoretically, there would be nothing to stop, for instance, a racist movement that claimed to be fighting for rights of oppressed whites against blacks [or indeed of blacks against whites] from portraying itself as an anti-authoritarian struggle. Clearly, there must be an ethical content to this project of resistance to domination. There must be some notion of ethical limits. These contours can be provided, as we suggested, by the anarchist discourses of morality and rationality that have now been freed from their groundedness in an essential identity. These discourses have been ontologically reconstituted, but their content has been retained. We must look at the content of these ethical discourses, and how it can be redefined in a way that makes it valid for the anti-authoritarian project I have been trying to outline.

Anarchist Ethics

Classical anarchism as a theory of revolution no longer has any great relevance to today's struggles. The question of the state, for instance, is one whose importance has diminished. Foucault has questioned the very existence of the state as a unified institution, preferring to see it as a relatively dispersed series of practices. Even Deleuze and Guattari's analysis of the state sees it as a dispersed series of political and social signifiers rather than a centralized institution. Moreover, anarcho-feminists reject the state reductionism of classical anarchism, seeing it as a discourse that ignores other forms of domination, such as patriarchy—in the same way, perhaps, that the economic reductionism of Marxism ignored state domination.[20] The struggles that anarchism fought are now dead struggles, and the subjects that it sought to liberate—the lumpenproletariat, the peasants, etc.—no longer exist as essential revolutionary identities. So what relevance does anarchism have for our purposes? As a revolutionary philosophy based on an essentialist idea of man, and aimed at overthrowing the state and establishing a free society based on natural principles in its place, it has little real relevance. But as an ethical strategy, and a strategy of resistance against domination and the place of power, it still has immense importance. Anarchism is, fundamentally, an ethical critique of authority—almost an ethical duty to question and resist domination in all its forms. In this sense it may be read against itself: its implicit critique of authority may be used against the authoritarian currents which run throughout its classical discourse. In other words, this ethical "core" of anarchism can perhaps be rescued, through the logic already outlined, from its classical nineteenth-century context. For instance, as I have already indicated, the critique of authority may be expanded to involve struggles other than the struggle against state domination. Perhaps, also, anarchism's traditional rejection of the authoritarian class reductionism of Marxism, and its opening of revolutionary subjectivity to those excluded by the Marxist analysis—the peasantry and the "lumpen-proletariat"—can be used against its own essentialist ideas of what constitutes man and humanity. This would open it·to a plurality of identities. Perhaps anarchism should be read as a series of possible contradictions which can be used against one another and which can produce new possibilities. Kropotkin argues that "inner contradiction is the death of ethics."[21] I would argue, contrary to this, that inner contradiction is the very *condition* of ethics. For something to be ethical it can never be absolute. Poststructuralism rejected morality because it was an absolutist discourse intolerant of difference: this is the point at which morality becomes unethical. Ethics, for Derrida, must remain open to difference, to the other. In other words, it cannot close itself off to that which contradicts it. However, contradiction is not used here in its dialectical sense, as something that will be overcome in a higher morality. Rather, contradiction is used here in the sense of the war model, or Deleuze and Guattari's rhizome—to mean an antagonism which cannot be resolved, and which generates further possibilities and conditions for ethical thinking.

Freedom and Equality

This logic may be applied to the central ethical principle of anarchism: the essential interrelatedness of freedom and equality. To its great credit, anarchism rejected the classical liberal idea that equality and liberty are naturally contradictory terms that limited one another.[22] According to liberal thinking, individuals could never have maximum equality and maximum liberty: there was always a trade-off between the two, so that the more equality one had, the less liberty one had, and vice versa. Anarchists argued that this was based on a fundamental distrust of human nature; rather freedom and equality were entirely compatible. In fact, they are essential to one another, as Bakunin argues:

> I am free only when all human beings surrounding me—men and women alike—are equally free. The freedom of others, far from limiting or negating my liberty, is on the contrary its necessary condition and confirmation. I become free in the true sense only by virtue of the liberty of others, so much so that the greater the number of free people surrounding me the deeper and greater and more extensive their liberty, the deeper and larger becomes my liberty.[23]

In other words, for anarchists, freedom is not contained in its narrow, negative sense as "freedom from." Freedom is seen in its positive, social sense as "freedom to," and therefore it is increased through its interaction with the freedom of others. Freedom is fundamentally social, then, and can only exist when there is an equality of freedom.

Now, what if one were to suggest, contrary to the anarchist position, that freedom and equality are not essentially compatible? This suggestion would not, however, be made on the basis of the liberal argument, which claims that equality and liberty are essentially incompatible. To say that freedom and equality are inherently incompatible is just as much an assumption as claiming that they are naturally compatible: both arguments are based on an essentialist idea of human nature. We could instead argue that equality and liberty are neither essentially contradictory, nor essentially compatible—they are not *essentially* anything. Rather, they must be freed from essentialist arguments altogether. This would leave them open to antagonism. To say that they are antagonistic terms, however, does not imply an essentialism. We are not arguing that equality and freedom can never be compatible, but rather that compatibility is not essential to their terms and is not, therefore, guaranteed—it is something that must be discursively constructed, perhaps through the logic of empty signification. If they can be freed from their essential basis in human nature, then these ethical terms can be seen as existing in an antagonistic relationship, in which one interacts with the other and produces the other in a different way. In other words, the relationship between these two antagonists is not one of essential interrelatedness, or essential separateness, but rather one of *contamination*, in which each term contaminates and changes the meaning of the other. This relationship will not be decided in advance, as it was in anarchist and liberal discourses, but rather will be continually reinterpreted and redefined by the political interventions that engage with this question.

The relationship between equality and freedom is central to the ethical problem that we are trying to address. It goes to the heart of the question of the ethical contours of the anti-authoritarian project. Imagine, for instance, a xenophobic political movement which claimed to be anti-authoritarian, which did so upon the grounds of freedom of expression, and which saw any attempt to resist this expression as a denial of its freedom, as an encroachment on its rights. One only has to look at the current debates on racism and political correctness for an example of this. Does this not force us to reevaluate the question of equality and freedom: a movement or theory which denies racial, or sexual, equality to others, and claiming, in doing so, to be exercising its own freedom. Should equality be affirmed at the expense of freedom, or should freedom—the freedom possibly to espouse discriminatory and intolerant ideas—be defended at the expense of equality? The anarchist notion of the essential relatedness of freedom and equality does not hold in this situation because we are forced to see equality and freedom as limits upon one another. How, then, can this misappropriation of the idea of freedom be resisted without actually denying freedom itself?

If the discourse of freedom is used against the idea of equality, as it is in this situation, then it still nevertheless involves a notion of equality: freedom of expression is still part of the discourse of equality—the equal right of all groups to express themselves. Laclau's discussion of *particularism* and *universalism* in the discourse of multiculturalism, deconstructs these terms in a similar way: groups within a multicultural society who assert their difference and particularism in opposition to universalism are, nevertheless, depending upon a universal notion of equal rights in doing so.[24] In the same way, the traditional opposition between freedom and equality is deconstructed and made undecidable because the two terms depend on each other. Moreover, the "freedom" asserted by an intolerant political movement or theory is the freedom to oppress and exclude others—so in this sense it is not freedom that is being expressed here at all, but rather a discourse of domination. Because freedom has been connected discursively with equality, it cannot be used against equality and, therefore, to deny equality—sexual, religious, racial, etc.—in this way, is also to deny freedom. It is on this ground, then, that intolerance can be resisted.

This is not, as we have said, an essential ground: it is not based on a notion of human nature, or on an essential interrelatedness between freedom and equality. Rather, it is based on a discursively constructed relationship of contamination between the two terms.

Singularity

Perhaps the politico-ethical question might shift altogether from the relationship between equality and freedom, to one of *singularity*. Singularity might allow one to combine freedom and equality in a nondialectical way that retains a certain antagonism between them. Singularity would imply a notion of respect and freedom for difference—for anything singular—without this freedom encroaching on the freedom of others to be different. It would involve, then, an equality of freedom for difference and individuality.

This idea of singularity as equal respect for difference allows us to bridge the ethical gap between poststructuralism and anarchism. If there were a minimum ethic that these two anti-authoritarian discourses shared it would be a respect for individuality and individual difference. Perhaps anarchism's central ethic was, as Bakunin said, "the freedom of every individual unlimited by the freedom of all."[25] He argues that "the respect for the freedom of someone else constitutes the highest duty of men . . . this is the basis of all morality, and there is no other basis."[26] The trouble for poststructuralists was that this freedom inevitably meant a further domination. Because it was grounded in essentialist ideas it was inevitably limited to certain identities, or to certain aspects of identity, excluding others. However, as I suggested, this idea of respect for the freedom of others can be rescued from its essentialist foundations through the logic of empty signification, and become thus de-transcendentalized.

It is precisely this de-transcendentalized notion of ethics that poststructuralism implies but never really makes explicit. Nancy Fraser, one of Foucault's critics, argues that what Foucault lacks is some commitment to a notion of ethics: "good old-fashioned modern humanism or some properly de-transcendentalized version thereof, begins to appear increasingly attractive."[27] Now it is on this point that Fraser is wrong. While poststructuralists like Foucault would reject "good old-fashioned humanism" for the reasons presented above, there is nothing in poststructuralism that precludes the possibility of a de-transcendentalized ethical strategy of some sort. As we saw in the chapter on Foucault, there *is* ethical engagement there. The only criticism of poststructuralism that could be made is that it does not make this commitment strongly or explicitly enough, and this is for fear of bringing back the moral absolutism that it is trying to eschew.

It could be argued, then, that poststructuralism does have a minimum ethics, and this would be, as Todd May argues, that "one should not constrain others' thought or action unnecessarily."[28] In other words, poststructuralist ethics involves resistance against the domination of the individual, against any form of authority that imposes upon the individual limits and constraints. It implies,

then, a respect for individuality and individual difference. This is an ethics
which implicitly, yet undoubtedly, runs throughout Foucault's work, despite his
rejection of humanist essence and repressive power—factors which, if his critics
are to be believed, made any ethical sensibility impossible.[29] There is also the
implicit defense of the rights of the individual discussed in the chapter on
Foucault, as well as an attack on the lack of reciprocity in the way that
institutions and institutionalized discourses deal with individuals. This
condemnation of unequal power relations has much in common with anarchism.
Stirner's work, also, is an explicit attack on the essentialist ideas, and the
political institutions based on them, which mutilated individuality by imposing
"human" norms upon it. Deleuze and Guattari wrote about the oppressive
Oedipalization of the individual and the way that this limited individual
difference and closed off the possibilities of becoming. Derrida, while not as
explicitly political as those above, tried to create a theoretical space for the
recognition of difference and plurality, which had been denied by metaphysical
unities of logocentric discourse. Moreover, he spoke of an ethical, and even
judicial, sensibility of respect for singularity. Foucault also said that theory
should always be respectful of the singular: this is Foucault's ethics.[30]

So it may be argued that poststructuralism shares with anarchism a
commitment to respect and recognize autonomy and difference: a minimum
ethics of singularity. And perhaps it is upon this singularity that a de-
transcendentalized ethical ground—or rather a nonplace—can be constructed; an
ethics that will inform the project of resistance to authority. Moreover, bringing
together poststructuralism and anarchism through the ethics of singularity has
shown, contrary to the received wisdom, that it is quite possible to have a notion
of respect for human values without a concomitant theory of humanism or a
foundation in human essence.[31]

Politics beyond Identity

Moreover, the idea of singularity works against essentialist discourses by
constructing a notion of identity that is constitutively open. As we have seen in
the discussion of Lacan, identity is constituted through a lack—through a
structural emptiness blocking its full constitution as an identity, leaving it
incomplete and thus open to different articulations. However the ethics of
singularity comes closer to expressing this openness and flux of identities: it
rejects the idea of an essential, stable identity because this is seen, as I have
argued, as a way of dominating and excluding that which differs from this
"universal" identity. Singularity is a respect for what is different, for what is
singular, and this implies a defense of difference against universalizing and
essentialist identities and the political discourses based on them. It could be
considered a rhizomatic term—a term that deconstructs both the different and
the same, producing a nondialectical notion of difference. It resists the idea of a
stable universal identity because this is seen as merely a way of dominating
other identities. Also, singularity resists the "binarization" of thought and

identity because this is only a dialectical absorption of the other into the structure of the same. Throughout this discussion I have argued that the binarization of political thought—the grouping of a plurality of struggles into simple oppositions of man/state, man/power, etc.—merely reaffirms the place of power. We have seen this in the Manichean logic of anarchism. Stirner, for instance, argues that to affirm immorality against morality, or crime against law, is not really resistance at all, but rather only reaffirms the dominance of what it is supposed to resist. Lacan showed that the Law is actually reproduced, rather than resisted, by its transgression. Derrida also rejects such oppositional thinking, showing that it based on an essentialism that is counterproductive, and that it only reaffirms the dominant hierarchy of thought. Foucault, too, argues that such simple binary transgression limits the possibilities of our thinking, in particular our political thinking:

> The problem is not so much that of defining a political 'position' (which is to choose from a pre-existing set of possibilities) but to imagine and to bring into being new schemas of politicization. If 'politicization' means falling back on ready-made choices and institutions, then the effort of analysis involved in uncovering the relations of force and mechanisms of power is not worthwhile.[32]

In other words, the political task today is not to posit a certain identity in opposition to power, but rather to dismantle the binary structure of power and identity itself; to disrupt the theoretical and political logic which reproduces this opposition and which limits thinking to these terms.[33] So perhaps anti-authoritarian thought should try to operate outside this oppositional structure of identity and free itself from its obligation towards certain essential identities of resistance.

We seem to be surrounded today by a multitude of new identities and lifestyle politics—"S/M" gays, "separatist" lesbians, "transgenders," etc. We are faced with a proliferation of new particularistic demands—the demands of some feminist groups for "women's only" services and facilities, or the demands of gays for their own "space," their own political representation, their own "gay only" events, etc. Everywhere there is the assertion of a particular, differential identity with its own demands for exclusive social, political, and cultural rights. However, as we have seen, the political field is a rhizomatic system, with multiple connections forming between different identities—even if they are in opposition—thus opening up ever new and unpredictable possibilities. Therefore, to posit a particular identity of opposition—to think solely in terms of the oppression of women by men, gays by straights, blacks by whites, etc.— is to severely limit our political possibilities. Perhaps this is why there is certain inanity and definite sense of boredom that goes along with identity politics, with waving the banners of "feminist struggles," "gay struggles," "black struggles," etc. There is a certain litany of oppressions which most radical theories are obliged to pay homage to. Why is it that when someone is asked to talk about radical politics today one inevitably refers to this same tired, old list of struggles and identities? Why are we so unimaginative politically that we cannot think outside the terms of this "shopping list" of oppressions? Is this not precisely the kind of essentialist and oppositional thinking that Foucault exhorts us to avoid? Why are we assuming that being black or gay or female is necessarily an identity of resistance? Is this not an essentialist assumption? Binary political thinking is based, as Nietzsche would argue, on a culture of *ressentiment* that often reproduces the structures of oppression. It falls into the trap of place, and thus goes against the ethics of anti-authoritarianism. One sees this in the way that certain feminist discourses demonize men, in much the same way that male chauvinist ideas once denigrated women. Oppositional logic of this sort merely reaffirms the structures of oppression that it is supposed to resist. This authoritarian logic is made inevitable by essentializing female identity—by positing an identity which is intrinsically "good" and "truth-bearing," but which is oppressed by male identity. Wendy Brown analyses this culture of ressentiment in modernist feminism: the valorisation of women because of their oppression.[34] Female identity is thus defined as "oppressed" and "good" in opposition to male identity seen as intrinsically "oppressive" and "bad." It is precisely this sort of puerile oppositional thinking that the anti-authoritarian project resists.

Moreover, it is this oppositional thinking which, as Stirner argues, mutilates individuality. How would this logic deal with a woman who did not necessarily identify herself as a women, or who did not see herself as oppressed, necessarily, by men; or a black who did not identify with being black? Would they be denied a political voice or political credibility? Does this oppositional thinking not posit a stable identity to which certain political implications are essential: does it not close off identity to flux and becoming? There have been numerous cases, for instance, where transgender women have been excluded from various feminist and lesbian groups because they were somehow not "women" enough, because they were still seen as men and, therefore, could not have any idea of what it feels like to be a "real" woman, suffering "real" oppression. It is this sort of authoritarian essentialism which completely discredits oppositional political thinking. Singularity allows us to think beyond these oppositions, and to theorize that which does not fit so neatly into its structures of "difference." This is not to say, of course, that women, gays, blacks, and Asians are not oppressed or excluded in certain ways and that there are not legitimate anti-authoritarian struggles surrounding these issues. But to base struggles purely on an essential identity—on "blackness" or "gayness"— and to exclude from these struggles others who do not conform to these "identities" entirely for that reason, goes against the ethics of anti-authoritarianism. We should be getting away from such an unimaginative politics, and thinking in ways that deterritorialize this logic. The danger of positing difference is that it becomes essentialized, allowing oppositional structures to be built upon it. This does not mean that a politics of difference and plurality be abandoned; it means simply that it resist the temptation of essentialism, that it become open to other differences—open even to the possibilities of the Same. Singularity allows us to do precisely this: to theorize non-essentialist difference. This is the ethical task of the anti-authoritarian project.

Ethics of Postanarchism

It is on this ethical question of essential identities that anarchism can again be read against itself, with interesting results. Anarchism's defense of autonomy and individuality can operate against its notion of an essential identity, and its essential morality and rationality. The idea of autonomy in anarchist discourse is based on an essential identity, and the moral and rational imperatives associated with this: one is autonomous within the limits of an essential humanity and within universal moral law. However, autonomy can also mean autonomy from the moral and rational imperatives associated with this very idea of an essential human identity. This contradiction is evident in Kropotkin's work on ethics. He argues, on the one hand, that morality must be based on established truths and firm rational foundations, making it impossible to doubt.[35] However, he also says that morality should not become an injunction or a categorical imperative.[36] He wants a "new morality" which is non-transcendental and which respects individual rights.[37] Yet he wants this non-transcendental law to be based on "organic necessity," on the universal law of organic evolution.[38] For Kropotkin there is no contradiction here because he sees the basis of individuality and moral autonomy to be this universal organic law. As we have seen from a poststructuralist critique, however, any discourse or identity based on universal and essential foundations necessarily conflicts with the notion of autonomy and individuality.

This contradiction points to certain limitations in anarchism's idea of autonomy. There are two possible interpretations of autonomy available to anarchists. One is based on the idea of the true, essential self, which has moral authenticity as its ultimate goal. It is this essentialist, dialectically mediated idea of the self that I have rejected. The other is, perhaps, more in line with the ethics of singularity: instead of authenticity being an end goal, it is more of an ongoing process of questioning and reinterpretation, and it is always subject to change.[39] This latter notion of subjectivity rejects the unquestioned allegiance to the moral codes that the classical anarchists were, in reality, demanding. It demands to know why one should accept a particular moral condition just because it is based on natural law or is rationally founded: and it is this questioning, this demand to know *why*, this refusal to accept anything on its own terms, which is itself distinctly ethical. So, rather than a morally-authentic self—a notion of the self dialectically subordinated to universal moral and rational laws—there is an alternate idea of the self being morally authentic precisely through the questioning of this very idea of authenticity. This latter interpretation posits an identity that is structurally open, contingent, and morally-autonomous. I have referred to an anarchism of subjectivity, rather than an anarchism based on subjectivity. This is a postanarchist notion of autonomy—and it is this idea of autonomy that has greater relevance for anti-authoritarian thought.

The structural openness of the logic of *postanarchism* allows us to disrupt the unity of political thought by freeing it from "essential" foundations, and thereby opening it to contingency and multiple interpretations. So in that case postanarchism should not be taken as a coherent political identity, or a

teleologically determined, unified body of revolutionary thought. Such totalizing logic has proved disastrous for anti-authoritarian politics. Rather, postanarchism should be seen as a series of ethical strategies for resistance to domination. It is this constitutive openness which, paradoxically, provides its own ethical limits: it remains resistant to discourses and struggles which are intolerant and restrictive. However this ethical resistance to intolerance is always undecidable: it must always question itself. If it is just a mere application of a limit, then it itself becomes unethical.

This radical openness perhaps defines the ethical limits of a non-essentialist democratic politics. This democratic ethic of radical pluralism is possible because it does not start by presupposing an essential identity as its foundation and limit. Rather than a democratic pluralism based on identity, it is a democratic pluralism *of* identity. So rather than democratic pluralism starting with an identity, identity itself starts with democratic pluralism—with a radical openness. This is the democracy both demanded, and made possible, by the politics of postanarchism.

Conclusion

This book has attempted to make radical anti-authoritarian thought more "democratic." The conceptual impetus for this came out of a comparison between anarchism and poststructuralism, a comparison which exposed, in a fundamental way, the problems central to anti-authoritarian thought. The tension between these two anti-authoritarian discourses, then, provided both the dynamic for the discussion, and the analytical tools with which these problems could possibly be resolved. The problem most pertinent to the discussion is the problem of essentialism. I have argued that without a thorough critique of the essentialist categories that bind it, there can be no hope for radical politics. Unless anti-authoritarianism is made aware of its own potential for domination, then struggles against authority continue to risk perpetuating it. In order to avoid the place of power, radical politics must be allowed to be conceived in different ways, in ways that do not rely on essentialist foundations to justify them. The epistemological privilege granted by the uncontaminated point of departure can no longer serve as a ground for a critique of domination. The politics of resistance against domination must take place in a world without guarantees. Nietzsche exhorts us to "Build your cities on the slopes of Vesuvius! Send your ships into unchartered seas!"[40] Freed from both the comforting guarantees and the stifling limits of essentialist discourses, anti-authoritarian thought may now explore these unchartered seas.

The point here, however, has not been really to construct a new politics, but rather to show that the old politics of "place"—defined by essentialist ideas and oppositional thinking—has reached its conceptual limits. It is to show the way in which Enlightenment-humanist ideas, exemplified by anarchism—freedom, revolution, morality, and rationality—create the conditions for their own modification. Nor does the unmasking of the limits of these ideas mean that the old politics should be completely abandoned. It simply contends that politics can no longer be confined within these traditional terms and categories. There will always be something that exceeds the political definitions and boundaries laid down for it, something unpredictable, often antagonistic, fleeting and contingent, something that we had not quite reckoned on. This is the outside to politics, its limitless limit. This discussion, by pointing to the limits of what we normally consider to be the political, by pointing to the potential for domination in any political movement, has tried to remain faithful and open to this contingency. This openness is precisely what is meant by *politics*.

Notes

1. As Bakunin says: "In a word, we reject all privileged, licensed, official, and legal legislation and authority, even though it could arise from universal suffrage, convinced that it could only turn to the benefit of a dominant and exploiting minority, and against the interests of the vast enslaved majority. It is in this sense that we are really Anarchists." See *Political Philosophy*, 255.

2. As we have seen, anarchism based itself on a fundamental distinction between the natural order of human essence, and the artificial, political order of power and authority, and while the natural order was oppressed and stultified by power, it remained essentially uncorrupted by it. It was outside the world of power and authority.

3. Schurmann, *Heidegger On Being And Acting*, 6.

4. Schurmann, *Heidegger On Being And Acting*, 5.

5. Schurmann, *Heidegger On Being And Acting*, 7.

6. Schurmann, *Heidegger On Being And Acting*, 6.

7. Needless to say some modern anarchists do not exactly embrace this postmodern logic of uncertainty and dislocation. John Zerzan argues that without a notion of an autonomous subjectivity as well as a belief in the possibility of free rational communication and the power of language to liberate the world—all of which poststructuralism has questioned—there can be no possibility of agency or emancipation, and this leads only to nihilism and relativism. He sees what he calls "postmodernism" as a moral and political catastrophe. See John Zerzan "The Catastrophe of Postmodernism," *Anarchy: A Journal of Desire Armed* (fall 1991): 16-25. We have heard this argument that equates poststructuralist ideas with nihilism and relativism many times before (particularly with respect to Foucault) from various Habermasian and communitarian quarters. I have tried to show throughout the discussion that, contrary to this claim, poststructuralism does not lead to nihilism and it does allow political engagement. In fact it could be argued that poststructuralism better facilitates political and ethical engagement than the Enlightenment based politics represented by Zerzan, which remains trapped within structures and categories that are irrelevant to today's politics. Not all anarchists however, reject these ideas out of hand. Some have been more open to them, realizing their emancipative potential. See Phillip Winn, "Anarchism and Postmodernism: Towards Non-Hierarchical Knowledge(s)," *Anarchist Age Monthly* 23 (November 1992), 27-30.

8. Nietzsche, *The Gay Science*, 181.

9. Laclau and Zac, "Minding the Gap," 19.

10. Quoted in Marshall, *Demanding the Impossible*, 558.

11. The empty signifier, Laclau argues, is a signifier without a signified. Signification, according to Saussure, depends on a system of differences that are relational. Each identity is constituted only through its difference from all the other identities. This

system of differences must have limits otherwise the differences would become infinitely dispersed and, therefore, meaningless. It must be a closed totality for signification to take place. If there are limits, however, there must be something beyond those limits—limits are only defined by a beyond. The limits of signification are thus an arbitrary exclusion of the other, an arbitrary closing off of the system of differences. This radical exclusion causes an ambivalence inside the system of difference—the identity of each element in the system is constituted only by its difference from the other identities; but also these differences are equivalent to one another in the sense that they fall on one side of the line of exclusion. In order for this exclusion to be signified, the various elements in the system have to cancel their differences and form, Laclau argues, "chains of equivalence." The system becomes pure being, pure systematicity, which requires the creation of empty signifiers in order to signify itself. Signifiers must empty themselves of their fixedness to a particular signified in order to represent this system of pure Being, which is rather like the Lacanian Real: it is something which cannot be signified, but rather points to the limits of signification themselves. It signifies the very breakdown of signification itself—as Lacan would argue a signifier only functions through its failure to completely represent something. The identity of pure Being, it must be remembered, can never be completely realized because it is based on an undecidability between difference and equivalence. In other words, the logic of this systematicity means that a particular signifier, in order to represent the system, is emptied from its content—freed from its fixity to a particular signified and a particular foundation—and, thus, becomes an empty signifier. See Ernesto Laclau, "Why do Empty Signifiers Matter to Politics?" in *The Lesser Evil and the Greater Good: The Theory and Politics of Social Diversity*, ed. Jeffrey Weeks (Concord, Mass.: Rivers Oram Press, 1994), 167-178, 167.

12. Stirner, *The Ego,* 179.

13. Bakunin, *Political Philosophy,* 146.

14. Bakunin, *Political Philosophy,* 157.

15. Baldelli has a notion of "ethical capital," where certain virtues, or at least virtuous tendencies, are rooted in a natural conception of human society. See Giovanni Baldelli, *Social Anarchism* (Harmondsworth: Penguin Books, 1972), 29-41.

16. Carol Erlich, "Socialism, Anarchism and Feminism," in *Reinventing Anarchy: What Are Anarchists Thinking About These Days?,* ed. Howard J. Erlich (London: Routledge & Kegan Paul, 1979), 259-277. Not all feminist theories, however, reject authority. Some feminists, like Gearhart, call for the establishment of a matriarchy—female domination—to replace the patriarchy. I would argue that it is this sort of logic which reaffirms the place of power and domination and which we are seeking to avoid. See Sally Miller Gearhart, "The Future—If There is One—Is Female," in *Reweaving the Web of Life: Feminism and Non-Violence,* ed. Pam McAllister (Philadelphia: New Society Publications, Philadelphia, 1982), 266-288.

17. Carol Erlich, "Introduction—to Anarcho-Feminism," in *Reinventing Anarchy,* 233-236.

18. Bookchin, a contemporary anarchist, argues that differences will be resolved in a dialectically produced principle of unity. Thus, struggles are dialectically determined in such a way that their identities are effaced in the idea of unity. I would argue that it is this sort of totalizing and essentialist political logic that should be rejected. See Murray Bookchin, *Post-Scarcity Anarchism* (Berkeley: The Ramparts Press, 1971), 285.

19. Ernesto Laclau, "Politics and the Limits of Modernity," in *Universal Abandon: The Politics of Post-Modernism,* ed. Andrew Ross (Minnesota: University of Minnesota Press, 1988), 63-82.

20. Erlich, "Anarcho-Feminism," 234.

21. Kropotkin, *Ethics,* 27.

22. The paradoxical relationship between liberty and equality in political philosophy is explored by Hilb. See Claudia Hilb, "Equality at the Limit of Liberty," in *The Making of Political Identities*, 103-112.

23. Bakunin, *Political Philosophy*, 267.

24. Ernesto Laclau, ed.,"Subject of Politics, Politics of the Subject," in *Emancipation(s)* (London: Verso, 1996), 47-65.

25. Bakunin, *Political Philosophy*, 268.

26. Bakunin, *Political Philosophy*, 156.

27. Nancy Fraser, *Unruly Practices*, 58.

28. Todd May, "Is Poststructuralist Political Theory Anarchist?" 178.

29. The treatment of the mad for instance, Foucault regarded as intolerable: "The repressive role of the asylum is well known: people are locked up and subjected to treatment . . . over which they have no control." See "Revolutionary Action," 228.

30. Foucault, "Is it Useless to Revolt?" 9.

31. Hooke argues with reference to Foucault that it is quite possible to have some notion of human rights and values without grounding it in a humanist discourse, or in the figure of Man. See Alexander Hooke, "The Order of Others: is Foucault's anti-humanism against human action?" *Political Theory* 15, no. 1 (1987): 38-60.

32. Foucault, "The History of Sexuality," in *Power/Knowledge*, 190.

33. Foucault was against, for instance, the naive politics that saw the prisoner as an innocent freedom fighter; rather Foucault wanted to question the opposition between innocence and guilt, between the criminal and the normal.

34. Brown argues that much feminist hostility towards a postmodern rejection of foundations, as well as an attachment to oppositional politics, is an example of the culture of "ressentiment," in many feminist theories: "I want to suggest that much North American feminism partakes deeply of both the epistemological spirit and political structure of *ressentiment* and that this constitutes a good deal of our nervousness about moving toward an analysis as thoroughly Nietzschean in its wariness about truth as post-foundational political philosophy must be. Surrendering epistemological foundations means giving up the ground of specifically *moral* claims against domination—especially the avenging of strength through a moral critique of it—and moving instead into the domain of the sheerly political: 'wars of position' and amoral contests about the just and the good in which truth is always grasped as coterminous with power, as always already power, as the voice of power." Brown thus employs a war model of analysis here—an affirmation of struggle and antagonism—as an antidote to the sickness of a ressentiment-inspired oppositional politics that has inhabited much feminist discourse. See Wendy Brown, *States of Injury: Power and Freedom in Late Modernity* (Princeton, N.J.: Princeton University, 1995), 45.

35. Kropotkin, *Ethics*, 22.

36. Kropotkin, *Ethics*, 25.

37. Kropotkin, *Ethics*, 29.

38. Kropotkin, *Ethics*, 30-31.

39. George Crowder, *The Idea of Freedom in Nineteenth-Century Anarchism* (Microfiche – 1987), 262.

40. Nietzsche, *The Gay Science*, 22.

Bibliography

Allen, Barry. "Government in Foucault." *Canadian Journal of Philosophy* 21, no. 4 (1991): 421-440.

Althusser, Louis. *For Marx*. Trans. Ben Brewster. London: New Left Books, 1977.

Althusser, Louis, and Etienne Balibar, eds. *Reading Capital*. London: Verso, 1979.

Arac, John, ed. *After Foucault: Humanist Knowledge and Post-Modern Challenges*. London: Rutgers University Press, 1988.

Bakunin, Mikhail. *From Out of the Dustbin: Bakunin's Basic Writings 1869-1871*. Ed. Robert M. Cutler. Ann Arbor, Mich.: Ardis, 1985.

————. *God and the State*. New York: Dover Publications, 1970.

————. *Marxism, Freedom and the State*. Trans. K. J. Kenafick. London: Freedom Press, 1984.

————. *On Anarchism*. Ed. Sam Dolgoff. Montreal: Black Rose Books, 1980.

————. *Political Philosophy of Mikhail Bakunin: Scientific Anarchism*. Ed. G. P. Maximoff. London: Free Press of Glencoe, 1953.

————. *Selected Writings*. Ed. Arthur Lehning. London: Cape, 1973.

————. *Selections: Bakunin on Anarchy*. Ed. Sam Dolgoff. New York: Knopf, 1972.

————. *Statism and Anarchy*. Trans. and ed. Marshall S. Shatz. Cambridge, U.K.: Cambridge University Press, 1990.

Baldelli, Giovanni. *Social Anarchism*. Harmondsworth, U.K.: Penguin Books, 1972.

Barry, Andrew, ed. *Foucault and Political Reason: Liberalism, Neo-Liberalism and Rationalities of Government*. Chicago: University of Chicago Press, 1996.

Beiner, Ronald. "Foucault's Hyper-Liberalism." *Critical Review* 3, no. 9 (1995): 349-370.

Benvenuto, Bice, and Roger Kennedy. *The Works of Jacques Lacan: An Introduction*. London: Free Association Books, 1986.

Berlin, Isaiah. *Karl Marx: His Life and Environment*. London: Oxford University Press, 1963.

Bernauer, James, *Michel Foucault's Force of Flight: Towards an Ethics of Thought*. Atlantic Highlands, N.J.: Humanities Press International, 1990.

Bernauer, James, and David Rasmussen. *The Final Foucault*. Cambridge, Mass.: MIT Press, 1988.

Best, Steven, and Douglas Kellner. *Postmodern Theory: Critical Interrogations*. Hampshire: Macmillan, 1991.

Boaz, David. *Libertarianism: A Primer*. New York: Free Press, 1997.

Bogue, Ronald. *Deleuze and Guattari*. London: Roultedge, 1989.

Bookchin, Murray. *Post-Scarcity Anarchism*. Berkeley, Calif.: Ramparts Press, 1971.

————. *Remaking Society*. Montreal: Black Rose Books, 1989.

Bornstein, Stephen, David Held, and Joel Krieger, eds. *The State in Capitalist Europe: A Casebook*. Winchester, Mass.: Allen & Unwin, 1984.

Bottomore, Tom, ed. *A Dictionary of Marxist Thought*. 2d ed. Cambridge, Mass.: Blackwell Reference, 1991.

Boyne, Roy. *Foucault and Derrida: The Other Side of Reason*. London: Unwin Hyman, 1990.

Brown, Wendy. *States of Injury: Power and Freedom in Late Modernity*. Princeton, N.J.: Princeton University Press, 1995.

Butler, Judith. *Subjects of Desire: Hegelian Reflections in Twentieth Century France.* New York: Columbia University Press, 1987.

Callinicos, Alex. *Is There a Future for Marxism?* London: Macmillan Press, 1982.

Caputo, John. "Beyond Aestheticism: Derrida's Responsible Anarchy." *Research in Phenomenology* 18 (1988): 59-73.

Caputo, John, and Mark Yount. *Foucault and the Critique of Institutions.* University Park, Pa.: Pennsylvania State University Press, 1993.

Carroll, John. *Break-Out from the Crystal Palace. The Anarcho-Psychological Critique: Stirner, Nietzsche, Dostoyevsky.* London: Routledge & Kegan Paul, 1974.

Carter, April. *The Political Theory of Anarchism.* London: Routledge & Kegan Paul, 1971.

Clark, John. *The Anarchist Moment: Reflections on Culture, Nature and Power.* Montreal: Black Rose Books, 1984.

————. "Marx, Bakunin and the Problem of Social Transformation." *Telos* 24 (winter 1979): 80-97.

————. *Max Stirner's Egoism.* London: Freedom Press, 1976.

Clifford, Michael R. "Crossing (out) the Boundary: Foucault and Derrida on Transgressing Transgression." *Philosophy Today* 31 (fall 1987): 223-233.

Colombat, André Pierre. "A Thousand Trails to Work with Deleuze." *Substance* 66 (1991) 10-23.

Connolly, William. "Beyond Good and Evil: the Ethical Sensibility of Michel Foucault." *Political Theory* 21, no. 3 (August 1993), 365-388.

————. *Identity/Difference: Democratic Negotiations of Political Paradox.* Ithaca, N.Y.: Cornell University Press, 1991.

————. *Political Theory and Modernity.* Oxford, U.K.: B. Blackwell, 1988.

Cornell, Drucilla, ed. *Deconstruction and the Possibility of Justice.* New York: Routledge, 1992.

Coward, Rosalind, and John Ellis. *Language and Materialism: Developments in Semiology and the Theory of the Subject.* London: Routledge & Kegan Paul, 1977.

Creagh, Ronald. "La deference, l'insolence anarchiste et la postmodernitie." *L'homme et la societe* 1-2 (June/July 1997): 131-148.

Critchley, Simon. *The Ethics of Deconstruction: Derrida and Levinas.* Oxford: Blackwell, 1992.

Crowder, George. *Classical Anarchism: The Political Thought of Godwin, Bakunin and Kropotkin.* Oxford: Clarendon Press, 1991.

————. *The Idea of Freedom in Nineteenth-Century Anarchism.* 1987. Micro-form.

Dean, Mitchell. "Foucault's Obsession with Western Modernity." *Thesis Eleven* 14 (1986): 44-61.

Deleuze, Gilles. *Foucault.* Trans. S. Hand. London: Althone Press, 1988.

————. *Nietzsche and Philosophy.* Trans. H. Tomlinson. London: Althone Press, 1992.

Deleuze, Gilles, and Felix Guattari. *Anti-Oedipus: Capitalism and Schizophrenia.* Trans. R. Hurley. New York: Viking Press, 1972.

————. *A Thousand Plateaus: Capitalism and Schizophrenia.* Trans. B. Massumi. London: Althone Press, 1988.

Deleuze, Gilles, and Claire Parnet. *Dialogues.* Trans. H. Tomlinson. New York: Columbia University Press, 1987.

Dematteis, Philip. *Individuality and The Social Organism: The Controversy Between Max Stirner and Karl Marx.* New York: Revisionist Press, 1976.

Derrida, Jacques. *Dissemination.* Trans. B. Johnson. Chicago: University of Chicago Press, 1981.

————. *Margins of Philosophy.* Trans. A. Bass. Brighton: Harvester Press, 1982.

————. *Of Grammatology.* Trans. G. C. Spivak. Baltimore: Johns Hopkins University Press, 1976.

————. *Positions.* Trans. A. Bass. Chicago: University of Chicago Press, 1981.

————. *Specters of Marx: The State of Debt, the Work of Mourning & the New International.* Trans. P. Kamuf. New York: Routledge, 1994.

————. *Speech and Phenomena, and Other Essays on Husserl's Theory of Signs.* Trans. D. Allison. Evanston, Ill.: Northwestern University Press, 1973.

————. *Spurs: Nietzsche's Styles.* Chicago: University of Chicago Press, 1978.

————. *Writing and Difference.* Trans. A. Bass. Chicago: University of Chicago Press, 1978.

Dews, Peter. "The Paradigm Shift to Communication and the Question of Subjectivity: Reflections on Habermas, Lacan and Mead." *Revue Internationale de Philosophie* 49 (1995): 483-519.

————. "The Tremor of Reflection: Slavoj Zizek's Lacanian Dialectics." *Radical Philosophy* 72 (July/August 1995): 17-29.

Diprose, Rosalyn, and Robyn Terrell, ed. *Cartograhies: Post-Structuralism and the Mapping of Bodies and Spaces.* Sydney, Australia: Allen & Unwin, 1991.

Dolan, Frederick M. "Political Action and the Unconscious: Arendt and Lacan on Decentering the Subject." *Political Theory* 23, no. 2 (1995): 330-352.

Donzelot, Jacques. "The Poverty of Political Culture." *Ideology and Consciousness* 5 (1979): 73-86.

Draper, Hal. *Karl Marx's Theory of Revolution VI: State and Bureaucracy.* New York: Monthly Review Press, 1977.

Dreyfus, Hubert L., and Paul Rabinow. *Michel Foucault: Beyond Structuralism and Hermeneutics.* Chicago: University of Chicago Press, 1982.

Ellingham, Francis. "John Clark and Stirner's Negativity." *Ego* 41 (1978): 3-5.

————. "Social Totalitarianism." *Ego* 29 (spring 1972): 10-12.

Eltzbacher, Paul. *Anarchism: Exponents of Anarchist Philosophy.* Trans. S. Byington. London: Freedom Chips Bookshop, 1960.

Engels, Freidrich. *Anti-Duhring.* Moscow: Progress Publishers, 1969.

Erlich, Howard J., ed. *Reinveting Anarchy, Again.* San Francisco, Calif.: AK Press, 1996.

————. *Reinventing Anarchy: What Are Anarchists Thinking These Days?* London: Routledge & Kegan Paul, 1979.

Ferguson, Kathy E. "Saint Max Revisited: A Reconsideration of Max Stirner." *Idealistic Studies* 12, no. 3 (September 1982): 276-292.

Feuerbach, Ludwig. *The Essence of Christianity.* Trans. G. Eliot. New York: Harper, 1957.

Feuerbach, Ludwig. *The Fiery Brook: Selected Writings of Ludwig Feuerbach.* Trans. and ed. Zawar Hanfi. New York: Anchor, 1972.

Fine, Bob. "Struggles Against Discipline: The theory and politics of Michel Foucault." *Capital and Class* 1 (1981): 75-95.

Fons Elders, ed. *Reflexive Water: The Basic Concerns of Mankind.* Canada: Condor Books, 1974.

Foucault, Michel. *The Archaeology of Knowledge.* Trans. A. M. S. Smith. London: Tavistok, 1974.

————. *Discipline and Punish: The Birth of the Prison.* Trans. A. Sheridan. London: Penguin Books, 1991.

————. *The History of Sexuality VI: Introduction.* Trans. R. Hunter. New York: Vintage Books, 1978.

————. "Is It Useless to Revolt?" *Philosophy and Social Criticism*, 8, no. 1 (1981): 1-9.

————. "Kant on Enlightenment and Revolution." Trans. C. Gordon. *Economy and Society* 15, no. 1 (1986): 88-96.

————. *Language, Counter-Memory, Practice*. Oxford: Basil Blackwell, 1977.

————. *Madness and Civilisation*. Trans. R. Howard, New York: Vintage Books, 1988.

————. "Omnes et Singulatim." In *The Tanner Lectures on Human Values II*. Salt Lake City: University of Utah Press, 1981.

————. "On Attica: An Interview." *Telos* 9 (spring 1974): 154-161.

————. *The Order of Things: An Archaeology of the Human Sciences*. London Tavistok, 1970.

————. "The Politics of Crime." Trans. M. Horowitz. *Partisan Review* 43, no. 3 (1976): 453-466.

————. *Politics, Philosophy, Culture: Interviews and Other Writings, 1977-1984*. Trans. A. Sheridan. Ed. L. D. Kritzman. New York: Routledge, 1988.

————. *Power/Knowledge: Selected Interviews and Other Writings 1972-77*. Ed. Colin Gordon. New York: Harvester Press, 1980.

————. "War in the Filigree of Peace: Course Summary." Trans. Ian Mcleod. *Oxford Literary Review* 4, no. 2 (1976): 15-19.

Fraser, Nancy. "Foucault on Modern Power; Empirical Insights and Normative Confusions." *Praxis International* 1, no. 3 (1981): 272-287.

————. *Unruly Practices: Power, Discourse, and Gender in Contemporary Social Theory*. Minneapolis: University of Minnesota Press, 1989.

Freedman, Robert, ed. *Marxist Social Theory*. New York: Harvest Books, 1968.

Friedman, Jeffrey. "Postmodernism Versus Postlibertarianism." *Critical Review* 5, no. 2 (spring 1991): 145-158.

Gallop, Jane. *Reading Lacan*. Ithaca, N.Y.: Cornell University Press, 1985.

Gandal, Keith. "Michel Foucault: Intellectual Work and Politics." *Telos* 67 (spring 1989): 121-134.

Gasché, Rodolphe. *Inventions of Difference: On Jacques Derrida*. Cambridge, Mass.: Harvard University Press, 1994.

————. *The Tain of the Mirror: Derrida and the Philosophy of Reflection*. Cambridge, Mass.: Harvard University Press, 1986.

Giddens, Anthony. *Capitalism and Modern Social Theory: An Analysis of the Writings of Marx, Durkheim and Max Weber*. Cambridge, U.K.: Cambridge University Press, 1971.

Godin, William. *Anarchist Writings*, ed. Peter Marshall. London: Freedom Press, 1968.

Goldman, Emma. *Anarchism and Other Essays*. 2d ed. New York: Mother Earth Publishing, 1911.

Goodway, David, ed. *For Anarchism: History, Theory and Practice*. London: Routledge, 1989.

Gordon, Colin, ed. "Question, Ethos, Event: Foucault on Kant and Enlightenment." *Economy and Society* 15, no. 1 (February 1986): 71-87.

————. *The Foucault Effect: Studies in Governmentality*. Chicago: University of Chicago Press, 1991.

Graham, Marcus, ed. *Man: An Anthology of Anarchist Ideas, Essays and Commentaries*. London: Cienfuegos Press, 1986.

Griffin, John. *A Structured Anarchism*. London: Freedom Press, 1991.

Grisham, Therese. "Linguistics as an Indiscipline: Deleuze and Guattari's Pragmatics." *Substance* 66 (1991): 36-52.

Gutting, Gary, ed. *The Cambridge Companion to Foucault.* Cambridge, U.K.: Cambridge University Press, 1994.

Habermas, Jurgen. *Autonomy and Solidarity: Interviews.* Ed. Peter Dews. London: Verso, 1986.

—————. "Foucault's Lecture on Kant." *Thesis Eleven* 14 (1986): 4-8.

—————. *Moral Consciousness and Communicative Action.* Trans. C. Lenhardt. Cambridge, Mass.: MIT Press, 1990.

—————. *The Philosophical Discourse of Modernity: Twelve Lectures.* Trans. F. Lawrence. Cambridge, Mass.: MIT Press, 1987.

—————. *The Theory of Communicative Action V1.* Trans. T. McCarthy. Boston: Beacon Press, 1984.

Hardt, Michael. *Gilles Deleuze: An Apprenticeship in Philosophy.* Minneapolis: University of Minnesota Press, 1993.

Harrison, Frank. *The Modern State: An Anarchist Analysis.* Montreal: Black Rose Books, 1987.

Hegel, Georg Wilhelm Friedrich, *The Philosophy of Right: The Philosophy of History.* Trans. T. M. Knox. Chicago: Encyclopaedia Britannica, 1952.

Hobbes, Thomas. *Leviathan.* Oxford: Basil Blackwell, 1947.

Honneth, Axel, ed. *Communicative Action: Essays on Jurgen Habermas' Theory of Communicative Action.* Trans. J. Gaines. Cambridge, U.K.: Polity Press, 1991.

Hooke, Alexander. "The Order of Others: Is Foucault's Anti-humanism against Human Action?" *Political Theory* 15, no. 1 (1987): 38-60.

Hoy, David. C. *Foucault: A Critical Reader.* New York: Basil Blackwell, 1986.

—————. "Splitting the Difference: Habermas's Critique of Derrida." *Praxis International* 8 (January 1989): 447-464.

Hoy, Terry. "Derrida: Postmodernism and Political Theory." *Philosophy and Social Criticism* 4, no. 3 (1993): 243-260.

Hunt, Lester H. "Politics and Anti-Politics: Nietzsche's View of the State." *History of Philosophy Quarterly* 2, no. 4 (October 1985): 453-468.

Jessop, Bob. *State Theory: Putting the Capitalist State in its Place.* Cambridge, U.K.: Polity Press, 1990.

Kafka, Franz. *Metamorphosis and Other Stories.* London: Minerva, 1992.

Kearney, Richard. "Derrida and the Ethics of Dialogue." *Philosophy and Social Criticism* 19, no. 1 (1993): 1-14.

Kelly, Aileen. *Mikhail Bakunin: A Study in the Psychology and Politics of Utopianism.* New Haven: Yale University Press, 1987.

Koch, Andrew. "Max Stirner: The Last Hegelian or the First Poststructuralist." *Anarchist Studies* 5 (1993): 95-107.

—————. "Poststructuralism and the Epistemological Basis of Anarchism." *Philosophy of the Social Sciences* 23, no. 3 (1993): 327-351.

Kolakowski, Leszeck. *Main Currents of Marxism V1: The Founders.* Trans. P. S. Falla. Oxford: Clarendon Press, 1978.

Krell, David. and David Wood, eds. *Exceedingly Nietzsche: Aspects of Contemporary Nietzsche-Interpretation.* London: Routledge, 1988.

Krimerman, Len, ed. *Patterns of Anarchy: A Collection of Writings on the Anarchist Tradition.* New York: Anchor Books, 1966.

Krips, Henry. "Power and Resistance" *Philosophy of the Social Sciences* 20, no. 2 (1990): 170-182.

Kropotkin, Peter. *Ethics: Origin and Development.* Trans. L. S. Friedland. New York: Tudor Publishing, 1947.

—————. *Fields, Factories and Workshops Tomorrow.* London: Allen & Unwin, 1974.

————. *The Great French Revolution 1789-1793.* London: William Heineman, 1909.

————. *In Russian and French Prisons.* London: Ward & Downey. 1887.

————. *Mutual Aid: A Factor of Evolution.* Ed. Paul Avrich. New York: New York University, 1972.

————. *Revolutionary Pamphlets.* Ed. Roger N. Baldwin. New York: Benjamin Blom, 1968.

————. *The State: Its Historic Role.* London: Freedom Press, 1943.

Krupnick, Mark, ed. *Displacement: Derrida and After.* Bloomignton: Indiana University Press, 1983.

Lacan, Jacques. *Ecrits: A Selection.* Trans. A. Sheridan. London: Tavistok, 1977.

————. *The Four Fundamental Concepts of Psycho-Analysis.* New York: W. W. Norton, 1981.

————. "Kant with Sade." *October* 51 (winter 1989): 55-95.

————. *Language of the Self: The Function of Language in Psychoanalysis.* Ed. Anthony Wilden. Baltimore: John's Hopkins Press, 1968.

Laclau, Ernesto. *Emancipation(s).* London: Verso, 1996.

————. *New Reflections on the Revolution of Our Time.* London: Verso, 1990.

————, ed. *The Making of Political Identities.* London: Verso, 1994.

Laclau, Ernesto, and Chantal Mouffe. *Hegemony and Socialist Strategy: Towards a Radical Democratic Politics.* London: Verso, 1989.

Lash, Scott. "Genealogy and the Body: Foucault/Deleuze/Nietzsche." *Theory, Culture and Society* 2, no. 2 (1984): 1-17.

Lechte, John. *Fifty Contemporary Thinkers: From Structuralism to Postmodernity.* London: Routledge, 1994.

Lefort, Claude. *Democracy and Political Theory.* Minneapolis: University of Minnesota Press, 1988.

————. *The Political Forms of Modern Society: Bureaucracy, Democracy, Totalitarianism.* Ed. John B. Thompson. Cambridge, U.K.: Polity Press, 1986.

Lenin, Vladimir Ilich. *The State and Revolution: The Marxist Theory of the State and the Tasks of the Proletariat in the Revolution.* Rev. ed. Moscow: Progress, 1965.

Love, Nancy S. *Nietzsche, Marx and Modernity.* New York: Columbia University Press, 1986.

Machan, Tibor R. *Liberty for the Twenty-First Century: Contemporary Libertarian Thought.* Lanham, Md.: Rowman & Littlefield, 1995.

Madison, Gary, ed. *Working through Derrida.* Illinois: Northwestern University Press, 1993.

Marshall, Peter. *Demanding the Impossible: A History of Anarchism.* London: Harper Collins, 1992.

Marta, Jan. "Lacan and Post-Structuralism." *The American Journal of Psychoanalysis.* 47, no. 1 (1987): 51-57.

Martin, Luther H., Huck Gutman, and Patrick Hutton, eds. *Technologies of the Self: A Seminar with Michel Foucault.* Amherst: University of Massachusetts Press, 1988.

Marx, Karl and Friedrcih Engels. *Collected Works.* Trans. R. Dixon. London: Lawrence & Wishart, 1975.

Marx, Karl, Friedich Engels, and Vladimir Ilich Lenin. *Anarchism and Anarcho-Syndicalism.* Moscow: Progress Publishers, 1972.

Marx, Karl. *Critique of Hegel's 'Philosophy of Right.'* Ed. Joseph O'Malley. Cambridge, U.K.: Cambridge University Press, 1970.

————. *Capital.* Ed. Friedrich Engels. New York: International Publishers, 1967.

————. *Grundrisse.* Ed. and trans. David McLellan. New York: Vintage Books, 1973.

Massumi, Brian. *A User's Guide to Capitalism and Schizophrenia: Deviations from Deleuze and Guattari.* Cambridge, Mass.: MIT Press, 1992.

Masters, Anthony. *Bakunin, The Father of Anarchism.* London: Sidgwick & Jackson, 1974.

May, Todd. *Between Genealogy and Epistemology: Psychology, Politics and Knowledge in the Thought of Michel Foucault.* University Park: Pennsylvania State University Press, 1993.

—————. "The Community's Absence in Lyotard, Nancy, and Lacoue-Labarthe." *Philosophy Today* 37, no. 3 (1993): 275-284.

—————. "Is Poststructuralist Political Theory Anarchist?" *Philosophy and Social Criticism* 15, no. 2 (1989): 167-181.

—————. "Kant the Liberal, Kant the Anarchist: Rawls and Lyotard on Kantian Justice." *The Southern Journal of Philosophy* 28, no. 4 (1990): 525-538.

—————. *The Moral Theory of Poststructuralism.* University Park: Pennyslvania State University Press, 1995.

—————. *The Political Philosophy of Poststructuralist Anarchism.* University Park: Pennsylvania State University Press, 1994.

—————. "The Politics of Life in the Thought of Gilles Deleuze." *Substance* 66 (1991): 25-35.

McAllister, Pam, ed. *Reweaving the Web of Life: Feminism and Non-Violence.* Philadelphia: New Society Publications, 1982.

McKenna, Andrew J. *Violence and Difference: Girard, Derrida and Deconstruction.* Urbana: University of Illinois Press, 1992.

Megill, Allan. *Prophets of Extremity: Nietzsche, Heidegger, Foucault and Derrida.* Berkeley: University of California Press, 1985.

Merquior, José Guilherme. *Foucault.* London: Fontana Press, 1985.

Miliband, Ralph. *The State in Capitalist Society.* New York: Basic Books, 1969.

Miller, David. *Anarchism.* London: J. M. Dent & Sons, 1984.

Miller, James. *The Passion of Michel Foucault.* New York: Simon & Schuster, 1993.

Minson, Jeffrey. *Genealogies of Morals: Nietzsche, Foucault, Donzelot and the Eccentricity of Ethics.* London: Macmillan, 1985.

Mouffe, Chantal. *The Return of the Political.* London: Verso, 1993.

Moussa, Mario, and Ron Scapp. "The Practical Theorizing of Michel Foucault: Politics and Counter-Discourse." *Cultural Critique* 33 (spring 1996): 87-112.

Negri, Antonio. *The Politics of Subversion: A Manifesto for the Twenty-First Century.* Trans. J. Newell. Cambridge, U.K.: Polity Press, 1989.

Newman, Stephen L. *Liberalism at Wit's End: The Libertarian Revolt against the Modern State.* Ithaca, N.Y.: Cornell University Press, 1984.

Nietzsche, Friedrich. *Beyond Good and Evil.* Trans. R. J. Hollingdale. London: Penguin Books, 1990.

—————. *Birth of Tragedy, and the Case of Wagner.* Trans. W. Kaufmann. New York: Vintage Books, 1967.

—————. *The Gay Science.* Trans. W. Kaufmann. New York: Vintage Books, 1974.

—————. *On the Genealogy of Morals.* Ed. and trans. Walter Kaufmann. New York: Vintage Books, 1989.

Norris, Christopher. *Derrida.* London: Fontana Press, 1987.

Nozick, Robert. *Anarchy, State and Utopia.* Oxford: Basil Blackwell, 1974.

Parker, S. E. "Enemies of Society." *Ego* (formerly *Minus One)* (October-December 1967): 1-4.

Pasquino, Pasquale. "Political Theory of War and Peace: Foucault and the History of Modern Political Theory." Trans. P. Wissing. *Economy and Society* 27, no. 1 (February 1993): 77-88.

Paterson, R. K. W. *The Nihilistic Egoist Max Stirner*. London: Oxford University Press, 1971.

Patton, Paul. "Conceptual Politics and the War-Machine in Mille Plateaux." *Substance* 44-45 (1984): 61-80.

———. "Taylor and Foucault on Power and Freedom." *Political Studies* 37, no. 2 (1989): 277-281.

———, ed. *Nietzsche, Feminism and Political Theory*. London: Allen & Unwin, 1993.

Patton, Paul, and Megan Morris. *Michel Foucault: Power, Truth, Strategy*. Sydney, Australia: Feral Publications, 1979.

Perez, Rolando. *On An(archy) and Schizoanalysis*. New York: Autonomedia, 1990.

Peters, Michael. "What Is Poststructuralism? The French Reception of Nietzsche." *Political Theory Newsletter* 8 (1996): 39-55.

Poulantzas, Nicos. *Political Power and Social Classes*. London: Verso, 1978.

Purkis, Jon, ed. *Twenty-First Century Anarchism: Unorthodox Ideas for a New Millennium*. London: Cassell, 1997.

Pyziur, Eugene. *The Doctrine of Anarchism of Michael A. Bakunin*. Milwaukee: Marquette University Press, 1955.

Rabinow, Paul, ed. *The Foucault Reader*. New York: Pantheon Books, 1984.

Rappaport, Elizabeth. "Anarchism and Authority." *Archives Europeenes de Sociologie* [European Journal of Sociology] 17, no. 2 (1976): 333-343.

Ricardo, Miguel-Alfonso, ed. *Reconstructing Foucault: Essays in the Wake of the 80s*. Amsterdam: Rodopi, 1994.

Ross, Andrew, ed. *Universal Abandon: The Politics of Post-Modernism*. Minnesota: University of Minnesota Press, 1988.

Ryan, Michael. *Marxism and Deconstruction: A Critical Articulation*. Baltimore: Johns Hopkins Press, 1982.

Saltman, Robert. *The Social and Political Thought of Michael Bakunin*. Connecticut: Greenwood Press, 1983.

Santagali, Salvatore. *The Social and Political Thought of Max Stirner*. (Ph.D. Thesis) London School of Economics, 1989.

Sax, Benjamin C. "Foucault, Nietzsche, History: Two Modes of the Genealogical Method." *History of European Ideas* 11 (1989): 769-781.

Schrift, Alan. "Between Church and State: Nietzsche, Deleuze and the Genealogy of Psychoanalysis." *International Studies in Philosophy*, 24, no. 2 (1992): 41-52.

———. "Nietzsche and the Critique of Oppositional Thinking." *History of European Ideas* 11 (1989): 783-790.

———. "Reading, Writing, Text: Nietzsche's Deconstruction of Author-ity." *International Studies in Philosophy* 17, no. 2 (1985): 55-64.

———. "Reconfiguring the Subject as a Process of Self: Following Foucault's Nietzschean Trajectory to Butler, Laclau/Mouffe, and Beyond." *New Formations* (summer 1995): 28-39.

———. *Nietzsche's French Legacy: A Genealogy of Poststructuralism*. New York: Routledge, 1995.

Schurmann, Reiner. "'What Can I Do?' In Archaeological-Genealogical History?" *Journal of Philosophy* 82 (1985): 540-547.

———. "On Constituting Oneself as an Anarchist Subject." *Praxis International* 6, no. 3 (1986): 294-310.

————. *Heidegger on Being and Acting: from Principles to Anarchy*. Trans. C.-M. Gros. Bloomington: Indiana University Press, 1987.

Seitz, Brian. "Constituting the Political Subject, Using Foucault." *Man and World* 3 (October 1993): 443-455.

Shepherdson, Charles. "History of the Real." *Post-Modern Culture* 5, no. 2 (1995) <http://jefferson.village.virginia.edu/pmc/contents.all.html>

————. "The Intimate Alterity of the Real." *Post-Modern Culture* 6, no. 3 (1996) <http://jefferson.village.virginia.edu/pmc/contents.all.html>

Sheridan, Alan. *Michel Foucault: The Will to Truth*. London: Tavistok, 1980.

Simons, Jon. *Foucault and the Political*. London: Routledge, 1995.

Simpson, Julia. "Archaeology and Politicism: Foucault's Epistemic Anarchism." *Man and World* 27, no. 1 (1994): 23-35.

Smart, Barry. *Foucault, Marxism and Critique*. London: Routledge & Kegan Paul, 1983.

Smith, Joseph and William Kerrigan, eds. *Interpreting Lacan*. Princeton, N.J.: Yale University Press, 1983.

Stauth, George. "Revolution in Spiritless Times: An Essay on Michel Foucault's Enquiries into the Iranian Revolution." *International Sociology* 6, no. 3 (1991): 259-280.

Stein, A. L. "Literature and Language after the Death of God." *History of European Ideas* 11 (1989): 791-795.

Stirner, Max. *The Ego and Its Own*. Trans. S. Byington. London: Rebel Press, 1993.

Surin, Keith. "The Undecidable and the Fugitive: Mille Plateaux and the State-Form." *Substance* 66 (1991): 102-113.

Thiele, Leslie Paul. "The Agony of Politics: The Nietzschean Roots of Foucault's Thought." *American Political Science Review* 84, no. 3 (1990): 907-925.

Thomas, Paul. *Karl Marx and the Anarchists*. London: Routledge & Kegan Paul, 1980.

Thomson, Ernie. *Feuerbach, Marx and Stirner: An Investigation into Althusser*. Santa Barbara: University of California, 1991. Microfiche.

Tifft, Larry. "The Coming Redefinitions of Crime: An Anarchist Perspective." *Social Problems* 26, no. 4 (1979): 392-402.

Tifft, Larry and Louis Stevenson. "Humanistic Criminology: Roots from Peter Kropotkin." *Journal of Sociology and Social Welfare* 12, no. 3 (1985): 488-520.

Tifft, Larry, and Dennis Sullivan. *The Struggle to Be Human: Crime, Criminology and Anarchism*. London: Ceinfuegos Press, 1980.

Tucker, Robert, ed. *The Marx-Engels Reader*. 2d ed., New York: Norton, 1978.

————. *The Marxian Revolutionary Idea*. London: Allen & Unwin, 1970.

Turkle, Sherry. *Psychoanalytic Politics: Jacques Lacan and Freud's French Revolution*. 2d ed., London: Free Association Books, 1992.

Walzer, Michael. "The Politics of Michel Foucault." *Dissent* 30 (fall 1983): 481-490.

Weeks, Jeffrey, ed. *The Lesser Evil and the Greater Good: The Theory and Politics of Social Diversity*. Concord, Mass.: Rivers Oram Press, 1994.

Woodcock, George. *Anarchism: A History of Libertarian Ideas and Movements*. Harmondsworth: Penguin, 1962.

Woolsey, W. William. "Libertarianisms: Mainstream, Radical, and Post." *Critical Review* 8, no. 1 (1994): 73-84.

Worsley, Peter. *The Three Worlds*. London: Weidenfeld & Nicholson, 1984.

Zerzan, John. "The Catastrophe of Postmodernism." *Anarchy: A Journal of Desire Armed*. (Fall 1991): 16-25.

Zizek, Slavoj. *For They Know Not What They Do: Enjoyment as a Political Factor*. London: Verso, 1991.

————. *Tarrying with the Negative: Kant, Hegel, and the Critique of Ideology.* Durham: Duke University Press, 1993.
————. *The Sublime Object of Ideology.* London: Verso, 1989.

Index

Engels, Friedrich, 17, 24
enjoyment. *See jouissance*
Enlightenment, the, 55, 58, 61–62, 71,
    83, 121, 129. *See also* humanism
epistemology, 72
equality, 167–69
Erlich, Carol, 165
essence. *See* human essence
essentialism: in anarchism, 51;
    Deleuze and Guattari's critique,
    105–9; Derrida's critique, 117–
    18, 120, 123–24; poststructuralist
    critique of, 6–7, 14, 105; problem
    of, 2–4, 12, 13; Stirner's rejection
    of, 57–60, 62–64, 69–72. *See also*
    binary logic
ethics: of alterity, 126–27; in classical
    anarchism, 164–65; in
    deconstruction, 126–27; in
    Foucault, 169; for a politics of
    resistance, 162, 164–70, 173–74;
    in poststructuralism, 169–70
ethnic identity, 3
excess, 89–90, 97, 124–25
exteriority, 108. *See also* Outside (to
    power)

fascism, 166
feminism, 165, 172, 177n. 34
Ferguson, Kathy, 67
Feuerbach, Ludwig, 8, 39, 57–59
figure of resistance, 89, 92, 107–11
fixed ideas, 59, 61, 64
Foucault, Michel, 9, 75; on
    anachronism of revolution, 79–
    80; concept of power, 76–83, 85–
    89, 143; critique of humanism,
    82–83, 85–86; critique of
    "repressive hypothesis," 83; on
    morality, truth, and knowledge,
    81–82, 169–70; notion of ethics
    for, 169; paradox of, 91–92; on
    place of power, 76–77, 80–81; on
    resistance to power, 79–80, 87–
    92, 97; on Stalinism, 33, 76; on
    the state, 77–79; transgressing the
    self, 90–91; use of war model,
    80–81, 91–92
foundationalism, 97, 105. *See also*
    essentialism

Fraser, Nancy, 87, 88, 89, 169
freedom, 4, 28, 68–69, 90–91, 167–69

Gasché, Rodolphe, 123
gay politics, 95n. 80, 171–72
genealogy, 80–81
The German Ideology (Marx), 22, 59
GIP (Information Group on Prisoners),
    94n. 40
God: death of, 89, 162; man as, 85, 119
Godwin, William, 42
governmentality, 78
Guattari, Felix, 9, 97; the abstract state,
    98–100; critique of essentialism,
    105–9; critique of representation,
    101–3, 105, 110; on desire, 100–
    103, 109–11; figures of
    resistance, 107–11; fragmentation
    of the subject, 120, 121; machinic
    subjectivity, 103–4; non-
    authoritarian thought, 104–7, 108,
    110–11; notion of the Outside,
    107–8, 151; on Oedipal
    representation, 101–3
Gulag, 33, 76

Habermas, Jurgen, 149–51
harmony model of society, 41–42, 43,
    44–45, 46–7, 50
Hegel, G. W. F., 17–18
hegemony, 148
Heidegger, Martin, 120, 161
hermeneutics, 127
hierarchies, 105
Hobbes, Thomas, 43, 45–47
homosexuality, 86, 96n. 80, 172
human nature, 42, 60; for Marx, 60
human subjectivity, 5, 39, 40, 46, 51,
    117, 143, 145; as anarchism's
    place of resistance, 5, 39–40, 47,
    49–50; as authoritarian discourse,
    103–4; for Lacan, 140; machinic,
    103–4; non-essentialist idea of,
    173–74; for Stirner, 140–41; as
    uncontaminated point of
    departure, 5
humanism: Derrida's critique of, 119–
    22; Foucault's critique of, 82–83,
    85–86; in Marx, 59–60; problem

About the Author

Saul Newman is a Postdoctoral Fellow in the Division of Society, Culture, Media, and Philosophy at Macquarie University, Australia. His research interests are in the area of contemporary and poststructuralist political philosophy—in particular, theories of power, desire, identity, ideology, psychoanalysis, and the possibilities of political action today. He has extensive research links with the Center for Theoretical Studies at the University of Essex, United Kingdom, and has also been a Visiting Fellow in the Critical Theory Institute at the University of California, Irvine. He is widely published, with work appearing in journals such as *New Formations, Theory and Event*, and *Philosophy and Social Criticism*. He holds a Ph.D. in political science from the University of New South Wales, and a B.A. in politics, philosophy and history from the University of Sydney. Among his other interests are literature, film, boxing, American muscle cars, and diving.